The Next Great War in the Middle East

RUSSIA PREPARES TO FULFILL THE PROPHECY OF GOG AND MAGOG

S. DOUGLAS WOODWARD

FOREWORD BY JOHN PRICE, AUTHOR OF *THE END OF AMERICA*

OTHER BOOKS WRITTEN BY
S. DOUGLAS WOODWARD

Are We Living in the Last Days?
Decoding Doomsday
Black Sun, Blood Moon
Power Quest Books 1 and 2
Lying Wonders of the Red Planet
Blood Moon
Is Russia Destined to Nuke the U.S.?

The Final Babylon
(Co-written with Douglas W. Krieger and Dene McGriff

Uncommon Sense
(Co-written with Douglas W. Krieger)

CONTRIBUTING AUTHOR
TO THE FOLLOWING BOOKS

Pandora's Engine
God's Ghostbusters
Blood on the Altar
The New Tactics of Global War

THE NEXT GREAT WAR
IN THE MIDDLE EAST

Russia Prepares To Fulfill
the Prophecy of Gog and Magog

A Geopolitical and Expositional Analysis
on the Imminent Russian and Islamic Attack
on the United States, Saudi Arabia, and Israel –
And How U.S. Foreign Policy Decisions
Are Leading to the Destruction of America

S. DOUGLAS WOODWARD

FAITH HAPPENS
OKLAHOMA CITY

The Next Great War in the Middle East

Published in the United States of America

Version 1.1, January 10, 2016

Faith Happens
Woodinville, WA 73142

Web site: www.faith-happens.com
Contact the author at doug@faith-happens.com

All quotations of scripture are from the King James Version of the Bible unless otherwise noted.

Because of the dynamic nature of the Internet, web addresses provided here may have changed.

Photographs are from Wikipedia Commons unless other sources are noted. Copyright of photographs from news sources is cited as available.

Cover design by the author.

ISBN-13: 978-1523230068

ISBN-10: 1523230061

TABLE OF CONTENTS

This book is dedicated to three amazing men of God
who have contributed so much to my ministry
and my personal spiritual life:

Billy Graham

Francis Schaeffer

Hal Lindsey

FOREWORD

By John Price, Author
The End of America

Recent public opinion polls confirm that increasing numbers of Americans believe that we are now living in what the Bible describes as "the end times". In his latest book, *The Next Great War in the Middle East,* S. Douglas Woodward convincingly demonstrates that Americans' impressions of our troubled world today are correct and aligned with the Scripture. The author, who has penned an impressive series of books based on factual analysis and prophecy, makes a significant contribution to our understanding of these troubled days in this current publication. Like the Sons of Issachar, Doug helps us understand our times (I Chronicles 12:32).

The Next Great War in the Middle East contains an in-depth look at what Russia is doing in the Middle East, what America is not doing, and what the consequences of both are likely to be. Although challenged by some present-day "pop" prophecy speakers, Woodward returns to classic scholarship demonstrating the identity of Gog and Magog to be Russia. He cites currently available military statistics to show that *"Russia looks the part (of Gog) more than ever before"*. For Americans confused by what they read and hear coming from the battles swirling around Syria and ISIS, Woodward's book is their answer. The book demonstrates that Russia entered the Syrian conflict for strategic reasons which, from Russia's viewpoint, make perfect sense. Likewise, he shows why America's globalist geopolitical philosophy today underlies its failure to engage and support Israel. Ultimately, this fatal flaw will result in America's demise.

Having recently punted away its best opportunities, Woodward carefully outlines the options left for the U.S. After delineating these unattractive alternatives, he notes, *"The options intensify the probability of the Ezekiel 38-39 conflict, the Battle of Gog and Magog."* Bible students know that Ezekiel reveals in these two chapters a coming invasion of Israel by Gog (Russia), Persia/Medes (Iran) and other nations all of which are today Muslim, though the prophecies were written many centuries before the Quran. When the Ezekiel 38-39 invasion of Israel commences, he writes, *"Israel will be virtually alone with no superpower to defend it, other than the God of Israel."*

Americans who follow the news should have no trouble believing that the U.S. will abandon Israel when it is invaded by Russia, Iran and other Muslim nations. The current administration has ignored, disregarded, mistreated and betrayed Israel on frequent occasions. Imagine if the Ezekiel invasion started tomorrow morning and Israel cried out to America for help. Do we really think that the current Commander-in-chief would order American armed forces to defend Israel with deadly force? Not likely.

Woodward proves by careful original language analysis of prophetic verses that Gog (Russia) and its allies will launch an attack on America (seen by the prophets as *The Daughter of Babylon*) during *the same period of time* as its invasion of Israel. I completely agree. Jeremiah (50:51) refers to the destruction of the Daughter of Babylon as God's vengeance for this nation's betrayal of Israel when Gog and the Muslim invaders descend from the north to sweep Israel into the sea. The Prophets tell us that Gog, along with the Kings of the Medes (Iran), will not only conspire to invade Israel (Ezekiel 38 and 39), they will also be used by the Lord to annihilate the Daughter of Babylon (Jeremiah 51:11, 28). Doug's book makes the case that much of what the U.S. has been doing in Syria and purportedly against ISIS is, in fact, aimed at Russia, attempting to blunt, if not eliminate, its influence in the Middle East.

Since God promises in His Word that those who curse Israel will themselves be cursed (Genesis 12:3), a nation which stabs Israel in the back cannot expect to survive. Thus, this book helps us understand that when Russia and Iran invade Israel, God will permit them to take out America, the primary traitor of Israel, described by Woodward as *"a nation unwill-*

ing or unable to come to the aid of Israel in its predicted future war against Gog and its company."

Doug Woodward has researched and authored what I consider to be a major addition to prophetic analysis. In Ezekiel 38 we read:

> *[10] Thus saith the Lord God; It shall also come to pass, that at the same time shall things come into thy mind, and thou shalt think an evil thought:*

> *[11] And thou shalt say, I will go up to the land of unwalled villages; I will go to them that are at rest, that dwell safely, all of them dwelling without walls, and having neither bars nor gates,*

> *[12] To take a spoil, and to take a prey; to turn thine hand upon the desolate places that are now inhabited, and upon the people that are gathered out of the nations, which have gotten cattle and goods, that dwell in the midst of the land.*

> *[13] Sheba, and Dedan, and the merchants of Tarshish, with all the young lions thereof, shall say unto thee, Art thou come to take a spoil? hast thou gathered thy company to take a prey? to carry away silver and gold, to take away cattle and goods, to take a great spoil?*

When I wrote *The End of America* in 2009, I assumed that the verses describing the *"land of unwalled villages"* were references to Israel. Woodward carefully unpacks the prophecies to show that *"on that day"* when Gog invades Israel it will *also* attack the land resting *"carelessly"* and *"dwelling confidently"*, which is the Daughter of Babylon. He sees the Ezekiel invasion and the assault on the Daughter of Babylon as happening *"almost simultaneously"*. His analysis is not only Biblically based, it is centered on geopolitical reality. American Defense Department strategists should study this book and prepare accordingly. In failing to comply with our written promise to Israel (as signed at Camp David), America's not coming to Israel's defense will be our undoing.

Doug Woodward also convincingly warns Christian authors who imply the end of days remain decades away, that what we witness daily mirrors exactly the Bible's forecasted harvest of those final days. He writes *"the apocalypse is not comfortably distant"*. Just so.

I am pleased to recommend S. Douglas Woodward's latest book, as it is truly an eye-opener on matters prophetic. His words could not be truer: *"The alarm clock triggering the bomb we call World War III continues to tick away."*

Tick. Tick. Tick.

John Price
December 2015

INTRODUCTION

IT WAS ALL SO SIMPLE THEN

Once upon a time, students of Bible prophecy were uniform in their perspective regarding a number of pivotal assumptions about the so-called "prophetic scenario." Debates on the matter of Bible prophecy mostly had to do with timing and whether the rapture of the Church would happen in the beginning, middle, or end of the Great Tribulation period most often identified with Daniel's 70th week.

As a result of the success of Hal Lindsey's *Late Great Planet Earth* and Tim LaHaye and Jerry Jenkins *"Left Behind"* series, most evangelicals in America, to be more specific, those who believed in what is called "futurism" (that is, those that believe there remain many Bible prophecies related to the Second Advent awaiting fulfillment), agreed on the following points:

- *The power base of the antichrist would be "Rome" and a revived Roman Empire.* Europe would grow so strong it would exceed the United States in diplomacy, economics, and military power. Europe would grow into a one-world system. The possibility that the "New World Order" would be behind the transition was not usually included in the prophetic presentation.

- *The antichrist would be a descendant of Jewish ancestors* (perhaps through the tribe of Dan), but also claim European ancestry (perhaps including both Greek and Roman forebears).

- *The United States was universally seen to be "missing in action" during the end times.* Hal Lindsey, Grant Jeffrey, David Jeremiah, and many other prophecy pundits discounted the U.S., seeing moral corruption, reduced military spending, loss of individual freedoms, and increased influence of socialism all accounting for our undoing.

- *The rapture of the Church would precede the worst geopolitical events described by the Bible*, including the apocalyptic plagues, natural disasters such as earthquakes, and the eruption of massive wars across the globe. Since American prophecy writers saw our country as predominantly a Christian nation, it was assumed that the rapture would contribute mightily to the decimation of America too.

- *Mystery Babylon was considered the Roman Catholic Church.* Luther and Calvin believed this to be true. John Wesley, the founder of the Methodist Church agreed. Many modern evangelical leaders tended to confirm this view too. The zenith of this judgment in our day came when Dave Hunt, another famous prophecy writer, published his magnum opus, *A Woman Rides the Beast* (1994). The 600-page book chronicled the atrocities of Rome against Protestants. The notion that the False Prophet, the second beast of Revelation 13, would be the Roman Pope was commonplace. Many held Roman Catholicism would win out once Protestants returned to the fold.

- *The return of Israel to its historic land was considered the high water mark of fulfilled prophecy.* The "dry bones" came together in 1948 and survived numerous wars. The teaching of dispensationalists, like author Lindsey and highly esteemed works of scholars John Walvoord, Dwight Pentecost, and Charles Ryrie, as well as more recently renowned author and teacher Chuck Missler, pastor and author Mark Hitchcock, and scholar Randall Price, all emphasize that Israel is the "mega-sign" that signals we live in the last days.

- *The archenemy of Israel, Gog and Magog, would be realized through the power of the Soviet Union.* The "red menace" would eventually combine forces with the Islamic states surrounding Israel, and come against tiny Israel. This great war would most likely kick-off the Great Tribulation, highlighted by massive persecution of Jews and Christians (those "left behind" for one of several reasons, mostly because they got on board too late). This war would also premiere the Antichrist making a peace treat with Israel for protection.

- *The Battle of Gog and Magog would be "next up" right before Daniel's 70th Week (and the Great Tribulation) commenced.* Many prophecy scholars expounded the scripture citing the Grand Prophecy of Ezekiel 38-39 contending it would be prominently displayed on our radar screens since it was destined to occur in the very near-term. While some argued the construction of a new Jewish temple in Jerusalem would be the necessary pre-condition for Jesus' return, most others suggested that the Gog and Magog conflagration would set the stage for that monumental event; and in fact, it was absolutely essential so the Temple Mount would be cleared (and no longer declared off limits) to allow the future Jewish temple's construction.

HOW THE WORLD (AND BIBLE PROPHECY) HAS CHANGED

Since 1970, however, many geopolitical realities have transpired that diminished the probability these conclusions would prove true. In effect, the traditional prophetic scenario *did not stand the test of time.* Evaluating the assumptions one-by-one, we can readily see how each of these premises fails to obtain allegiance today:

- *The growth of Islam,* especially the impact of extreme Muslim beliefs neatly summarized in one word, *jihad,* increases the fears of Westerners that Mohammed and not Jesus will be the dominating religious figure of the twenty-first century. Protecting Islam now seems to be the new byword of the political left including the current President, with Christianity passé and the silent majority of white Anglo-Saxon protestants considered obscurantist at best, and at worst, Islamophobic.

- *The Soviet Union began to crumble* with the fall of the Berlin Wall in 1989, and soon thereafter it was fully confirmed when the revolution against communism in Russia booted Mikhail Gorbachev out of office. By 1991, many political experts regarded Marxism to be an ideology of the past. If Gog was a Russian, which was now doubtful, he certainly wasn't going to be a communist. Perhaps this counterfeit Gog, defrocked from his Marxist priestly vestments, might instead find his way back to his thousand-year-old roots in the Russian Orthodox Church. Strange how that has seemingly come to pass.

- *The European Union never found its footing.* The Euro as a combined unified currency increasingly falters. The socialism of Europe has broken the bank, so to speak, with too many benefits for too many geriatrics and too few youngsters to pay taxes into the system. The demographics of Europe show it to be a civilization rapidly trending downward, with married couples having too few children to replace themselves. For a number of nations including Greece and Cyprus, with others holding on for dear life like Spain, Ireland, Portugal, and Italy, prospects seem bleak. (The openness of Europeans to embrace Syrian refugees can be explained by this demographic decline and the fact that many Syrians are already educated in Western ways).

- *The decline of the United States has been greatly exaggerated.* While many prophecy experts predict the U.S. economy is ready to collapse at any moment, this has proven to be more fear mongering than fact. The U.S. military, from a conventional weapons perspective (land, naval, and air) continues to reign globally. True, U.S. "policing actions" have grown more problematic as we have seen in the South China Sea (2015) and in the Middle East. But if we are talking about projecting power, the U.S. is the only horse to ride with eleven carrier groups (compared to one apiece for Russia and China), and over 80 nuclear powered *boomers* (subs that carry nuclear ballistic missiles) and *attack submarines* (that carry torpedoes and cruise missiles) primarily targeting enemy shipping. Likewise, U.S. aircraft continue to outpace almost all the competition, although recently Russian aircraft have just about drawn even with the U.S. as the universal fighter, the F-35, has disappointed many experts.

- *The timing of the rapture of the church is fervently debated.* During the past two decades a new theory of the rapture known as the "pre-wrath" rapture, has grown popular especially with younger people who doubt that Americans are likely to see special treatment when it comes to escaping the Great Tribulation. Many former "pre-Tribbers" are embracing this view or going even further, acknowledging they are now "post-Trib". Consequently, the timing of the rapture has become a test for orthodoxy among the old-line Dispensationalists. Battle lines as well as swords have been drawn. Acrimony runs hot.

- *The Roman Catholic Church is no longer seen as the only source of evil in the Christian world.* Many who continue to espouse Bible prophecy as a key element of orthodox Christianity worry that new teachings about prosperity and the "seeker-friendly church" has become the latest apostasy capturing the minds and ministries of evangelical pastors and theologians. Conservative leaders have become the most recent victims of "modern theology" spouting historic Christian liberalism (now entering its third century) by denying the inerrancy of the Bible, the orthodox understanding of the deity of Christ, and proposing "centering prayer" as a key element of an true oxymoron – *Christian Buddhism.* New Age Spirituality, made famous in the 1970s by a number of writers (who used to be counted as just plain cockamamie), has infiltrated what was once the secure bastion of biblical orthodoxy.

- *Many now question Israel as the axiomatic mega-sign of fulfilled Bible prophecy.* Those that hold to the rebirth of Israel as a demonstration of God's unswerving commitment to His historic people and whose protection amounts to a sacred obligation for Bible-believing Christians, are considered simple-minded "Christian Zionists with no sense of how vile (so they say) the Jews can be." Furthermore, Zionism has become a bad word for many – purportedly a form of bigotry denying Palestinians have rights too. Championing Israel has become equated with prejudice and political incorrectness. What used to be called "replacement theology" is finding a home among a number of prophecy teachers who now doubt that God has distinctive programs for Israel and for the Church. A number of authors have grown "enlightened" and embrace a view that dramatically discounts Israel's once exalted status in the minds of many American evangelicals. Israel is regarded as an occupier and oppressor.

- *The new candidate for Gog and Magog are the Turkish peoples.* Specifically, many popular prophecy pundits now consider Ankara to be the power player in the Islamic world. Those who consider Turkey to be the home of the Islamic antichrist would include successful authors Joel Richardson, Walid Shoebat, and even the popular Jewish author and speaker Avi Lipkin. Likewise, for a number of years respected godparent of eschatology Chuck Missler has proposed that the "Eastern leg" of the Roman Empire might be the home of a "Roman" antichrist. Many of the newly popular proponents draw strength from Missler's conversion, adopting the view that Islam will be the predicted one-world religion and Babylon will be rebuilt on the Euphrates, growing to become the capital for Antichrist. Those that espouse Turkey as the best candidate to fulfill the prophecy concerning the land of Magog (Ezekiel 38-39), assert this view for numerous (some not-so-obvious) reasons cited here:

  ✓ The seven churches of Revelation were in ancient Turkey, i.e., Anatolia.

  ✓ Noah's ark came to rest in Turkey (Mount Ararat) and *"as it was in the days of Noah so it shall be in the days of the Son of Man."* (Matthew 24:37)

- ✓ Pergamum in Turkey was "the seat of Satan" according to Revelation 2:13 (although its famous temple was dismantled and moved to Berlin during the time of Adolf Hitler).

- ✓ Meschech and Tubal are located in Turkey. Magog comprises a region between the Black and Caspian Seas. *"Son of man, set thy face against Gog, the land of Magog, the chief prince of Meshech and Tubal, and prophesy against him"* (Ezekiel 38:2).

- ✓ Ankara is considered more "true north" of Jerusalem than is Moscow.

- ✓ Turkey is sometimes considered the protector of Islam. Proponents claim the Ottoman Empire reigned for almost 1,000 years, from the tenth century until the twentieth. Presumably, Turkey, like Rome, will revive to be the final great empire of the last days.

In response, Turkey does possess a significant military contingent; however, its strongest suit is its member status in NATO – not that it holds military weapons of superior strength (its WMD are controlled by NATO), a massive and accomplished army (it ranks tenth in the world), or that it controls economic or political influence in any sector, which it avowedly does *not*. History may be on Turkey's side, but history, after all is passé. Turkey only stirs up controversy, allegedly supporting ISIS (illegally buying their oil). Turkey seems harmless to everyone but the Kurds who live in its southeastern region.

While I personally cannot comprehend the relevance of a number of these arguments supposedly demonstrating Turkey fulfills the Ezekiel prophecy regarding Gog and Magog, (as cited above and promulgated by its advocates), my approach in this book relies much more on arguments for the alternative candidate; that is, a *positive* polemic for why Russia remains the best candidate to be Ezekiel's Gog, not a *negative* assessment of Turkey's capacity to fulfill the attributes of God as Ezekiel describes him. On the other hand, I will cite the factors that make the "Turkish theory" highly problematic, reasons I consider axiomatic to geopolitical reality.

- *Finally, in the past decade, a different major war will become the predicted "next event" that underscores the imminency of the Lord's anticipated return.* Well-respected lecturer, author, and friend Bill Salus, has written two important books, *Israelestine*

(2008) and *Psalm 83 (2013)*, which pre-empted the Battle of Gog and Magog as the *next* great war in the Middle East. Salus powerfully argues (and his view has grown to be part and parcel of most eschatology author's scenarios today), that the nations listed in Psalm 83 must be eliminated or at least vanquished in such a way that Israel would grow to be rich and at peace. His view is that Israel will soon flourish in peace and security. It will become the "land of unwalled villages". It will literally drop its guard, considering unnecessary the walls that protect it today. The borders of Israel described in the last portion of Ezekiel (chapters 40-48) would be greatly expanded (from the Nile to the Euphrates). The "inner ring" of nations such as Syria, Iraq, Jordan, and even Egypt will hold no threat to Israel. Perhaps two to three decades from now, when Israel believes itself invulnerable and owns the Arab wealth, Gog will muster its hordes and attack Israel to "take a spoil". Only then will Gog and Magog become the "next great war."

IS PSALM 83 THE NEXT GREAT WAR?

In my considered opinion, the question of whether the Psalm 83 war is the *next great war* of the Middle East depends not so much upon whether Psalm 83 describes war in our times (between Israel and its neighbors), but upon *how we interpret one particular passage from the prophet Ezekiel, specifically Ezekiel 38:10-13.* From premises drawn from this passage, supporters of Psalm 83 (it being the supposed *next great war)* promulgate several notions that require fulfillment before the war of Gog and Magog could occur. For the reader's convenience, to quote the scripture in question:

> *¹⁰ Thus saith the Lord GOD; "It shall also come to pass, that at the same time shall things come into thy mind, and thou shalt think an evil thought:*
>
> *¹¹ and thou shalt say, I will go up to the land of unwalled villages; I will go to them that are at rest, that dwell safely, all of them dwelling without walls, and having neither bars nor gates,*
>
> *¹² to take a spoil, and to take a prey; to turn thine hand upon the desolate places that are now inhabited, and upon the peo-*

> *ple that are gathered out of the nations, which have gotten cattle and goods, that dwell in the midst of the land."*
>
> [13] *Sheba and Dedan, and the merchants of Tarshish, with all the young lions thereof, shall say unto thee, "Art thou come to take a spoil? Hast thou gathered thy company to take a prey? To carry away silver and gold, to take away cattle and goods, to take a great spoil?"* (Ezekiel 38:10-13)

The first premise to which I draw the reader's attention concerns how Gog will come against a land that *needs no walls for protection.* Ezekiel mentions Israel in verse 8 of the chapter as, "dwelling in the land" against (or near to) the "mountains of Israel" where the people will dwell safely.

> *After many days thou shalt be visited: in the latter years thou shalt come into the land that is brought back from the sword, and is gathered out of many people, against the mountains of Israel, which have been always waste: but it is brought forth out of the nations, and they shall dwell safely all of them. (Ezekiel 38:8)*

The conventional prophetic view (from Hal Lindsey forward) along with those who support the Psalm 83 "next war" thesis, supposes that Israel is *also the land referenced in verse 11*, and therefore, Israel *must not be threatened* since the people must dwell safely. Given that Israel continues to be threatened today by its hostile neighbors, this would seem to suggest that something dramatic must occur to nullify this threat and supply Israel with peace and tranquility. Proponents for the Psalm 83 war thesis propose the answer lies within the words of Psalm 83. In this Psalm, Israel fights against the many nations (peoples and tribes) surrounding it on three sides, to demonstrate that the *Jehovah (Yahweh) is the name of the Lord.* The Psalmist (in this case Asaph who did prophesy for the Lord) says Israel fights this battle (or battles) *"that men may know that thou, whose name alone is JEHOVAH, art the most high over all the earth"* (Psalm 83:18). Jews and Christians alike, all those who believe firmly that the Bible sanctions no compromise in designating the identity of the LORD God, would never accept that Jehovah and Allah are two names for the same entity. Whether Psalm 83 refers to wars past or future (or perhaps most likely, *currently going*), Jehovah is the LORD and only He deserves our praise. I stand firmly with the Psalm 83 proponents in this regard.

However, the stark reality remains that Israel still lives behind a 417-mile-long wall for protection, a wall that serves as a compelling point in favor for an indefinite delay of the war of Gog and Magog until *after the Psalm 83 war*. In other words, the proposed Psalm 83 war must occur so that Israel takes down the wall (or opens its gates), no longer threatened by Palestinian terror. As long as the long wall remains and is well guarded, *the Battle of Gog and Magog cannot take place*. Or so the argument goes.

The second premise follows from the first; namely the assumption that Israel comprises the focus of the passage and therefore Israel must be *the land of unwalled villages*. It has been and is still taught by most everyone that Israel *must live at ease first* – that is, it must dwell safely. This is true for almost all futurists regardless of the sequence they suppose between (1) a Psalm 83 conflagration and (2) the Battle of Gog and Magog. Furthermore, it is assumed that after Israel wins this war it enriches itself with the spoils of the forecasted war, because the motivation of Gog appears to be "to take spoils" from the land of unwalled villages. Thus, Israel must possess great wealth. Consequently, given the standard assumption the land of unwalled villages is Israel, Israel must also become *a dominating empire in the Middle East*. It will acquire the wealth of its neighbors. It will dwell securely. Never mind that this political incorrectness extends beyond any situation that the world could possibly allow Israel to enjoy (that is, to possess the wealth of its Islamic neighbors). Nevertheless, since these geopolitical objections carry little to no weight for most eschatology teachers (those futurists who subscribe to this line of thinking), Israel's becoming a dominating empire in the Middle East continues to be seen as the most plausible prophetic scenario.

However, Israel remains the same nation that took the Temple Mount in the Six-Day War of June 1967 and then immediately returned it to the Islamic trust known as the WAQF (fearful of the global Arab response if Israel occupied this Islamic – and Jewish – sacred site). To this author, not only does it seem out of character for Israel to take such aggressive measures, it constitutes geopolitical suicide. I believe there is a much more plausible scenario that both recognizes geopolitical realities and better fits the scriptural witness if we consider the whole counsel of God. The prophecies of the Battle of Gog and Magog – as well as the extensive prophecies in Jeremiah, Isaiah, and Zechariah concerning the daughter of Babylon – lead me to envision a very different scenario.

Nevertheless, according to the "Psalm 83 war" thesis considered in conjunction with the conventional view concerning the interpretation of Ezekiel 38, *Israel will grow rich while Gog grows envious* – and eventually feels enticed to steal that wealth. That is, the proposed future vast riches of Israel motivate Gog to seize Israel's post-Psalm 83-war wealth. This seems to be the most plausible scenario *if Israel is the land of unwalled villages.*

The third premise that figures into the favored scenario relates to the *implied holder of the riches.* The conventional view of Ezekiel 38:13 sees "Sheba and Dedan, the Merchants of Tarshish, and the young lions" *protesting* what is happening when Gog goes on the attack. From the standpoint of the conventional view of scholars for almost fifty years, these nations sit on the sideline and wonder aloud what Gog is doing. The spoil being sought, according to this view, *belongs to Israel.* It comprises the wealth acquired during the Psalm 83 war. As we will discuss later in this book when expositing the passage in Ezekiel, the astonishment of "Sheba and Dedan, the Merchants of Tarshish, and the young lions" comes not from protesting what appears to be the object of Gog's attack, i.e., Israel, but rather *Gog's attack upon them!* That is the key thesis advanced here. The spoil that Gog seeks in verse 13 actually comprises the wealth of the "third parties" identified in this passage, and not Israel. Verse 13, and in fact the whole passage from verse 10 to 13 comes across as "an aside" – a parenthetical comment, as in "Oh, and by the way while I'm telling you about what will happen to Israel, let me tell you about what will happen to Saudi Arabia, England, and its colony the United States."

The U.S. in particular, as well as Saudi Arabia, possesses great wealth. England too remains one of the most dominating financial powers in the world. It you combine these two nations with the support given by Saudi

Arabia (through the enforcement of the Petro-dollar), this trio of nations amounts to the "axis of economy" that drives the world system. The Anglo-American alliance, through its colossal marketplaces (namely Wall Street and the City of London) along with the dominating power of Saudi Arabia in OPEC, encompasses more than any other financial alliance, the wealth of the world. The U.S., England, and Saudi Arabia, has vast "cattle and goods", "silver and gold", (and other vast natural resources) as well as the U.S. comprising a nation gathered from the lands all over the world. It too fits the description Ezekiel provides, and thus, constitutes a candidate for the attack of Gog, especially since "taking the U.S. military out of the way" would be militarily necessary before Gog could bring his armies against Israel. Although economics will not be a subject discussed in this book, it should be stressed at the outset that the single greatest way for the BRICS nations (Brazil, Russia, India, China, and South Africa) to overcome the infamous international bankers would be to "break the bank" – literally destroy the World Bank and the International Monetary Fund, backed by the U.S. and U.K. systems, and eliminate the staggering amount of debt held by BRICS. In 2013, Brazil, India, and South Africa owed more than $1.2 trillion dollars, with less than $1 trillion in their central bank reserves. U.S. and U.K. bankers can block payments to the BRICS nations. Russia and China remain throttled and controlled by the Anglo-American nexus. The BRICS bank remains "dollar-denominated".[1]

Some might object that the U.S. has already deserted Israel and will not stand alongside Israel to oppose its enemies. But in truth this comprises a reactionary perspective from we conservatives who hold Israel dear. We are frustrated that the current administration has not prioritized Israel's security above other U.S. actions in the Middle East, vis-à-vis the Iranian "deal". While it is quite true that the U.S. has not been strongly supportive of Israeli interests, particularly as it has pressed Israel to accept a "two-state solution"; nevertheless, reckoning the U.S. has "abandoned Israel completely" overstates U.S. policy. Despite the obvious – that the U.S. is far less enthusiastic about supporting Israel than it used to be – it is geopolitically unthinkable that the U.S. would sit idly by and "do nothing" as long as the U.S. possesses vast military assets and retains some proximity to the region. Additionally, the Jewish lobby remains too influential to allow the U.S. to "sit the next one out". Furthermore, the U.S. government, even this administration, knows it stands to lose its foothold completely in the Middle East if Israel ceases to exist. The U.S. would not intentionally sit on the sidelines. U.S. participation, however, might not be an option.

If the U.S. were attacked with nuclear weapons, the danger for Israel would become enormous. Gog would then feel free to muster its company and commence the campaign against Israel. The U.S. would no longer be the "only remaining superpower" protecting Israel. Israel would be on its own – humanly speaking, entirely on its own – except for the greatest superpower of all, the LORD God of Israel. Of course, that is what the Bible predicts.

WHY THIS BOOK HAS BEEN WRITTEN

Indeed, it is this topic that constitutes the subject matter for which I write and from which I derive the name for this book. It is not my principal intention to criticize directly the theory regarding a future Psalm 83 war. Furthermore, I will not critique the case for the Psalm 83 war point-by-point; that is, I will not offer detailed counter-arguments for why I believe it does not reflect what will happen in the months (and years) ahead. Such an approach quickly grows tedious for most any reader.

Indeed, I would stipulate that the Psalm 83 war thesis might wind up being exactly right regarding what will happen soon in Israel. Proponents could be correct. Psalm 83 may forecast that a great war lies just beyond the horizon. Having said that, I still challenge the premises of the "Psalm 83 perspective", but primarily from the observations discussed below, drawing from geopolitical realities in the world today and considering other scripture besides Psalm 83 (specifically prophecies from Ezekiel, Jeremiah, Isaiah, Zechariah, and Joel) that, when assembled, logically invalidate a *future* Psalm 83 war. Consider these possibilities:

- The war of Psalm 83 may already have been underway since the time of the Jewish War of Independence in 1948 or beginning with the 1967 Six-Day War. The wars against the "inner ring" of Islamic nations surrounding Israel have always ended with Israel stronger militarily with greater leverage over its neighbors. This could be the fulfillment of the confrontations listed there. The distinction between the "inner ring" (Syria, Iraq, Jordan, Egypt) and the outer ring (Iran, Libya, Sudan, Turkey, and former Islamic Russian states like Turkmenistan, Kurdistan, Azerbaijan), has been a distinction draw before, and the question raised, "Why is the inner ring not mentioned in the Gog and Magog war?" Were they previously conquered by Israel or are they included in the "many people with thee" Ezekiel mentions in passing in verse 38:6?

- The premise of a future Psalm 83 war, as a necessary precondition to the war of Gog and Magog, comprises a near-impossibility based on geopolitical factors that should become apparent as we proceed through this book. Indeed, we must consider the geopolitical realities and interpret the Bible's prophecies in light of what is happening in the world today. Pursuing the opposite approach – developing a scenario from one prophetic passage in the Bible and then "fitting the facts" into that scenario has failed time and again. Remember that the Jews of Jesus' day also had a scenario for who their Messiah would be, what the circumstances of his coming look like, and what they expected him to do (i.e., to vanquish their enemies). Their presupposed scenario ultimately caused them to miss Messiah's "visitation". The wrong scenario can lead us down the wrong path too – to be even a bit more emphatic, it can lead us *way down the wrong path.*

- The timing for the fulfillment of this prophecy entails a deferment of the prophetic timetable for the Lord's return at least two or three decades hence. I do not believe the Lord will tarry that long. There are too many fuses already lit which lead me to conclude that the explosion of apocalyptic events lies just ahead. The geopolitical realities of what is happening in Europe and the Middle East, the tension in the relationship between Russia and the United States, and the increased terrorist threats globally mandate a "breaking point" well before the year 2045 or even 2035 as the "Psalm 83" war thesis holds.

To venture further (and I tread carefully here), I contend that the implications of holding to the conventional view, whether supplemented by the Psalm 83 War position or not, have several especially negative effects on "preparing ourselves" and "watching for the Lord's return".

To be specific, the conventional view:

- *Suggests that the proximity of the apocalypse remains comfortably distant.* I do not believe this to be so. My conviction is that the timing of the Lord's coming appears very near term, within a few years or sooner, and not several decades from now. While it is standard Pre-Tribulation Rapture position that the rapture may happen at a time well before the Battle of Gog and Magog, there are many scholars who assert that the two may happen at virtually the same time. We will explore the timing of this war toward the end of this book.

- *Supposes that Israel's neighbors will be defeated by Israel in the Psalm 83 war and Islam will not pose any serious threat to God's people thereafter.* This Islamic threat will continue, in my assessment, affecting Israel, the U.S., Europe, and even Russia. Assuming a near-term defeat of Islam, which the Psalm 83 war implies, does not rightly size up the harrowing occurrences in the days soon to transpire. Perhaps ISIS will be defeated and declared a non-factor in 2016 or 2017 based upon the massive air assault by Russia and the coalition of nations headed by the U.S. But the likelihood for continued terrorist attacks both inside and outside Israel from this point forward will remain extremely high. Hamas, Hezbollah, and Al-Qaeda, all continue to plague the Western world, including Israel. One threat may be weakened or eliminated, but then several others take their place. Additionally, ad hoc attacks carried out by Palestinians in Jerusalem are almost a daily news item as 2015 comes to a close. True, a Psalm 83 war could change the facts on the ground. Far from providing peace, however, terrorism could intensify and pressure from the world community would likely condemn Israel at levels exceeding what we see in the geopolitical arena to this point. Israel would not live in peace by disposing of its Arab neighbors and eliminating the Palestinian threat – a threat that exists now in Israel will remain for the foreseeable future.

- *Supposes a political motive or mindset that remains quite foreign to the nation state of Israel today.* Israel would not seek to keep spoil obtained from a war with its neighbors. Israel remains content with its borders – *it does not seek additional territory just as fervently as it still refuses to compromise its existing borders.* Israel's enemies assert the Zionist agenda is to dominate the region and the world. That remains a scandalous conspiracy popularized by Hitler and echoed by anti-Semites and jihadists today. But evidence is still lacking after 80 years.

ORGANIZATION AND PRESUPPOSITIONS OF THIS BOOK

To pursue these subjects, I have divided the book into two parts: the first comprises a geopolitical assessment of events in the Middle East relying upon expert secular sources from recent Internet-based periodicals, paying particular attention to Russian and U.S. foreign policy as well as to Russia's military revitalization that increases its threat to Israel and the United States. Throughout my writing career, my methodology has been to cite sources that are not of the same mindset as I, or subscribe to the same apocalyptic *futurism,* as do I. Seeking independent sources logically strengthens my arguments and increases the usefulness of my writings to those outside the community of believers who do not share my assumptions regarding the veracity of Christianity and the coming Second Advent of Christ. My intent has always been to provide an apologetic approach, giving a reason for the hope that is within me. (1 Peter 3:15)

Additionally, my guiding principle (which I hope to follow in this endeavor) focuses on geopolitical issues which classical eschatology endeavored to expound. In contrast, today's prophetic teachers often overemphasize the sensational, the weird, and the paranormal, even promoting understandings of reality that reduce the credibility of our witness. Too many times we deal with topics that scare people away – that keep unbelievers from hearing the proofs inherent in Bible prophecy. This approach may sell books, but it compromises our mission to reach the world for Christ.

However, my commitment today is to write books that keep apocalyptic themes balanced with the broader teachings of the gospel, emphasizing that the coming Kingdom of God remains the byword of Jesus' message even while proposing present day events, as well as dramatic occurrences in nature, that could *possibly* constitute authentic signs of Jesus' soon return.

Furthermore, I caution that many prophetic teachers have wondered too far into conspiracy theories. While the Bible is based on the greatest conspiracy of all, Satan's seeking to overthrow Jehovah (and His son Jesus) hoping to sidetrack His plan for humankind, too many vocal conspiracy advocates label every horrific event in our world a "false flag". Not only do I question all conspiracy theories (while holding some to be true), I believe we should challenge every not-so-obvious theory championing conspiracy, examining the evidence cautiously before adopting it. For the more often we subscribe to conspiratorial explanations behind negative events in our world, the more we grow gullible and paranoid. Eventually we wind up subjecting all our beliefs – including our most sacred ones – to others' skepticism. As with the conspiracy theories we espouse, those who engage with us in public or private venues could conclude our affirmations of biblical faith are just as "over the top" as the conspiracy theories we regard to be true. At this point, we become lumped into "truthers," "birthers," and other disrespected theorists, thereby disqualifying all our opinions. While any given conspiracy theory may prove out to be true (and many are), concluding all such evils reinforce that our government is out to get us, or that every diabolical attack stems from an "Illuminati" plot or secret society scheme, only causes others to question our gullibility.

My mission is to assess and point out the "signs of the times", exposing how the events of our day do or don't fit into what the Bible teaches about the last days. I attempt to offer reasonable explanation and educated speculation supported by reliable, unbiased research that makes (1) biblical principles and prophecy relevant to our lives and (2) the Bible's claims believable.

As such, the second part of this book delves into the Bible in an expository manner to examine in detail why the Ezekiel's prophecy of Gog and Magog most likely references a conflict between Russia and the United States in contemporary times. In some sense this conflict can be seen as a prelude to the actual "battle" of Gog and Magog (a battle that appears, from Ezekiel's rendering, to be a short-lived contest in which *God* and not Gog comes out on top!) I will bring to the forefront new insights into the Gog and Magog conflict that are not a rehash of previous findings and assertions on the subject. And I seek to substantiate the frequently rejected, but historic position that *Russia is Gog.*

Finally, I emphasize that the U.S. and not just Israel is threatened by the "Red Storm Rising" to borrow from the title of the late Tom Clancy's celebrated book on a possible World War III scenario. The U.S. has invited its own destruction through a series of choices made during the past four administrations (from the end of the Reagan era to now). This conclusion may be painful but it is essential if we are to acknowledge and reverse the downward spiral of America and recover the ground we've lost.

If you are a reader that is a policy maker influencing our government or an executive guiding our major corporations, I entreat you to read carefully and consider what is written here. Unapologetically, I am not an academic with political science credentials or experience in the Foreign Service. But I am a serious researcher, an author of many books having studied theology and history extensively, and am most familiar with geopolitics in light of Bible prophecy having studied these matters for over four decades. And I have compiled for your convenience here, extensive information from dozens of sources that are considered reliable and responsible.

So, to these tasks I pledge my best efforts. If I convince you these things be so, I trust you will share this information with others and create a viral effect that can change the lives of many and alter the course of our once great nation. No task is more important in these times ahead.

THE NEXT GREAT WAR
IN THE MIDDLE EAST

Part One: Geopolitical Analysis

1: IS RUSSIA'S MILITARY TRULY A THREAT TO THE U.S.A.?

"Therefore, son of man, prophesy and say unto Gog, Thus saith the Lord GOD; In that day when my people of Israel dwelleth safely, shalt thou not know it? And thou shalt come from thy place out of the north parts, thou, and many people with thee, all of them riding upon horses, a great company, and a mighty army: And thou shalt come up against my people of Israel, as a cloud to cover the land; it shall be in the latter days, and I will bring thee against my land, that the heathen may know me, when I shall be sanctified in thee, O Gog, before their eyes." (Ezekiel 38:14-16).

DOES THE PROPHECY OF THE BATTLE OF GOG AND MAGOG VERGE ON FULFILLMENT?

STUDENTS OF BIBLE PROPHECY IDENTIFY THE BATTLE OF GOG AND MAGOG AS ONE OF THE MIGHTIEST SIGNS OF THE COMING DAY OF THE LORD AND THE RETURN OF JESUS CHRIST. JEWS ASSOCIATE the coming of Messiah with this "last battle" when a great power from the "northern quarters" comes forth to destroy the land of Israel. The principle character in the prophecy besides Israel is *Gog from the land of Magog*. It is he who will assemble nations that already surround Israel – brought together out of a mutual desire to destroy Israel – armies from northern Africa; from the areas we associate with Turkey, the Caucasus (southwestern Asia), and from Persia (today's Iran).

Scholars do not all agree that the leader of this great army will be Russia, although for over 150 years, even before the fall of the Ottoman Empire (1923) there have been biblical expositors that have proposed Russia fits the bill. One prominent scholar expressing this opinion was Wilhelm Gesenius (1786 – 1842), the noted Middle East ancient languages scholar, Lutheran teacher, and biblical critic.[2]

In our day, many advance the same supposition: that the "great bear" we know as Russia is destined to be Gog of the Ezekiel prophecy. Deep studies into the history of peoples and nations, their origins and movements, compel this author to agree. (We will take this up in part two of this book). From my vantage point, it is not a matter of "if" Russia is destined to fulfill the prophecy of Gog, but "when" she will do so.

There are a number of steps or stages that must be accomplished before Russia can be definitely identified with Gog, and thus fulfill the prophecy. Certainly one of them includes a large military presence in proximity to the area. Another is a series of alliances with the key nations identified in the prophecy. And finally, the leader or prince (as Gog is also identified by Ezekiel through the Hebrew word *Rosh*)[3] would need to be a vital military power, able to lead the varied peoples of the Middle East in an attempted conquest of Israel.

It has not been lost on conventional students of Ezekiel's prophetic vision that Russia looks the part more than ever before. As a result of the ongoing Syrian civil war, Russia has positioned itself to exert its will through military bases and naval assets in the area. Russia is the principal supporter of Syria's failing government of Bashar al-Assad. Just within the past few months, Russia has supplied sophisticated anti-aircraft and missile weapons to Iran (the S-300 ABM system). They have moved its revised brother, the S-400 in the Syrian theater under their control. New tanks and aircraft have also been introduced.

The last plank of the platform for Gog consists of a military that can dominate the region. *It does not have to have a global military presence.* But it must be capable of controlling political events in the area and eventually mounting an assault in conjunction with its regional allies against Israel. It may also need to assault its adversaries with missiles that, like the arrows from an expert archer, do not return to the archer without achieving their desired effect.[4]

From a geopolitical standpoint, for Russia to be Gog, not only would it need to be dominant in the Middle Eastern theater, its principal adversary must be reluctant to stand against it and unwilling or unable to come to the defense of Israel. This is exactly the picture that Ezekiel paints. The prophet talks of those who stand outside the fray and either are frozen into inaction, or are attacked themselves such that they are unable to come to help Israel. It takes little expository skill to conclude that Gog's adversary would come from those very nations, nations also mentioned in Ezekiel's prophecy: *"Sheba, and Dedan, and the merchants of Tarshish, with all the young lions thereof, shall say unto thee, 'Art thou come to take a spoil? Hast thou gathered thy company to take a prey? To carry away silver and gold, to take away cattle and goods, to take a great spoil?'"* (Ezekiel 38:13)

Once again, scholars are not in agreement who these nations are, but most argue that Sheba and Dedan are the inhabitants of the Sinai Peninsula, led today by Saudi Arabia. The merchants of Tarshish are European nations, most likely Spain, Portugal, and especially England that created powerful colonies in the new world to exploit its resources and grow to become trading partners and merchants in their own right. Of course, America was birthed primarily from England. *The Lion of England gave birth to the young lion of the United States.* Therefore, the *young lions* are most often regarded as these new world colonies. This author has written extensively on this subject, citing over 200 verses from several prophetic books in the Old Testament, which point to the United States as the future "daughter of Babylon" who will also be attacked by a great power from the north. (A summary is provided in Appendix B.)

The destruction of the "young lion", however, is not our focus in this study. (See the author's book, *Is Russia Destined to Nuke the U.S.?* 2015). Our focus here: identify Gog and how other nations, particularly Israel, will be targets of its aggression. So, hypothetically, does a dominant nation exist that can be considered an adversary of Russia that may have retreated from the region and grown less willing to support the nation of Israel? Is there a "restraining" nation holding Gog back, but if taken out of the way, frees Gog to attack Israel and fulfill Ezekiel's prophecy?

I assert that the United States of America is that nation. Its actions over the past two decades have led it to step back at this time from being the dominant foreign power and presence in the Middle East. And its current policy of establishing relations with Iran at the expense of upsetting relations with Israel and Saudi Arabia, seem to have put the U.S. in the exact state of mind that Ezekiel describes – a nation unwilling or unable to come to the aid of Israel in its predicted future war against Gog and its company. Indeed, on the surface all of these nations appear to have a passive response, *"Art thou come to take a spoil? Hast thou gathered thy company to take a prey?"* The question remains for this author whether their lack of support is because they are *unwilling* or because they are *unable* to respond. That comprises a detailed study that we will take up later in this book. (See the chapter "Where is the Land of Unwalled Villages?")

Figure 1 - A Russian ICBM Mobile Launcher

Therefore, coming back to the point of this chapter: is Russia's military truly capable of being a dominating presence in the Middle East? Can it replace the "power vacuum" left by the resignation of the U.S. after pulling out of Iraq? Would Russia assemble "its company" presumably of Islamic nations for which is serves as guard (Ezekiel 38:7) and bring them together in a unified battle plan against Israel? Is Russia's military a genuine threat to the United States?

We will explore the issue of Russia's military capability here based upon journalistic and expert papers mostly published within the last few months. Time is of the essence. The most current data from the pundits of geopolitics supplies the most conclusive evidence of what has happened today regarding Russia in the Middle East. Additionally, I should stress that the data sources from which I draw are secular sources, non-biased with no particular eschatological point of view (other than professing none and likely holding to a secular, non-theistic mindset). Finally, as the reader will note, the sources are generally considered by their peers to be reliable and responsible. No conspiracy theorists are cited here, although no assumption is made regarding beliefs these journalists and scholars hold to themselves and have not made public.

SOME EXPERTS DENY RUSSIA POSSESSES SUPERIOR MILITARY STRENGTH

Opinions vary widely on whether the Russian Military is a real threat to the United States. Analyst assessment prior to the Russian excursion in the Syrian civil war strongly suggested that Russia's military was in horrible shape and represented little threat to U.S. military and geopolitical strategies. One year ago, Jonathan Masters of the *Council of Foreign Relations* provided this dismal analysis of Russia's ability to update its military capabilities:

> Rearmament has been slow, and much of the military's equipment remains decades old. The once formidable Soviet navy is now little more than a coastal protection force, experts say. All of the navy's large vessels, including its flagship and sole aircraft carrier, the non-nuclear Kuznetsov, are holdovers from the Cold War. (By comparison, the United States has ten nuclear carriers and builds several new warships each year.) Russian air power [will remain] limited, at least in the short term. Aircraft manufacturer Sukhoi is de-

veloping several new advanced warplanes, including a fifth-generation "stealth" fighter (the T-50), but production has been sluggish in some cases, and most of the current air force dates from the 1980s.[5]

Dave Majumdar, the Defense Editor for *The National Interest* remains outspoken on the weaknesses of Russian armaments, mostly from the perspective of how old Russian weapon systems are. Majumdar points out that Putin is indeed committed to upgrading his weapons; however, the financial challenges he faces will certainly curb his spending. Majumdar builds his expert opinion on strategic and long-term factors, both economic and demographic. From his vantage point, Russia simply doesn't have the industrial base or the population to compete with the U.S. Says Majumdar:

> All in all, Russia's military has made tremendous progress since its post-Soviet low-point in the mid-1990s. But it has a long way to go before it completes its reforms, which could take until 2030—or later. Even then, Russia is not the Soviet Union—it doesn't have the population or industrial base to be that kind of juggernaut. And even when reforms are complete, Russia can't compete head-to-head with the U.S. and its allies. Certainly Moscow's military forces will continue to modernize, but Russian military might—other than its nuclear forces—is an illusion. It's a paper tiger.[6]

David Axe, in his May 27, 2015 article published by Reuters, "Russia's Navy: More rust than ready," provided this negative appraisal:

> Russia has struggled to maintain warm-water ports. Seizing Crimea helps ensure Moscow's access to ice-free waters for commercial and military shipping.
>
> But Russia's busy fleet schedule masks an underlying seagoing weakness. Moscow's warships are old and unreliable. Yet the government is finding it increasingly difficult to replace them with equally large and powerful new vessels.
>
> Russia is a geriatric maritime giant surrounded by much more energetic rivals. [7]

However, that analysis is on the verge of a dramatic reassessment, due to the Russian campaign in Syria to support the government of Bashar al-Assad as we will document momentarily. First, allow me here to provide the reader with some key statistics and geographical factors useful to assess Russia's military might.

AN OVERVIEW OF RUSSIA'S MILITARY CAPABILITY

Over the past 15 years, since the time that Vladimir Putin took the reins of Russia, the military has grown to be a much more formidable foe. From the Baltic Sea in the North to the Balkans in the South to the Black

SELECTED CONVENTIONAL MILITARY DATA

Country	Troops (active)	Tanks	Combat Aircraft	
RUSSIA	845,000	22,550	1,399	CSTO
ARMENIA	44,800	109	15	
AZERBAIJAN	66,950	433	44	
BELARUS	48,000	515	72	
GEORGIA	20,650	123	12	
KAZAKHSTAN	39,000	300	121	
KRYGYZSTAN	10,900	150	33	
MOLDOVA	5,350	0	0	
TAJIKISTAN	8,800	37	0	
TURKMENISTAN	22,000	680	94	Source: IISS: The Military Balance 2014
UKRAINE	129,950	1,150	231	
UZBEKISTAN	48,000	340	135	Julia Ro *cfr*

Figure 2 - Conventional Military Data of Russia's Alliance Treaty
(Source: Council on Foreign Relations)

and Caspian Seas further East, Russia maintains a strong buffer against foreign incursion. It does not have the buffer that it had when the Iron Curtain existed and the Warsaw Pact nations stood between Europe and Russia. Nevertheless, a significant distance stands between the most powerful nations of Europe (Germany and France) and Russia.

The one chink in this armor is the Ukraine which borders Russia and has been heavily influenced by the United States in a decade long attempt to recruit Ukraine into NATO. Indeed, the civil war in Ukraine today is fought in no small part because of Russia's long-term desire to buffer itself from Western influences at work in Eastern Europe: e.g., The Baltics, Poland, Czechoslovakia, Hungary, Bulgaria and the Balkans which keep Russia at a distance from its less than friendly neighbors. The chart above, Figure 2, points out that numerous members of a *Collective Security Alliance Treaty*, replacing the Warsaw Pact, have military assets that must be taken in account to assess the real size of

Figure 3 - Russia's Security Alliance
(Source: Council on Foreign Relations)

the Russian footprint in military matters. These mostly Islamic republics have pledged to work together, similar to NATO, in the event of an attack. These nations extend from South and Central Asia (formerly subsumed within the old Soviet Union), across the "top" of India, all the way to China. Note: even without including the Ukraine resources shown in the chart, Russia and its aligned treaty member states can) muster approximately 25,000 tanks, 1.1 million troops and 1,500 combat aircraft. This does not include Russian allies such as Iran.

Of course, the alliance has a vast territory to defend. Just focusing on the western and southern flanks of Russia and its partners, from the map above (Figure 3), one can readily see the challenge the Collective Security Alliance Treaty members face. But measuring Russian military might mean much more than merely looking at the numbers. Due to events in the Middle East over the past few months, there are many elements now exposed to Western analysts eager to study what the Russians really possess in the way of modern weapon systems.

As the negative assessment provided at the outset of this article states, many of the conventional weapons of Russia consist in old, outdated, Soviet-era munitions. But this fails to take into account weapons that Russia has been developing during the Putin era that have been under wraps until now. These new systems, combined with its highly capable nuclear weapons comprise the real threat from Russia's military.

SYRIA SHOWS OFF STUNNING RUSSIAN ARMS CAPABILITY

Responding to David Axe's negative assessment of Russia's navy, Garret I. Campbell from the *Brookings Institute* took the opposite point of view in his October 23, 2015 article, "Russia is Proving Western Military Punditry Wrong":

> Russia's navy has been called "more rust than ready." But Russia is, impressively, both retrofitting older vessels and procuring newer ones. And the navy has unveiled a significant capability: Its Caspian Sea corvettes and frigates can fire cruise missiles at targets over 900 miles away. This is a previously unknown capability. To put things in perspective, the two variants of the U.S. Littoral Combat Ship, Freedom and Independence, are substantially larger at roughly 2,900 tons and 3,100 tons respectively—but they do not possess any cruise missile or similar power projection capability. [8]

Campbell goes further, elaborating on the relevance of the Russian navy to the conflict in Syria:

> In fact, the Black Sea Fleet has proven invaluable for Russia and its Syrian partners. The Black Sea Fleet's flagship, the guided missile cruiser Moskva, and an accompanying number of surface combatants, have deployed off of Syria to provide air and missile defense from the Mediterranean. The criticism is that these are older vessels with aging technologies. Compared to many NATO vessels this is true, but they are more than adequate for the job they have been deployed for. Moreover, their employment portends both a Russian capability and an intent aligned to achieving Russian limited foreign policy objectives. Thus they represent a significant threat which cannot be dismissed by NATO naval planners. [9]

In fact, the conflict in Syria has provided Mr. Putin a golden opportunity to show off what his military capabilities really are. Majumdar cautions though that the show may not be a "show of force" but a selective show of only a few *high-tech weapons*, otherwise known as precision guided munitions (PGM).

> While the Russians are demonstrating high sortie generation rates in Syria—they are not using more than a handful of precision-guided weapons. Moreover, even the Su-30SM has not been spotted with modern air-to-air missiles—which is strange. It could be that while Russia developed weapons like the R-77, it has not fielded those weapons in quantity.[10]

However, just two days after Majumdar posted his critical article on Russia's supposed "half-baked effort in Syria", Mr. Putin took the wraps off a new cruise weapon, as Campbell noted, launching and successfully hitting a Syrian target from a thousand miles away. Known as the *Kalibr* Cruise Missile, and launched from the Caspian Sea instead of the near-by Mediterranean, Russia displayed surprising munitions sophistication for all the world to witness:

> By mounting a missile strike on Syria from warships nearly 1,000 miles away on Wednesday, the Russian military demonstrated an important new capability... Moscow has said they were *Kalibr* ship-launched cruise missiles, also known as 3M-14s or, in NATO parlance, SS-N-30s. They are a fairly recent addition to an established family of ship-launched missiles that are mostly intended for ship-to-ship or shorter-range missions. The new model, intended for land attacks, is reported to have a much longer range than its siblings, perhaps reaching 1,550 miles.[11]

Steven Lee Myers and Eric Schmitt of the *New York Times* provided as extended assessment of the changing perception of the Russian military in their October 14, 2015 article, "Russian Military Uses Syria as Proving Ground and the West Takes Notice." Their analysis:

> Two weeks of air and missile strikes in Syria have given Western intelligence and military officials a deeper appreciation of the transformation that Russia's military has undergone under President Vladimir V. Putin, showcasing its ability to conduct operations beyond its borders and providing a public demonstration of new weaponry, tactics and strategy...

> Taken together, the operations reflect what officials and analysts described as a little-noticed — and still incomplete — modernization that has been underway in Russia for several years, despite strains on the country's budget. And that, as with Russia's intervention in neighboring Ukraine, has raised alarms in the West.

> In a report this month for the European Council on Foreign Relations, Gustav Gressel argued that Mr. Putin had overseen the most rapid transformation of the country's armed forces since the 1930s. "Russia is now a military power that could overwhelm any of its neighbors, if they were isolated from Western support," wrote Mr. Gressel, a former officer of the Austrian military.[12]

Therefore, the fighting in Syria amounts to more than a mere show of force. It comprises an environment for Russia to battle test its weapons and to learn lessons through deploying its munitions in real world settings. The U.S. is well aware of this intention and its implication.

> American officials, while impressed with how quickly Russia dispatched its combat planes and helicopters to Syria, said air power had been used to only a fraction of its potential, with indiscriminate fire common and precision-guided munitions used sparingly. "It is clear the Russians are already harvesting lessons from the campaign to apply to their other military operations," said David A. Deptula, a retired three-star Air Force general who planned the American air campaigns in 2001 in Afghanistan and in the gulf war. "Essentially," he said, "Russia is using their incursion into Syria as an operational proving ground." [13]

Up to this point in time, the U.S. had assumed it held a measurable advantage in the use of such high tech munitions, incorporating PGMs in a majority of its bombing sorties through the inclusion of a "kit"—an upgrade—that turns dumb bombs into smart ones:

> Since the Gulf War, U.S. forces have greatly increased the percentage of PGMs used during the various wars of the past twenty-five years—particularly since the introduction of Joint Direct Attack Munitions (JDAM). The JDAM—which is a Boeing-built kit—enables U.S. forces to rapidly convert general-purpose bombs into all-weather PGMs at relative low cost. The JDAM—and other weapons like it—have enabled the Pentagon to move to a situation where more than eighty percent of the weapons dropped by U.S. forces are PGMs. [14]

While Russia understandably may have fewer PGM capable weapons, to assume they have next to none has proven to be a very faulty premise. After the terrorist attacks in Paris on November 13, 2015, and the downing of the Russian commercial aircraft over the Sinai Peninsula in Egypt, Metrojet Flight 9268, two weeks earlier on October 31, Russia has taken off the gloves, including the usage of munitions possessing "pinpoint accuracy." In an article published in the week of November 21, 2015, Marina Koren of *The Atlantic* quotes Russian Defense Minister Sergei

Shoigu, "The number of sorties has been doubled, which makes it possible to deliver powerful pinpoint strikes upon ISIL fighters all throughout the Syrian territory."[15] Russia is stepping up its air campaign both in quantity and in quality. Myers and Schmitt commented in their October 14 article that Russia was *flying as many sorties in a single day as the coalition bombers were flying in a full month.* In terms of effectiveness, Russia appears to have what it takes to exploit the opportunities it considers decisive to its national security interests and importantly, to project power within the sphere it considers most crucial to its economic well-being: The oil fields of the Middle East and the pipelines that carry this treasure to its destinations.

WHAT'S OLD IS NEW AGAIN

Indeed, Vladimir Putin is committed to modernizing his military across the board despite limited financial resources that certainly restrict him from acquiring everything on his wish list. Western sanctions, the falling price of oil, and the devaluation of the Ruble, all have played havoc with his checkbook. Consequently, his most aggressive pursuits outstrip his actual purchasing power.

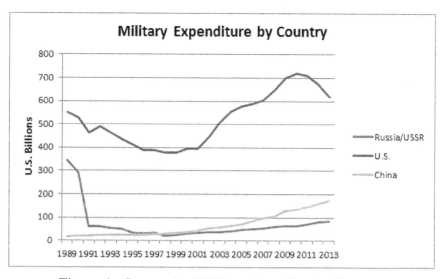

Figure 4 - Comparing Military Spending by Country

Although Russian President Vladimir Putin vowed to fully modernize the Russian military by 2020, it does not seem like an achievable task given the economic decline of Russia. Russia's economic difficulties due to Western sanctions forced Moscow to significantly cut back on some of its ambitious defense projects, including the development of the new fifth-generation bomber, the PAK DA.

Even though Russia is able to successfully carry out small military operations on the territories it is familiar with, such as Crimea and Georgia, a bigger war against a large rival military would be a great challenge to the Russian military that could bring deadly consequences for the Kremlin and its leadership.[16]

Nevertheless, the amount that Putin has spent on improving his military capability grows steadily while U.S. spending peaked in 2010 and is heading downward. According to Master (from the Council on Foreign Relations), Russia has doubled its budget at $90 billion in 2013. China spent twice as much for defense at $188 billion and the U.S. seven times as much as Russia at $640 billion (Masters cites a prominent source: Stockholm International Peace Research Institute—SIPRI). It should also be noted that while Russia and China's expenditures are distinguished one from the other, the increased alliance between the two states – when combined – makes their respective investments much more worrisome.

What do these numbers comprise? These figures include funding for armed services, paramilitary forces, military space activities, foreign military aid, and military R&D. Master points out the same economic challenge Russia faces – dwindling oil and gas revenues. And he concurs that Putin's plan constituted a 10-year $700 billion weapons program, although it is now losing some momentum halfway through its administration. Of particular note are his highest priorities: "strategic nuclear weapons, fighter aircraft, ships and submarines, air defenses, communications and intelligence."[17] In the final analysis, however, whatever shortfalls the reduced funding has precipitated, it has not stopped Russia from dramatically improving its forward deployment well beyond its immediate borders and even beyond its vast regional domain into the Middle East.

Indeed, the fight in Syria has proven that Russia can mobilize its forces quickly. As for the "Fertile Crescent" (extending from Syria through Iraq to Iran), Russia is taking steps to establish itself for the long haul.

> The Russian advancements go beyond new weaponry, reflecting an increase in professionalism and readiness. Russia set up its main operations at an air base near Latakia in northwestern Syria in a matter of three weeks, dispatching more than four dozen combat planes and helicopters, scores of tanks and armored vehicles, rocket and artillery systems, air defenses and portable housing for as many as 2,000 troops. It was Moscow's largest deployment to the Middle East since the Soviet Union deployed in Egypt in the 1970s. "What continues to impress me is their ability to move a lot of stuff real far, real fast," Lt. Gen. Ben Hodges, the commander of United States Army forces in Europe, said in an interview.[18]

CAN RUSSIA COMPETE WITH THE U.S. IN THE MIDDLE EAST?

But has Russia fielded a military team that can effectively compete with the U.S. in the Middle East? Apparently, the answer resounds, "Yes!"

> Michael Kofman, an analyst with the *CNA Corporation*, a nonprofit research institute, and a fellow at the *Kennan Institute* in Washington who studies the Russian military, said that the operations over Syria showed that *Russia has caught up to the capabilities the United States has used in combat since the 1990s.* That nonetheless represented significant progress given how far behind the Russians had fallen.[19] [Emphasis added]

As this book was nearing completion, the *U.S. Office of Naval Intelligence* (ONI) completed an analysis of the Russian Navy, with a particular focus on its activity and capability in the Middle East, entitled "The Russian Navy: A Historic Transition" (published late December

2015). A summary statement from its Executive Summary reaffirms our Navy's awareness that Russia has committed itself to advance its capability in order to compete effectively with Western powers in regions where Russia holds strategic interests.

> On the basis of currently available data it is projected that the Russian Navy will retain its core missions. Although the national defense mission of the strategic and general purpose navy has remained, today's fiscal realities require that the decreased number of major naval platforms be multi-mission capable and armed with the latest capabilities in weapons; sensors; and command, control, communications, computer, intelligence, surveillance, and reconnaissance (C4ISR) systems. Russia has begun, and over the next decade will make large strides in fielding a 21st century navy capable of a dependable national defense, an impressive but limited presence in more distant global areas of interest, manned by a new generation of post-Soviet officers and enlisted personnel.

Anthony Capaccio filed an article on this ONI report, "Russia Deploys Advanced Cruise Missiles in Major Navy Reboot." (*Bloomberg Business*, December 30, 2015) Capaccio notes the key lies in employing the new class of cruise missiles demonstrated in the Syrian theater within the last few weeks. This is the KALIBR-class missile. The ONI report indicates that this new missile is "profoundly changing its ability to deter, threaten or destroy adversary targets." These missiles promise difficulties for our Navy due to their 1,553-mile range, supersonic speed that skims across the war (based on the older but formidable anti-ship missile, the *Sizzler*, with which Chinese submarines are equipped). Given the use of these types of weapons, "big does not mean better" in terms of the ability for Russian assets to stand up to large U.S. Naval platforms. And while this ONI report continues to emphasize that lack of finances constrains Russian plans for modernization and also suggests Russia does not share the same type of "projection of power" as the U.S., the reality is that Russia does not have to able to deploy its Navy globally to have an enormous impact on the West. Just look at Syria.

RUSSIAN FINANCING OF ITS MILITARY

Andrey Biryukov in his article for *Bloomberg*, June 2, 2015, "The Secret Money behind Vladimir Putin's War Machine" cites *Global Firepower*, a service that ranks "conventional" war-making capabilities of 129 countries. He points to the facts showing Russia ranks a strong No. 2 after the U.S., but clearly ahead of China, India, and the U.K. His primary point: Putin is moving his economy toward an intensified "military-industrial complex" (i.e., a war economy), which will shore up the economic weaknesses besetting the nation during the past two years. Biryukov asserts that much of the money going toward defense spending is "black" (off the books). Says Biryukov:

> Putin is allocating unprecedented amounts of secret funds to accelerate Russia's largest military buildup since the Cold War, according to data compiled by Bloomberg. The part of the federal budget that is so-called black – authorized but not itemized – has doubled since 2010 to 21 percent and now totals 3.2 trillion rubles ($60 billion), The Gaidar Institute, an independent think tank in Moscow, estimates.

> Stung by sanctions over Ukraine and oil's plunge, Putin is turning to defense spending to revive a shrinking economy. The outlays on new tanks, missiles and uniforms highlight the growing militarization that is swelling the deficit and crowding out services such as health care. Thousands of army conscripts will be moved into commercial enterprises for the first time to aid in the rearmament effort.

> "The government has two urgent tasks: strengthening security at all levels of society and promoting innovation to end the macroeconomic stagnation," said Ruslan Pukhov, director of the Center for Analysis of Strategies and Technologies and an adviser to the Defense Ministry in Moscow. "The solution to both problems is to intensify the development of the military-industrial complex."

In 15 years, Putin has increased military spending 20-fold. At $84-$90 billion (as itemized in the budget), it exceeds all other nations except for the U.S. and China.[20] The point not to be missed: When considering where the battle lines have been drawn in the Middle East, Russia has demonstrated not only that it can compete with the U.S. military, its increased deployment of its newest weapon systems could mean the *U.S. would have to back away due to the power of the Russian Bear in the region.* And that has dramatic consequences for the U.S. over both the short and long-term. True, the U.S. can project power almost anywhere in the world. Russia, however, only needs to project power in the most critical "choke-point" of the world economy and geopolitical situation. By exerting its influence in Syria, Iraq, and through its partner Iran, Russia now finds itself in the catbird's seat. The U.S. is indeed backpedaling having failed to topple Bashar al-Assad in Syria and having established a reputation for creating chaos after every war in which the U.S. engages in the Middle East (looking at Libya, Iraq, and Afghanistan).

Analyst Hugo Spaulding, published a highly intelligent paper on December 1, 2015, on the web site of *The Institute for the Study of War*, "Russia's False Narrative in Syria" which summarizes the situation critically in respect to the respective moves of Russia and its nullifying what Spaulding sees as productive U.S. to responses to work constructively in the Middle East. While I disagree with him that the U.S. has taken the proper steps to end the influence of ISIS and pressure Assad into resigning, I judge that Spaulding correctly assesses what Russia wants by its intervention in Syria. He views Russia's intention as clearly to end NATO and distance Europe from the U.S.:

> Russia also leverages its air campaign in order to advance its strategic objective to challenge and undermine NATO. Russia's establishment of its first airbase on the Mediterranean Sea represents a direct threat to NATO's southern flank. Russia continues to increase its force projection capabilities in the region by deploying advanced hardware that provides little value in the direct fight against ISIS, including air superiority fighters, its most advanced long-range surface-to-air missile system, and its flagship guided missile cruiser. Russian war-

planes nominally tasked with targeting terrorists have violated the airspace of NATO's southernmost member Turkey on multiple occasions in order to assert Russia's freedom of action in and around Syria. Turkey's downing of a Russian bomber on November 24 represented a direct challenge to these force projection efforts. Moscow has nonetheless used the incident in order to cast [false portray] Turkey and NATO as obstacles to the destruction of ISIS.

Furthermore, the strategy of "divide and conquer", from Spaulding's perspective, remains key to appreciate Russia's approach to influence the nations of the Middle East:

> The Kremlin claims the legitimacy of its intervention in Syria from its alliance with the Assad regime, which it refers to as the country's *"lawful authority."* Russia insists that Western anti-ISIS efforts are illegitimate because Assad has not given the West permission to operate in Syrian airspace. Russia's campaign to pull regional actors such as Egypt, Iraq, Jordan and Israel into its counterterrorism axis is part of a larger effort to weaken Washington's ties with traditional U.S. partners in the Middle East. Russia's decision to establish a joint Iranian-Syrian-*Iraqi* information coordination center *in Baghdad* in the buildup to its air campaign demonstrated its intent to threaten U.S. partnerships and bolster the international legitimacy of the Assad regime under the guise of building a counterterrorism coalition. Russia has frequently expressed its willingness to conduct airstrikes in Iraq if requested by the Iraqi government, an escalatory step that would curtail U.S. operations in the country. Russia may eventually use the pretext of anti-ISIS efforts to expand its regional military footprint to Iraq or Egypt. [Emphasis added]

The issue in the months ahead revolves around how long Russia can play this hand to continue to advance its goals of destroying NATO in Europe and removing all vestiges of U.S. influence in the Levant (the eastern Mediterranean region). Will European nations join with Russia? That has already happened. Will the U.S. determine that "if you can't beat'em, join'em" and buckle under the pressure to allow Russia to lead the coalition against ISIS? Or will it instead attempt to challenge Russia's military presence in Syria? The fact that the U.S. has already opted to favor Iran and the Shi'ites over the Sunnis, thinking them the best choice to stabilize the Middle East (which most analysts now recognize was the motive behind the Iran "Nuclear Deal"), only makes the Russian position stronger. Predictions from several years ago that the U.S. would support Israel in an attack on Iran's nuclear facilities has proven to be a pie-crust promise (easily made, easily broken). Diminished U.S. support for Israel and the recent (although quiet) backing for Iran not only betrays Israel, but also betrays our cherished principle as champion of freedom and liberty, as well as our long-term policy of "making the world safe for democracy." A different principle is clearly now in play: *The U.S. leads the world toward the New World Order.*

This principle sees Russian nationalism as a major obstacle that must be thwarted if the New World Order is to succeed. Of course, many would advance that American nationalism is also an enemy of the NWO. Thus, defeating nationalism both in Russia and the U.S., for advocates of the NWO inside the U.S government – including the advisor Zbigniew Brzezinski – constitutes a much higher priority objective than defeating ISIS. Once we understand the priorities of our Presidents – from Bush 41 to Obama – we may begin to understand the tangled web we've woven in the Middle East.

In the final analysis, for all intents and purposes, Russia's presence has as its goal an ongoing effort to push the U.S. as far out of the region as it can get away with. However we choose to assess its effectiveness, Russia's military possesses sufficient power to exert real pressure on the U.S., causing the U.S.-led coalition to avoid fighting over who controls of the Fertile Crescent. U.S. double-mindedness is apparent to all the players (Iran, Israel, Russia, and Syria). Even if ISIS were defeated, the U.S. already lost the chess match to the Russians. But then, the Russians always have been considered the better chess players.

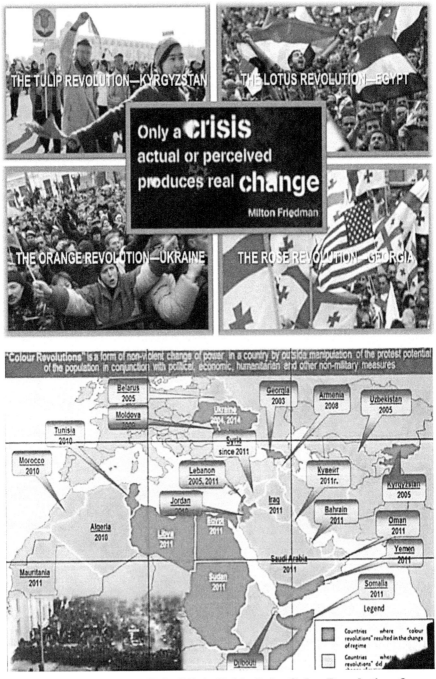

Figure 5 – Is the U.S. C.I.A. Behind the Color Revolutions?

2: WHY RUSSIA PURSUES SUPERIOR WEAPON SYSTEMS

DOES RUSSIA FEEL THREATENED BY THE UNITED STATES?

WHAT DRIVES THE RUSSIA MILITARY EFFORT? PART OF THE MOTIVATION APPEARS TO BE PURELY PRIDE BUT MORE IMPORTANTLY, A DEMONSTRATION TO THE WORLD (AND especially the United States) that Mr. Putin is not just full of bluster, but has achieved meaningful, concrete improvements in military capability. Unlike the U.S., which seeks to establish the New World Order (and is therefore rightly seen as a globalist nation), Putin is an avowed Russian nationalist and leads his country back to its former status of a full-fledged empire. Thus, it would be a colossal mistake to assume his efforts are nothing more than braggadocio or a childish reaction to hurt feelings resulting from Obama categorizing Russia as merely "a regional power."[21] The Russians see themselves as the good guys. They view the U.S. as power hungry. From their viewpoint, the U.S. seeks to impugn Russian strategic partners, creating chaos wherever the U.S. can't dominate in political and economic matters that best serve its interests.

According to Dmitry Gorenburg of CNA, a Virginia-based research institution, "Russian foreign policy appears to be based on a combination of fears of popular protest and opposition to U.S. world hegemony, both of which are seen as threatening the Putin regime."[22] Based upon his participation at a May 2014 Moscow Conference on International Security (MCIS), led by the Russian Ministry of Defense, Gorenburg writes:

> Defense Minister Sergei Shoigu and Foreign Minister Sergei Lavrov, argued that color revolutions are a new form of warfare invented by Western governments seeking to remove independently-minded national governments in favor of ones controlled by the West. They argued that this was part of a global strategy to force foreign values on a range of nations around the world that refuse to accept U.S. hegemony and that Russia was a particular target of this strategy.[23]

As noted in an earlier publication by this author, Moscow asserts that "color revolutions" are a device developed by the CIA to undermine former Soviet satellites and diminish Russia's regional influence. Such covert operations have purportedly been a tactic of the U.S. for decades, but especially so in the past 15 years as highlighted by the so-called "Arab Spring."[24] Certainly, there remains little doubt that since the 1950s forward, covert operations have been the mainstay of the CIA's mission. Tim Weiner's massive study on the CIA, *Legacy of Ashes* (2007), offers more than enough proof that Putin has rock-solid rationale to assume the U.S. will challenge Russia through employing clandestine operations.

IS A GLOBAL WAR FOR NATURAL RESOURCES COMING?

A slightly different take on what drives Putin comes from a Russian military analyst who proposes that the Ukrainian conflict was instigated by the United States with a more specific far-reaching goal in mind. Pavel Felgenhauer asserts the U.S. organized the tensions in the Ukraine to prevent Russia from preparing for a massive global war destined to commence within the next two decades. In February 2013, Felgenhauer cited the chief of the General Staff of Russia, Valeriy Gerasimov, who contended that this "great war" was certainly coming:

> "The so-called resource war. Sometime between 2025 and 2030 the world will face a complete catastrophe with an extreme lack of natural resources such as crude oil, gas, water and everything," Felgenhauer said...

> "In that regard, a world war or a series of regional wars would be unleashed, in which countries and people would fight for resources. And Russia would be attacked from all sides, as we [Russians] have a vast territory and a large variety of resources," the expert noted.

> Due to this, Russia "adopted a program of rearmament to rearm and prepare for this war," according to Felgenhauer.[25]

If it seems that Russia is paranoid, it is. The paranoia results, however, from centuries of attacks by many different opponents on all its vast flanks. Obviously, Russia has been and remains a big target. Its geographical position and its massive resources make it the world's "heartland." As such, it stands destined for endless conflict. It should be no surprise then to the Western world that Russia remains "on edge" – fearing attack from its adversaries.

NATO's top military commander, U.S. Air Force General Philip Breedlove, on April 30, 2015, made a number of relevant statements in his testimony to Congress:

> "Russian aggression is clearly visible in its illegal occupation of Crimea and its continued operations in eastern Ukraine… In Ukraine, Russia has supplied their proxies with heavy weapons, training and mentoring, command and control, artillery, fire support, tactical and operational-level air defenses.

> "We cannot fully grasp Putin's intent. What we can do is learn from his actions, and what we see suggests growing Russian capabilities, significant military modernization and an ambitious strategic intent."[26]

In their new book, *The New Tactics of Global War,* authors Benjamin Baruch and J.R. Nyquist argue that the "reinvigoration of Russia forces" is not happenstance, but the result of 50 years of planning and deception:

> We can see these principles being applied by Russia today, and there is little doubt that the stagnation in U.S. military programs clearly coincides with Russia's sudden "leap ahead." This is decidedly obvious with the upcoming deployment of 10 battalions of S-500 ABMs, the revolutionary new T-14 Armata tank, and the road mobile version of the SS-27 ICBM. The United States does not possess weapon systems comparable to these. The sudden emergence of Russian military superiority should surprise no one. This emergence may not be entirely obvious at the moment of this writing, but awareness of a shift in the balance of power is rippling like a shiver through the capitals of Europe.[27]

GOING NUCLEAR

Much of the Alliance's defensive strategy hinges on anti-ballistic missiles. Russia established an Aerospace Defense Command in 2011. The principle weapon for this network of medium to long-range surface-to-air missiles is the S-400. According to friend and expert on Russian military strategy, J.R. Nyquist, Russia employs over 11,000 such missiles all along its perimeter. Additionally, Russia boasts at least a ten-to-one advantage in tactical nuclear weapons over the United States in the European theater. (Tactical nukes

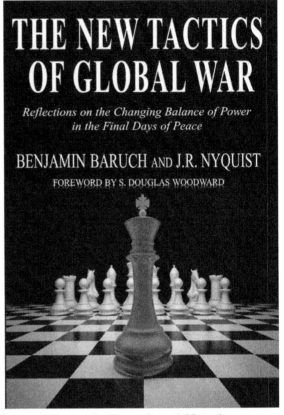

Figure 6 - Baruch and Nyquist,
The New Tactics of Global War

are usually classified as 1 kiloton or less in power, although they may range well beyond this metric. Generally, they are incorporated in artillery munitions and short-range missiles). Russia boasts of an even newer version of this missile, the S-500, which will be a dual-purpose missile. It can be used as an offensive as well as defensive weapon. Because it remains classified as an ABM (a defensive, "anti" ballistic missile), it is not counted in the number of "nukes" Russia possesses.

In my earlier study entitled, *Is Russia Destined to Nuke the U.S.?* I provided a summary assessment promulgated by acclaimed geopolitical and military experts prior to the summer 2015. Just five months ago, it was very difficult to find any academic or journalist who studies Russian geopolitical and military strategy that was willing to admit Russian nuclear capability constituted a serious threat to the United States. I noted in that small book how analysts downplayed Putin's threats to employ nuclear weapons:

> Western commentators that do opine suggest Putin's words are for internal consumption only—meaning that the Russian state doesn't intend to make good on its threat. For them, Putin seeks to create unity within his country through jingoistic language, deflecting the economic hardships the Russian people now face with a collapsing Ruble and dropping oil and natural gas revenues. The real question remains, however, whether experts are too quick to dismiss Putin's rhetoric. In other words, does Putin really need to strengthen his political position by talking tough? Or is another more sinister plan coming to into focus? [28]

No doubt it is a long-standing technique in *realpolitik* to build support at home by talking tough to your rivals in troubled times. Most U.S. Presidents receive higher marks in public opinion polls when we are *at war* or face that distinct possibility. Putin, however, has been popular throughout his "reign" (as Prime Minister or President) and for the most part remains so today. Many analysts believe that his steady drum beat touting supposed CIA covert operations harming Russian interests, leads most Russian citizens to conclude that they have no choice but to stand firm with their leader and project a strong collective profile against American aggression even though it is likely overstated through Russian propaganda.

CHANGES IN INFORMATION ACCESSIBILITY

Regardless of the spin Russian media places on national security issues, there is much greater freedom of information today than there was during the Cold War. Thanks to the Internet, Russian citizens have access to Western media too. There is hardly the same need for "Radio Free Europe" as there was in the Cold War. (On the other hand, RT TV, Russian Television U.S. featured on many cable networks, could be considered "Radio Free America" – supplying Russia's side of the story.)

Therefore, Putin won't stay in power forever playing the "U.S. is the boogie man card" unless evidence is consistently provided proving that the U.S. truly threatens Russia. Likewise, if there are dividends to be distributed from the war economy, at least in part, these must be enjoyed by the Russian populace at large. As the more shrewd analysts attest, moving to a full-fledged war economy may just be the ticket for the Russian people to have their cake and eat it too.

Today, five months after I published *Is Russia Destined to Nuke the U.S.?* expert assessment has modulated appreciably and articles now cite reasons to believe that especially in nuclear armaments, the Russians are at parity or in this area have superior capability to the United States. According to Master of the *Council on Foreign Relations* cited earlier:

> Russia's vast nuclear arsenal remains on par with the United States and is the country's only residual great power feature... Moscow has about 1,500 strategic warheads on deployed intercontinental ballistic missiles (ICBMs), submarines, and heavy bombers. These numbers comply with the so-called New START treaty[29] with the United States, which came into force February 2011. Russia is also believed to have some 2,000 non-strategic (also referred to as tactical, theater, or battlefield) nuclear warheads.

> Russia leaned on its nuclear deterrent as its conventional force languished in the years after the Soviet collapse. NATO's bombing of Yugoslavia in 1999 added to fears in the Kremlin that the U.S.-led alliance might impede Russia's ability to act in the region. Moscow appeared to lower its nuclear threshold in 2000, permitting the use of such weapons in response to major conventional attacks. By comparison, Soviet doctrine reserved nuclear weapons for use only in retaliation for a nuclear attack.[30]

Russia's nuclear weapons are land-based, submarine-based, and given the new KALIBR cruise missiles demonstrated in Syria, can be launched even from "old-fashioned" naval vessels. While the actual numbers of nuclear warheads and delivery systems are notoriously subject to "fudging", the most relevant factors pertain to Russian weapons (precision-guided munitions) which can penetrate U.S. defensive systems and strike multiple U.S. cities; or simply detonate weapons high above the North American continent creating an electronic magnetic pulse (EMP) that knocks out our electrical grid, disrupts our command and control systems, and potentially maims our military's ability to respond. Just this month (December 2015), famous journalist Ted Koppel published a new book called *Lights Out*, documenting the near-certain event of an EMP or cyber-attack on America's so-called "power grid." Says Koppel, "Our points of vulnerable access are greater than in all of previous human history… yet we have barely begun to focus on the actual danger that cyber-warfare presents." [31]

THE MOST STRATEGIC ASPECTS IN WEAPONS SUPERIORITY

Consequently, the issue isn't how many weapons a given nation state has in its arsenal – it's whether a select number of its devices can be deployed in a surprise attack, defeat defensive mechanisms protecting the targeted country, and most of all, whether that nation state stands ready and willing to use these weapons to gain economic or political advantage.

Indeed, as Koppel notes, we must be mindful that only a few nuclear devices exploded on or above American soil could send our economy into a destructive free-fall and increase our vulnerability to all sorts of subsequent attacks, whether carried out by terrorists or official agents of a foreign state. In other words, vulnerability does not come from a "weapons gap" (terminology made famous during the Cold War, e.g., a gap in which the Russians have more nukes than we do) but from *asymmetric* attacks by any number of enemies. Unfortunately, we no longer employ the military advantages leveraged fifty-years ago during the Cold War to threaten our enemies with nuclear attack. Furthermore, in the 1960s if a nuclear bomb were to hit us it would be easy to determine who dropped it. Likewise, another tactic of that time no longer true today: a nuclear war meant firing dozens if not a hundred or more missiles at your enemy.

This is not so in the twenty-first century. The strategic planning of to-day's Russian military assumes that *nuclear weapons can and will be used at some point in the future.* Tactical nukes or limited nuclear strikes can be carried out. The "threshold" for their use has been dramatically reduced. This is because military strategists believe weapons of mass destruction can be "managed" in a highly measured attack. And the source of the assault need not be obvious to those under attack.

That is why the so-called "suit case nuke" comprises such a stealthy threat. A small device that can destroy half-a-city, is an asymmetric weapon. Plus, despite claims to the contrary, the responsible party may not be apparent for days or even weeks after the fact. Neither can the victim of the attack assume they can "respond proportionately". In other words, Islamic terrorists might claim responsibility for a given nuclear detonation creating shock and a great number of deaths in one or more U.S. cities. But the supplier of that explosive device and the planners of its usage could be perfectly cloaked within government buildings half-a-world away in Tehran, Pyongyang, Beijing, or in Moscow.

J.R. Nyquist comments poignantly regarding what constitutes strength and weakness in light of the new tactics of global war:

> Nuclear warfare is not a question of economic power because in one hour you can destroy the economic power of the great-est country in the world by launching nuclear missiles at it. In fact, one nuclear bomb detonated in the stratosphere could trigger an EMP reaction into our power grid, and completely bring to a halt our economic system. Following such an at-tack, the United States would have no economy for a number of months. Therefore, we cannot measure our real strength by our financial or economic power, even if we assume that power is not compromised by indebtedness, which clearly is the case today. [32]

Ivan Eland, a liberal but respected authority on national security inter-ests,[33] pointed out in 2008 that the U.S. should not put its own cities at risk from nuclear attack to protect European states from Russian aggression. From his perspective, the United States has defined "its security as requiring intrusions into Russia's traditional sphere of influence. By expanding NATO into Eastern Europe and the former Soviet Union, the United States has guaranteed the security of these allied countries against a nuclear-armed power, in the worst case, by sacrificing its [own] cities in a nuclear war. Providing this kind of guarantee for these non-strategic countries is not in the U.S. vital interest."[34]

Eland's comment would seem to go without saying. However, the world in which we live today demands we realize our Russian rival seeks to control the geopolitics of our globe to accomplish their nationalist aims. U.S. sentiment to create a "New World Order" is not high on Mr. Putin's agenda. Eland goes further to make his point explicitly clear, which I also find compelling:

> Providing [a] guarantee for these non-strategic countries [be they Eastern European or Middle Eastern] is not in the U.S. vital interest. Denying Russia the sphere of influence in [its] nearby areas traditionally enjoyed by great powers (for example, the U.S. uses the Monroe Doctrine to police the Western Hemisphere) will only lead to unnecessary U.S.-Russian tension and possibly even cataclysmic war.

CAN WE MEET RUSSIA HALFWAY TO AVOID NUCLEAR WAR?

Given these risks, are we willing to find ways to "get along" with Russia, even when it exerts its military might to bully its neighbors such as the annexation of Crimea and the ongoing disruption of Ukraine, where Russia antagonizes the Ukrainian leaders in Kiev (i.e., since most of the Ukraine wishes to remain independent and be admitted into NATO)?

Make no mistake, getting along does not necessarily mean we believe what the Russians tell us. Indeed, the insightful words of J.R. Nyquist stand out at the conclusion of his joint work with Baruch. Nyquist condenses his belief that the policies of Putin are in effect the continuation of a long-term plan equated with *The Perestroika Deception*, which was a book by Anatoliy Golitsyn. Nyquist is widely recognized as an expert on these issues, so I take his opinion, while controversial, quite seriously. It is no small fact that the books Nyquist references were written many years before the collapse of the Soviet Union. In *New Tactics*, Nyquist advises in a conversation between Baruch and this author:

> If you are interested in a detailed picture, a good book is Anatoliy Golitsyn's *New Lies for Old* which should be studied backwards and forwards. This book was published in 1984, and it predicted the fall of the Soviet Union, and it predicted that it would all be organized from the top and would be fake; it would be a controlled collapse, engineered by the Communist Party for the purpose of altering the strategic balance through a bogus capitalist victory over communism. From this we can see that the whole thing was a ruse. Golitsyn made 140 falsifiable predictions and by 1992, almost 94 percent of those predictions had come true. That is an incredible statistic.[35]

> The other person who deserves study today is Jan Sejna. He wrote a book in 1982 entitled, *We will Bury You*. He was one of the top communist officials in the Eastern Bloc, a protégé of Khrushchev. It is enlightening to read his chapter on "The Strategic Plan," in which he describes the takeover of the United States from within and he also describes the faking of the collapse of the Warsaw Pact alliance as part of this strategy, confirming Golitsyn's warnings.

> The other book people should read is the 1987 book by Viktor Suvorov, *Spetsnaz*, paying particular attention to the chapter "Spetsnaz's First World War," in which he describes Grey Terror, an attack on the West by proxy terrorist forces, seeming to have no connection with Russia. These terrorists divert the security forces of the West in advance of a Russian strike.

As I stated above, the actual planners and suppliers of a nuclear weapon detonated in the United States, should it occur in the next decade, could be thousands of miles away when it happens, literally hiding behind walls and figuratively behind vocal terrorists who actually planted the bomb hoping to kill as many Westerners as possible, but who were not the primary party responsible for the attack. Indeed, the challenge we face today is to know who our enemy is. The truth is not so obvious. Therefore, good intelligence has never been more at a premium.

CONCLUSION

The U.S. has trimmed its defense spending considerably over the past four years. It doesn't appear that this downward trend will change unless a Republican is elected President. Back in 2011, Congress decided to trim almost $500 billion in defense procurement and operations over ten years. Things looked very positive for reducing the military budget back then:

> At the beginning of the year, a wave of protests swept away multiple Arab dictatorships. In May, U.S. Navy SEALS took out Osama bin Laden. In June, President Barack Obama announced the impending withdrawal of U.S. troops from Afghanistan. In December, the president celebrated the departure of the final American troops from Iraq, assuring the nation that "we're leaving behind a sovereign, stable, self-reliant Iraq." [36]

Four years later, the tables have turned against the U.S. Our leaders and its military finds itself (1) unable to oust Bashar al-Assad at the head of the Syrian state while bumping up against the Russian Air Force in the war against ISIS; (2) unable to declare victory in Iraq or Afghanistan since a decade of training hasn't made those regimes capable of standing on their own two feet; and (3) exposed to a potential threat of a war with China in the Pacific over "freedom of the seas." All of these issues loom large as 2015 comes to a close. Needless to say, our military stands at a heightened state of readiness.

However, it is not necessarily my position that we require more defense spending. Monies spent *to police the world should be reduced*. Endless fighting in the Middle East needs to be looked at with fresh eyes and detached from policies of previous administrations. Instead, of utmost importance is instituting a foreign policy that recognizes the realities of Russian interests – including a willingness to accommodate its regional priorities to a limited extent. We must also recognize that Muslims living in Islamic nations will continue to resist Western "colonial powers"

57

(Britain, France, and the United States) in our attempts to control the lives of Arabs, Egyptians, and Iranians. Since Churchill carved up the Middle East along arbitrary lines after World War I, Islamic populations have rejected most attempts from the West to secularize their cultures and place "puppets" in leadership positions that support the American agenda. (See Appendix A for an important discussion on this most crucial geopolitical issue). It's time for us to "wise up" by rejecting the globalism foisted upon the world by our Executive Branch and find an approach that respects the sovereign rights of all nations.

On the other hand, this does not mean America can be isolationist, that we can or should "vacate the premises", and then leave the Russians and the native Muslims to their own devices. We are tempted to do this. It is as if upon the first clap of thunder we grow worried. As the storm's intensity heightens, we feel tempted to hide in the bowels of the ship. At the height of the tempest, we are convinced we found the safest spot. The securest place, however, is clearly not to hole up deep within the confines of what a sinking ship.

The U.S. does play a vital part in "keeping the world safe" – most of the world counts on us to provide stability, politically as well as economically. The United States also has a generation-long commitment to protect Israel, a nation that shares our moral and political values and from which we draw most of our religious traditions. Furthermore, we have economic reasons why we need oil and gas in the Middle East to remain available to the nations of Europe and to ourselves until alternatives to fossil fuels are worked into the global infrastructure.

It is not in American interests to allow Russia to capture and manage the oil fields of Iraq, Iran, Saudi Arabia, and the pipelines running from these lands through Syria and on into Europe. Perhaps most importantly, we must recognize that the nature of asymmetric threats to our nation's security altogether changes the rules of the game. We must find ways to reduce hostilities between ourselves and both Russia and China, to build a safer world instead of requiring they fall into line with our agenda for "globalization." Our leaders, whether public or behind the scenes, may think they know comprises "what's best" for the world. This has been true for a century. It has been the U.S. that advanced the League of Nations and then later, the United Nations. But Russia and China see things differently. They assert "democratic globalism" assumes Anglo-American dominance at the center of the world's political and economic decision-making. We can go further and affirm the power brokers we traditionally equate with western multi-national corporations and international bankers establish "global" priorities. Therefore, we shouldn't be surprised Russia and China spurn a secondary role assigned to them implicitly by American policy or by the so-called *shadow government* that exerts real influence on what happens globally, whatever we construe that shadow government to be.

If we do not see our way clear to accomplish these things, the apocalyptic vision of the war of Gog and Magog prophesied by the prophet Ezekiel, will become our inevitable fate. It will not take long before this prophecy comes to pass. Gog will assemble the hordes of soldiers spoken of by Ezekiel that surround the tiny state of Israel and will plot against it until it comes to "cover the land like a cloud" as Ezekiel depicts the attack: *"Thou shalt ascend and come like a storm, thou shalt be like a cloud to cover the land, thou, and all thy bands, and many people with thee."* (Ezekiel 38:9).

If the Bible proves true, and I am certain it will, the fate of Russia, Israel, the United Kingdom, and the United States are all determined by the war about which the great biblical writer Ezekiel prophesies, and which precedes (only by a short span of years) the coming of the Messiah to establish the Kingdom of God upon this earth.

3: AMERICA SPEAKS LOUDLY BUT CARRIES NO STICK

"We are getting to a place where there are very little, if any, options left. This administration has frittered away most opportunities—to the point that I know that they're not going to be in direct conflict with Russia, and Russia knows that."

Senator Bob Corker, Senate Foreign Relations Committee Chairman

REFUGEES AND SYRIAN CIVIL WAR

A S THE SUMMER OF 2015 CAME TO A CLOSE, THE HEADLINES WERE DOMINATED BY THE REFUGEE CRISIS IN SOUTHERN AND EASTERN EUROPE. OVER THE PAST FOUR YEARS, FOUR MILLION SYRIANS fled their homes to refugee camps. During this past summer, at least one million made their way from the Middle East into Europe as a result of Germany opening its doors (and borders) to those who sought to escape the murder and mayhem in their homeland. The stories of trains and buses stuffed to the gills were legion. Families walked hundreds of miles with their little children held tight to their chests, sleeping in the open air of the countryside, and disrupting the highways along the paths to the north. The crisis reached epic proportions.

The horrors of the Syrian civil war were the root cause of this mass migration. Over 250,000 have died from the fighting. Most Syrian casualties, however, were civilians killed by their own government. The regime of Bashar al-Assad massacred thousands of innocents through the indiscriminate use of rifle fire, artillery, bombs, and (probably) even chemical weapons. But the terror in Syria went beyond these heinous acts.

The emergence of ISIS during the past two years exacerbated the violence and death in both eastern Syria as well as western Iraq. The misery in this region knew no borders as these Muslim extremists sought to install a caliphate across Syria and Iraq. Countless numbers have been literally put to the sword by these Sunni extremists. The United States, war weary from over ten years of fighting in Iraq and Afghanistan, reluctantly supplied only meager amounts of air support to aid moderate Muslims who fight against ISIS as well as the Syrian government of Assad. Unwittingly perhaps, the U.S. provided far more military help to ISIS with weapons abandoned at the end of the Iraq War than it did the purportedly "moderate" rebels the U.S. eventually determined were worthy of its support. Rather than sending in American troops, the U.S. government tasked the ragtag and hastily trained "moderate" Syrian rebels to lead the fight on the ground. But by the time the U.S. finally acted with some resolve, the odds the rebels could succeed in their quest dwindled to "one chance in a million". Still, the U.S. government continued to throw money at fielding native ground forces. Since the entry of Russia into the Syrian civil war on September 30, 2015, however, the failure of this program has become plain for all to see, except – most importantly – the Obama Administration.

THE FECKLESS AMERICAN FOREIGN POLICY

Seldom if ever has U.S. Foreign policy been so feckless. Since 2012, the Obama Administration has called for Assad to step down, but to no avail. The U.S. has poured $500 million into training less than 100 fighters to oppose Assad. And now fewer than half-a-dozen of those trainees remain in the fray with the rest killed, captured, or executed. Concurrently, the Obama administration has distanced itself from Israel, the one democracy that had been proven to be an invaluable Middle East ally for decades. Additionally, in July 2015, the U.S. proudly negotiated a deal with Iran that not only enables Tehran to pursue nuclear technology (and likely create nuclear weapons sooner rather than later), it has opened the spigot of $150 billion previously frozen Iranian assets for transfer back to Iran. By so doing, (assuming that Iran's past behavior is a predictor of its future policy), the U.S. Government indirectly became the number one financier of global terrorism. What did the U.S. receive in exchange for inking the Iran "nuclear" deal that our President and his Secretary of State heralded?

- First, a pledge by Iran that they will not pursue nuclear weapons outright even though they can advance their nuclear know-how with minor restrictions.

- Secondly, a public promise they will continue to pursue advances in missile technology without restraint; that way, when Iran does perfect a nuclear weapon it will then have the means to deliver it... "*ballistically*" and with almost no warning.

- Thirdly, verification that Iranian promises not to cheat to be made good by self-inspection (yes, that's correct – they will inspect themselves to verify they are keeping their word). On those nuclear sites Iran doesn't self-inspect, where third parties are allowed in to take a look around, Iran must be given no less than two-weeks' notice before outside inspectors can scrutinize their operations.

It would be easy to hear the laughs and the jeers by alert U.S. citizens if it were not for being drowned out by the cheers of "death to the great Satan, America" and "death to the little Satan, Israel" led in Tehran – cheers evoked by the same Muslim government consummating the deal with Secretary of State John Kerry who (like his boss) seemed oblivious to Iran's obvious *bad faith*. I say *obvious* because many pundits, like this author, chose to take Iranian leaders at their word.

ENTER RUSSIA INTO THE POWER VACUUM

Against this backdrop Vladimir Putin and the Russian military stepped into the Syrian civil war, ostensibly to support its ally – the Assad regime – but implicitly to maintain its valuable warm water port of Tartous on the Mediterranean. The Russians rode into Damascus on a red horse to protect their strongest Mideast ally, the deadly dictator Assad, while safeguarding their own interests there.

The civil war has given Russia the opportunity to make its presence felt in tangible and tactical ways. While under the cover of taking the battle to ISIS, Putin expanded an air force base in Syria with 36 Russian fighters and fighter-bombers, a number of helicopter gunships, and who knows how many "boots on the ground." And don't forget the armored equipment including nine tanks at first report. What was the U.S. response when this occurred? There were several – all of them baffling.

- First, Obama's press secretary lamented that the Russians would bring more instability into the region (which is impossible since the situation couldn't be more chaotic).

- Secondly, an admission that we don't know exactly what the Russians are up to in Syria. One spokesperson for the U.S. government said, "they keep popping up everywhere." [37]

- And then finally a questionable admission: "the Russian presence may prove helpful to quell the growth of ISIS."

These widely varied reactions demonstrated that the U.S. strategy, whatever it was, had broken free of its moorings and was now adrift with no steerage. The Obama Administration forfeited to Russia the initiative to fix a problem it helped cause in the first place.

Indeed, as a reminder, it wasn't that long ago that Putin bailed out Obama who had proclaimed Assad's "moving a whole bunch of chemical weapons around" was a red line that if crossed, would "change his calculus" intimating it would surely bring the wrath of the U.S. military down upon his regime.[38] Assad crossed the line. Obama was frozen in his tracks. John Kerry made an offhand remark which caught the attention of the Russians about how "forfeiting his chemical weapons could resolve the problem with Assad." Fearing that the U.S. was going to commence military action, Putin proposed overseeing the dismantling of the chemical weapon arsenal and Obama leapt at Putin's proposal, keeping the U.S. military out of Syria. In so doing, Obama demonstrated that he could surpass himself and his performance in Libya. Now he would no longer lead from behind. He would not lead whatsoever. He would just "make way". Assad was free to pursue the management of the Syrian civil war his way (including the annihilation of his political enemies, tens of thousands of his own citizens, and inciting a million Syrians to flee the country) with Russia one-step away from locking up the Middle East for its purposes, unchallenged by the U.S. military.

A LITANY OF LOST OPPORTUNITIES

Recapping what the U.S. accomplished during this timeframe: First, Assad continued to ignore the U.S. demand that he step down. With that failure securely under its belt, the U.S. turned its attention away from Syria as well as Iraq to achieve its ill-conceived deal with Iran while concurrently pulling almost all its remaining troops out of Afghanistan. With this action, the U.S. made the Middle East safe for no one except despots, death squads, and tyrants. Obama has insisted the deal stopped Iran from pursuing nuclear weapons. Still unsigned as this book is published, Iran does not appear willing to comply with the terms of the treaty, even though it is tilted heavily in its favor.

Unless a sudden about-face ensues with a plan to reenter the region with a substantial U.S. military force (not just air power, but U.S. "boots on the ground" with essential supporting equipment), it would be correct to say that the U.S. *has backed out of the "fertile crescent."* Today, Russia sells it weapons to Iran, Syria, and lately, even Saudi Arabia who also feels betrayed by its long-term ally, the United States. Russia entrenches itself in Syria more firmly than ever. Its inevitable encore: station additional troops and military equipment there. Indeed, on December 1, 2015, we learned that Russia created yet another airbase in Syria. Lucas Tomlinson, writing for *Fox News*, reported the following:

> Russia has expanded its military operations in Syria to include a second airbase as well as other posts, according to a U.S. official briefed on the latest intelligence from the region – even as President Obama expresses muted optimism that Russian President Vladimir Putin eventually will "shift" his strategy and work with the West.
>
> Moscow's presence has grown to a total of four forward operating bases, including recently added bases in Hama and Tiyas. But the most concerning to the Pentagon is the second airbase in Shayrat which can support fixed-wing aircraft, greatly expanding Russia's capability for airstrikes, which began on Sept. 30. "The Russians are operating helicopters out of Shayrat airport, but they are making [preparations] to land fixed-wing aircraft," another U.S. official confirmed to Fox News.
>
> Shayrat is located 25 miles outside of the Syrian city of Homs, an hour drive from neighboring Lebanon.
>
> Since September, Russia has based its warplanes and helicopters at Basel al-Assad airbase in Latakia, one of the last remaining

Assad strongholds along the Mediterranean coast. While the Pentagon cannot confirm any Russian military jets have landed at Shayrat, there are reports Russia has landed aircraft in the past few hours.

Russia's two other forward operating bases are used to land its attack helicopters employed to defend the Assad regime against Syrian rebels.

But when asked if the move to expand to a second airbase was defensive in nature in case Syrian rebels succeed in destroying the Latakia base, one of the U.S. officials pushed back. "This is an expansion, not a defensive move at all," the official said. He said Syrian rebels were nowhere close to taking the Russian airbase in Latakia.[39]

Recall that these latest military achievements transpire on the heels of Russia annexing Crimea, 18 March 2014. It supported the Russian-speaking Ukrainians in their rebellion in the Donbas region of Ukraine to provide further assurance that Crimea would remain under Russian control. After its total departure from Iraq and near "bug out" from Afghanistan, the U.S. may choose to focus its energies in Eastern Europe, poking Putin in the eye again by continuing to support the western leaning government in Kiev. Western sanctions against Russia remain in place although with only lukewarm support from our European allies, most of whom do not bother paying their dues to NATO either. Meanwhile, Germany slowly moves further away from Washington and closer to Moscow, reasserting itself as Europe's perennial leader even as it underscores its independence from American influence. Both German and Italian leaders enjoy good relationships with Mr. Putin and after the recent terrorist attacks in France, Italy along with France have joined Russia in coordinated air attacks on rebel positions in Syria. In fact, across Europe ties with the U.S. weaken. Only in Northeast Europe do nations there recognize the European Union is a paper tiger, unable to muster a defense against Moscow aggression. Specifically, only Poland and the Baltic states have faith that the U.S. will stand with them against Russia.

Therefore, under Barack Obama, the U.S. can boast that it has simultaneously lost its footing in the Middle East, diminished its prestige throughout most of Europe, while heightening animosity with its Russian rival. Indeed, throughout 2015, Russia has continually amped up its threats to use its nuclear arsenal to counter alleged U.S. clandestine operations – operations that Putin contends threaten the Russian state. What does this harsh talk mean? Most pundits suggest Putin "preps" his people for war against the West.

Syria has taught us just how dramatic the alterations in American foreign policy are. Recognizing the tragedy of the refugees and the thousands who have been killed, Syria stands as a benchmark indicating the United States will be much more selective about where it will exert its influence around the globe. Perhaps reversing the famous quotation of Theodore Roosevelt, we could aptly summarize the shift in American policy with these words: "The U.S. speaks loudly but carries no stick."

Consequently, a failure to act decisively leaves the U.S. facing even greater threats from both radical Islam and a revitalized Russia. Losing our foothold in the midst of the battle for Syria foreshadows dire consequences for our nation. Bible prophecy students recognize what has been transpiring. The battle described in Ezekiel 38-39 – of Gog from the land of Magog – appears destined to commence soon. As 2015 comes to a close with the U.S. essentially neutralized in the Middle East, Russia makes ready to gather up the armies of Islam along with its own forces to launch a massive attack on the one remaining obstacle to controlling all of the Middle East... Israel. The only question now is not *if* but *when* Russia decides to act. The probable trigger event – an Israeli attack on a "nuclear-weapons-capable Iran" – seems a most probable near-term major event that could lead to global war. The hush you hear is the world holding its breath.

HOW THE U.S. AND RUSSIA SWAPPED FOREIGN POLICY

As the Syrian situation settles into a steady state of bombing rebel groups of various shapes and sizes by the uncoordinated forces of Russia and the Western coalition, an interesting and dramatic change has become clear: Russia and the United States have exchanged their respective signature strategies, at least in a very key respect. This "great reversal" is *not* so much the fact that Russia has a clear strategy in Syria while the U.S. strategy there is anybody's guess. While that is certainly true, the "reversal" involves a much more worrisome observation.

Russian policy sees official state governments, however oppressive, as providing law and order. Indeed, law and order prevailed in autocratic Syria until the "Arab Spring" broke out in 2011; then chaos ensued as various terror groups and rebels opposing al-Assad gained strength and began fighting government troops. The numbers were not in their favor. Assad's forces numbered over 300,000. The rebels had only a few hundred. The rebels cried out for help in 2012. Sunnis from Saudi Arabia, Qatar, and the Arab Emirates provided considerable funds to them. But the U.S. dithered around until 2014 unsure whether it should supply weapons to the rebels or not. Although thousands were being killed every week, stopping genocide was not the U.S. policy as it had been in the Balkans under Clinton. It took ISIS' beheading of American citizen James Foley, August 20, 2014, before the U.S. commenced its bombing of ISIS. This did not stop or even slow down the Islamic State as it soon returned to Iraq, took over Mosul, and began to solidify its position there. In the opinion of U.S. Ambassador to Syria, Robert Ford, the U.S. had waited two years too long. In 2014, he resigned his post based on what he perceived as U.S. indecision and broken promises. Ford said that the Syrian people that had clamored for the U.S. to help oust Assad felt betrayed. ISIS proclaimed to those disheartened that the U.S. could not be counted on to support their desire for democracy. ISIS was their only hope. [40]

The uprising of millions of Syrians calling for the removal of Assad was beaten down by Assad's continuous massacre of bullets, bombs, and then chemical weapons. The revolution required people to stoke its fires – but by this time the majority of those people had departed. The Syrians that remained (generally the upper Middle Class and Upper Class) were keen to see peace and tranquility return, even if it meant keeping Assad. Indeed, the Syrians that remained in Damascus had reconciled themselves to needing an autocrat. For its part, Russia had been on the sidelines supplying weapons (along with Iran) to Assad since 2012, but their personnel had not gotten directly involved. This changed in the fall of 2015. Russian bombers began operations at the end of September. Massive air attacks followed. Reports claimed the Russians were completing more sorties in a single day than the coalition was in a full month. As it sent in airplanes, tanks, and naval vessels, Russia demonstrated its presence would serve as the harbinger of law and order – finally providing relief to the traumatized population of Damascus. No doubt it would prop up a dictator that had brutalized its people. But it would bring stability to Damascus and ensure the government of Bashar al-Assad persevered.

By entering the fray of the ongoing Syrian civil war in 2015, Russian policy *would now mirror the cold war policy of the U.S that for 60 years traditionally buttressed authoritarian dictatorships* that overtly suppressed communist revolution (think Vietnam, Guatemala, Chile, and Nicaragua). The U.S. was well known for undergirding fascism through covert CIA operations, suppressing opposition, and jailing political prisoners. Under the banner of protecting democracy in the face of communist revolution, U.S. policy from Eisenhower, Kennedy, Johnson, and indeed every U.S. President, was a no-holds-barred attack on Marxism. By so doing, the U.S. aided these "republics" to maintain some degree of stability, created an economy that favored those who supported the puppet government put in place by the U.S., and safeguarded U.S. corporate interests.

We were often called fascists and for good reason: law and order was enforced by a strong police force and military without consistent regard for human rights, justice, and the rule of law. Civil rights were generally a non-issue for U.S. overseers, whether they operated as diplomats (who may have been covert CIA agents) or staff operating in the stead of USAID (often unwitting supporters of technically unlawful U.S. programs and intrigue). The American public had little idea how unethical and illegal U.S. actions often were. It was all done in the name of protecting "liberty" and making the world safe for democracy.

Nevertheless, it did provide for a semblance of peace and tranquility. And (in most instances) it kept communism from carrying the day in the Western Hemisphere.

WHITHER FASCIST STATES OR FAILED STATES? THE "OBAMA DOCTRINE" UNVEILED

Now, based on what's happening in Syria, it's Russia that has adopted political and military assistance for an authoritarian dictator, arguing that the alternative for Middle Eastern nations can only be anarchy (and not democracy). Based upon U.S. actions during the Obama Administration, the evidence mounts that the U.S. appears to prefer the creation of a *failed state* – and this U.S. policy plays into the hands of Islamic revolutionaries who seek to overthrow tyrannical dictators. Once again, the U.S. insists its actions are motivated for the good of the people, for their rights, for overcoming oppressive leaders, and for supporting representative democracy. But the evidence that the U.S. really accomplishes these goals lacks much credence. What is compelling instead: U.S. support for the "Arab Spring" became a de facto "Obama Doctrine" (i.e., unwittingly create chaos through failed states across the Middle East). The State Department demanded dictators "must go" (e.g., Mubarak, Gadhafi, and Assad). But in each case, when regime change had occurred it only added to the chaos plaguing the Middle East. From Libya to Iraq, U.S. actions fail to substantiate its claims that America had the means to institute peace and prosperity, let alone American-style individual freedoms to the citizens of Libya, Egypt, Iraq, and now Syria.

Now it appears that the U.S. is only left with contrasting approaches that constitute a diabolical choice played out in the politics of our world: Despite its status as the sole remaining global power (a moniker quickly becoming outdated), it must now seek to (1) either back a sociopath strong man at the helm in third world countries who murders his citizens to maintain control, or (2) accept the anarchy resulting from violent radicals who fight among themselves killing one another and murdering civilian bystanders in the process, all in the name of defeating the goals of the opposing world power. Thus, creating democracy in the midst of chaos is not really an option. Strike the shepherd and the sheep scatter. American "nation building" has *morphed into the greatest myth of modern times.*

Vladimir Putin stated his preference without equivocation in his interview with CBS' Charlie Rose October 11, 2015 on *60 Minutes*. In considering what has happened in Libya after the fall of Muammar Gaddafi, it is hard to argue with Putin: "Gaddafi's death was a landmark, but three years later, it cannot be convincingly called a good one. Three years on, **Libya is still as much of a mess as ever. Fighting is split** among Arab nationalists, Islamists, regional militias and more." [41]

In Libya with Gaddafi, in Egypt with Mubarak, or in Syria with Assad, (likewise in Iraq with Maliki and Afghanistan with Karzai, two nations where we have had a huge military presence for over ten years), President Obama's administration has demanded tyrannical, murderous, or just old-fashioned corrupt heads-of-state step down from their posts. Using the imprimatur "establish democracy", President Obama (from my cynical perspective, only superficially) championed values Americans cherish, calling for *reform and personal freedoms* in these troubled lands. The unintended consequences, however, of his approach have proven to consistently throw the Middle East into turmoil, as his loud proclamations and pronouncements (and in many cases, ineffective actions taken too late) have tossed the existing leaders under the bus without ensuring the new bus driver could operate the vehicle. The phoenix does not rise from the ashes – no Thomas Jefferson steps up to bring order to the chaos.

In Syria, however, the price of failure to help the rebellion against the dictator Assad has been the highest so far: 250,000 civilians have been killed during the Syria civil war. Over the past two years, the U.S. has spent $500 million attempting to build an anti-Assad rebel contingent to fight Assad and pressure him out of office – all to no effect.

However, U.S. citizens did get something for their money. Our anti-regime fighters who would supposedly wage war against Assad after first defeating ISIS (the sequence was important and has proven to be exactly backwards), would be our former mortal enemies – Al Qaeda.

WHEN ENEMIES BECOME FRIENDS - AT LEAST "SORT OF"

To the surprise of most Americans, the U.S. supports the Syrian Al-Qaeda – Jabhat Al-Nushra. Along with other "moderates" who are virtually aligned ideologically with Al-Qaeda, they receive U.S. military assistance. All are headquartered alongside each other in the Syria province of *Homs*. Given their physical proximity and their ideological consistency, admittedly it is hard to tell one group from another.

The on-line magazine, *The Interpreter* (which specializes in Russian-translated news "to get the Russian translation right") provided this recap of the players with whom the United States has supplied weapons, despite their deeper-seated anti-American perspective. *The Interpreter* gathered the information below from a trusted independent authority, the *Institute for the Study of War (ISW)*. Below is an excerpt from the full article (emphasis added):[42]

> **ISW:** The groups that control the Talbisa-Rastan rebel pocket north of Homs are: al-Qaeda affiliate Jabhat al-Nusra, Ahrar al-Sham (HASI), and other FSA-affiliated rebel brigades. Unfortunately, we don't have fidelity on what groups exactly were impacted by the airstrikes today [September 30, 2015, when the Russians initiated their bombing of rebel positions]...

> **Interpreter:** Any idea which rebel unit was hit today in Al Lataminah, Hama province? The "FSA" commander told Reuters that his unit was hit, and he had recently received anti-tank missiles from a "foreign power." Any idea what, specifically, they are referencing?

> **ISW:** Tajama'a al-Izza was hit in Al Lataminah. They are an FSA-affiliated **TOW anti-tank missile recipient** that is active in the provinces of Hama, Idlib, and Aleppo. The TOW missile recipients active in northern Syria are believed to receive these anti-tank missiles from the Turkish Military Operations Command (MOC). [Read: NATO through which the U.S. supplies weapons]

> **ISW:** These groups are minimal and are usually rooted out by other rebel brigades in the area. [Read: Al-Qaeda is now a good guy, ISIS is the enemy.]

Interpreter: It looks like a member of *Tahrir Homs* was killed today. Do you know anything about this man or the unit? Do you know the group's ideological leanings?

ISW: Yes, the airstrikes killed Lyad al-Deek of Tahrir Homs today. Harakat Tahrir Homs is technically a Free Syrian Army affiliate, however in 2015 the once "moderate" Free Syrian Army is largely nominal and is not a good indicator of a rebel group's ideological leanings. Tahrir Homs, like a lot of the battle hardened opposition remaining in Homs, *is an Islamist brigade that is a military ally of Syrian al-Qaeda affiliate Jabhat al-Nusra.* The relationship between Nusra and Tahrir Homs with regards to governance was thought of as "uneasy" when Nusra first started to assert itself (and its strict version of Shari'a) in Homs, however *they have likely grown closer as time has gone on and probably are currently participating in joint rebel governance structures together.*

The "net" readers should take away from this account: the Russians began their attacks on rebels supported by the U.S. Those rebels were Jabhat al-Nusra, the Syrian affiliate of al-Qaeda. ISIS was not Russia's primary target – at least according to U.S. media sources. But as time goes on, (and as we will see after the Paris terrorist attacks), ISIS would suddenly become the target of both Russian and Coalition bombing. The U.S charged the Russians misled the world by bombing "friendly" rebels and leaving ISIS be. The Russians could have responded publicly by stating that the U.S. had misled the world by saying the U.S. was fighting against ISIS when its real objective was overthrowing Assad. Neither party came clean on what their real goal was in Syria. And neither dared to admit that they were, in effect, fighting a dangerous proxy war that could likely lead to a global conflict.

JUST HOW POWERLESS IS THE U.S.?

Barbara Star, pentagon reporter for CNN, reports that the supply caravan to Syria continued into October, 2015: "U.S. military cargo planes gave 50 tons of ammunition to rebel groups overnight in northern Syria, using an air drop of 112 pallets as the first step in the Obama Administration's urgent effort to find new ways to support those groups." [43] *The Daily Beast* also confirms CNN's facts concerning the ongoing support for the questionable allies, pointing out the "investment" to supply weapons continues despite their magnificent ineffectiveness:

> The rebels attacked by Russian forces on Wednesday and Thursday were in western Syria, alongside al Qaeda affiliates and far from any ISIS positions. That suggests the rebels were not there to fight the self-proclaimed Islamic State, as the Obama administration called the top priority. Instead, they were battling the Assad regime as part of a still-active CIA program for rebels which has run in tandem with the disastrous and now-defunct train and equip Pentagon program. [44]

The Daily Beast confirms the grim situation for U.S. policy in the region in the article, "The U.S. Admits We can't Protect Syrian Allies from Russia's Bombs":

> The Obama administration has emphasized that its main fight is against ISIS, but since 2011 it has been calling for Assad's negotiated "transition" from power. The administration realizes that it's in a much stronger position to facilitate that transition if it underwrites the application of mild to moderate military pressure on Damascus—not enough to topple the regime but enough to keep it on the defensive. Russia, unsurprisingly, has decided to rob the U.S. of that leverage by attacking the anti-regime rebels. And Putin has calculated, *with good reason,* that the U.S. will do little to nothing to defend these proxies from Russian bombs. [45]

"With good reason" as in "the U.S. does not want to start World War III." *The Daily Beast* article continues with an assessment of how mired in the mud the U.S. is when it comes to doing anything about Russia and its military adventure in Syria:

> To even threaten to take action against Russian forces now would be perilous as the U.S. has opened talks with Russia about "de-confliction," referring to crafting military methods to protect each country's pilots and forces on the ground from being struck. On Thursday, Pentagon officials held an hour-long video conference call with their Russian counterparts in what Pentagon spokesman

> Peter Cook called "initial steps."
>
> Cook repeatedly refused to answer whether the U.S. would com
> to the aid of either CIA-vetted or U.S. military-trained Syrian re-
> bels, calling the prospects of Russian airstrikes "hypothetical,"
> even after other government officials had confirmed such attacks
> a day earlier and reports from rebels made clear what was hap-
> pening. [46]

This leaves Syria to face one of two unthinkable choices: accept Assad's authority and return to an autocracy of death, or allow ISIS to install its cut-throat caliphate throughout Syria after it routs the competing rebel groups and chases the U.S., France, and the rest of "the Coalition" away.

Likewise, the U.S. may also have only two unthinkable alternatives: (1) admit defeat and accept a Russian counter-revolution that eliminates ALL opposition to Assad (while praying it becomes another intractable situation for Putin's Russia, i.e., "Afghanistan"); or (2) determine it will declare all-out war on Syria and ISIS simultaneously, working in concert with Al-Qaeda's al-Nusra and other Islamic groups who hate America but hate Assad more. Such an approach would not only be unsavory to the war-weary American populace who have seen enough fighting against Al-Qaeda and the Taliban, it would be disastrous to take on Russia in this region. No American who understands the military parity Russia has achieved in relevant military capability, hopes to directly confront Russian air power. To do so could risk a nuclear exchange, not just using tactical "nukes" but strategic "ballistic" missiles as well. And that outcome would be inevitable if the U.S. chooses to venture down that path.

What should we do? As Robert Ford the former American Ambassador to Syria said in a *Front Line* documentary on the Syrian civil war broadcast on May 26, 2015: "We waited too long to act. There are no good op-tions."

WHEN ALL ELSE FAILS – DECAPITATE THE HEAD OF STATE

Looking elsewhere for other more improbable alternatives: the U.S. and its half-hearted coalition of European nations through NATO could in-

Russia through sterner sanctions. Or perhaps thinking
of the box, we might attempt the assassination of Putin.

...inker, Paul Craig Roberts apparently along with some
proposed this may be the only viable option available to New
...orld Order advocates (that enigmatic label often affixed to – I argue
rightly – many U.S. leaders, including both elected and appointed officials
at the highest levels as well as advisors behind the scenes):

> According to the former Assistant Secretary of the Treasury under
> Ronald Reagan, Paul Craig Roberts, Putin is in great danger of
> being assassinated. His role in exposing the dark workings of the
> elites has been so clear that the powers that be may decide to take
> him out just as they did with John F. Kennedy.
>
> In a recent interview [October 16, 2015][47] on the Alex Jones
> Show, Roberts said that in addition to trying to assassinate Putin
> the controllers will continue to persecute whistleblowers and any
> other kind of dissident that dares oppose the agenda of the
> elites. "I think Putin is in substantial danger of assassination,"
> Roberts said. "I hope he stops walking around the streets unpro-
> tected," said Roberts. [48]

Consider this additional "fringe" analysis from *The Real Agenda News*, an
alternative news and opinion source to the mainline media's all-too-
frequent role of supplying U.S. policy propaganda:

> Before speaking at the United Nations last month, Vladimir
> Putin was frank on a television interview where he said the U.S.
> had to "rise above the endless desire to dominate the world".
>
> In a news conference that took place back in earlier,[49] Putin ex-
> posed the truth behind the rise of terrorist groups in the Middle
> East and Northern Africa, where according to him, *the United
> States had helped arm and train groups allied with Al-Qaeda in
> Libya, Syria, Iraq and Afghanistan.*
>
> Putin's statements about the role of the US in the creation of ter-
> rorism in the Middle East went unanswered by the Americans.
> His multiple calls and offers to sit down with the Americans to
> negotiate the terms of a peace agreement in Syria, as it happened

in Ukraine, have also been ignored by western leaders.

In his speech at the UN, Putin doubled down on his challenge to the status quo and said that the world could not afford to continue tolerating the current state of affairs.

Back in 2014, Herbert E. Meyer, a former CIA official, suggested that the US should deal with Putin's role in Ukraine by taking him out through assassination. Meyer said that if Putin was too stubborn to acknowledge that his career was over, the only way to get him out of the Kremlin was feet-first, with a bullet hole in the back of his head."

If you think that the crisis in Ukraine and the military crisis in Syria have not been enough to bring about a new world war, wait and see what will happen if the US, through any of its secretive intelligence organizations even attempts to assassinate Putin. [*Emphasis added*] [50]

And, of course, assassination of foreign leaders has been against U.S. law for several decades and something that the CIA, at least officially, cannot do. If prior experience teaches us anything (specifically, CIA Director William Casey's attempt to assassinate the head of Hamas in Lebanon during the 1980s), the U.S. would have to ask a huge favor of Israel's Mossad to do the dirty work. Needless to say, in more ways than one, that would take *some nerve* given the present state of U.S.-Israeli relations.

FACING THE MUSIC

So it is that making mostly half-hearted choices in formulating its Middle East policy, the U.S. now finds itself not just with its pants pulled down, it has become apparent that it has no coveralls at all to hide what amounts to its most glaring foreign policy snafus at any time over the past six decades. At the very least, the current administration failed to understand the geopolitical principles established almost 370 years ago with the "Peace of Westphalia, 1648). Sovereign states are to be respected. Furthermore, to avoid war there must be balance of power in any region where conflict seems likely. When the U.S. pulled virtually all of its forces out of Iraq, it created a vacuum that Russia was only too happy to fill. (It would be akin to the U.S. pulling its 40,000 troops out of Korea, troops that stifle the aggression of North Koreas dictators and keep their military in check.) No such Western "block" now exists in the region to dispel Islamic revolution and stifle Russian adventurism in the region. Obviously, because of world opinion against it, Israel is not free to act against its unfriendly Islamic neighbors nor is it capable of dealing with Putin's military machine should it decide to move many more military assets into Syria, Iraq, or any other nation state in the region.

Nevertheless, the White House won't face the music or acknowledge the military disadvantage the West (especially the U.S.) now experiences:

> While there was plenty of criticism from the Republican side, there were no ideas on how the U.S. could proceed—Republicans said that the Obama administration had missed opportunities to help bring the long Syrian civil war to a close.
>
> "I don't even know what to say," said Senate Foreign Relations Committee Chairman Bob Corker. "We are getting to a place where there are very little, if any, options left. This administration has frittered away most opportunities—to the point that I know that they're not going to be in direct conflict with Russia, and Russia knows that."
>
> Added Sen. Jim Inhofe, previously the top Republican on the Senate Armed Services Committee, "The answer is not 'Go after Russia and start World War III.' I just don't know what the [solution is] – that's what we're working on now." [51]

BACK DOWN OR ESCALATE – PICK YOUR POISON

Thus, the U.S. seems left with little choice but to pick its poison: (1) Withdraw from northern Middle East "the fertile crescent" countries and give them over to Russia who will deal with ISIS (from Iran through Iraq to Syria) stabilizing the region by its decisive military dominance; (2) continue to fight a proxy war to buy time in which we cautiously *support Al-Qaeda* and the "moderate" Syrian rebels who align with them supplying only modest weaponry that cannot win against the Russians, or (3) elevate the military confrontation with the Russians to force equally negative alternatives back upon Putin – and attempt to regain some lost ground.

On the other hand, what would the unsavory choices be for the Russian leader? One option: retaliate against U.S. military aggression by intensifying his own. Option two: back down and retreat completely lest he face the dilemma of starting World War III. However, to the whole world and especially his countrymen, if Putin selected this option he would be like a dog with his tail tucked between its hind legs, forced to return to his mat in Moscow and dream about what could have been. For Russia and Mr. Putin, the initiative would be lost for a decade or more.

Therefore, it appears the world stands at the precipice of a black chasm, a monumental moment of gravest danger: that a U.S. – Russian "confliction" (*read* "stare down" or "face-off") threatens another world war akin to Berlin in 1961 or the "Missiles of October" (i.e., the Cuban missile crisis) of 1962. Nikita Khrushchev didn't survive those iconic Cold War foreign policy failures. The Kremlin got rid of Khrushchev just as it would Putin if he backs down and flinches first in this WWIII brinkmanship. No doubt the Russian Prime Minister knows this would be the consequence of a failure to stand firm.

To this analyst schooled in Bible prophecy: since neither power – the U.S or Putin – can ill afford to consider the consequences if they shrink from the conflict over Syria and ISIS, all of these unthinkable options mitigate against resolution through any manner of diplomacy. In short, the options intensify the probability of the Ezekiel 38-39 conflict, the *Battle of Gog and Magog.* This prophetic war, if Russia proves to be Gog, will lead the ultimate archenemy of Israel to come against it, being Gog's last remaining real opposition to total regional dominance and a return to the status of global superpower.

It should already be clear to most readers, in making a deal with Iran, the U.S. only achieved a delay to an inevitable conflict. Russia and the Shiites dominated by Iran, Iraq, and Syria (and Shi'ite Yemenis on Saudi Arabia's southern border) will join together to fight against a consortium of strange bedfellows: Israel and Saudi Arabia. Why not the U.S.? The United States (and the United Kingdom) may be attacked just ahead of this Middle East assault against Israel and the Saudis to neutralize Western involvement. As we will describe in detail later, Gog and its Islamic confederates may elect to strike the U.S. and the U.K. by surprise. Israel will be virtually alone with no superpower to defend it other than the God of Israel.

To conclude: there have been serious U.S. – Russian conflicts before, but never has direct confrontation been any more likely than today. To be sure, Obama is not Kennedy and Putin is not Khrushchev. Obama and Putin are motivated in varying ways and perceive the hand they have to play quite differently than the hands played out during the Cold War of the early 1960s. But what comprises the greater risk today involves the belief that the threshold of using nuclear weapons lies much lower than it did a half-century ago. Nowadays, military leaders have begun to believe that nuclear weapons are "manageable" and can be brought into play and detonated when deemed advantageous or in the event of an inescapable existential threat. Consequently, all the alternatives set before world leaders are just as deadly as they were fifty years ago; however, they are now much more applicable because many of these leaders no longer consider their use abhorrent.

The alarm clock triggering the bomb we call World War III continues to tick away. It's almost time for the America President and his Russian counterpart to pick their poison – and the rest of the world will live (or die) with the consequences of their choices.

4: OUR MISGUIDED MOTIVES IN THE MIDDLE EAST

"The Obama team contends that Iran will be a more *reliable partner* (Obama used the word "responsible") in stabilizing the Middle East than Egypt, Saudi Arabia, Kuwait, and Jordan."

Herbert London, November 2015

THE U.S DOESN'T REALLY WANT TO DESTROY ISIS

AMERICAN CITIZENS RIGHTLY SUPPOSE THAT OUR PRESIDENT AND HIS ADMINISTRATION WOULD DO EVERYTHING IN THEIR POWER TO ELIMINATE THE THREAT OF ISIS IN THE MIDDLE EAST. Tragically, for misguided reasons, this is simply not the case.

The top priority in today's U.S. geopolitical and military strategy for the Middle East constitutes a very different and ill-advised motive. *President Obama's stated goal: seek regime changes across the board, eliminating the old autocrats – from the late murderous Muammar Gaddafi to the heinous president of Syria, Bashar al-Assad.* His priority is not to destroy ISIS, even though three years ago his stated intent was to "degrade and destroy them." As far as ISIS is concerned, President Obama's plan has at best "evolved" to allow ISIS room to maneuver so that it, along with other rebel groups will keep the pressure on Assad. Taking a step back to gain further perspective, we can conclude that the core tenets of U.S. strategy to bring peace to the Middle East is to eliminate the old order which we once fervently supplied and supported with our foreign aid, military technology, and covert operations conducted by our special forces.

Why would Assad's resignation take precedence over destroying ISIS? To understand this motive, we must come to grips with the real reason why the U.S. has attacked ISIS half-heartedly for so long, (enabling ISIS to carry on its revolution of terror). At a deeper level Washington's strategy owes to the fact the U.S. seeks to weaken Russia's hold on the Middle East and to dampen its hope to reestablish the Russian empire. By the

81

U.S. crippling Assad's rule, Russia would no longer have its Syrian base of operations in Tartous, on the Mediterranean. Without the threat of Russia shoring up the predominantly Shia northern quarters of the Fertile Crescent (Iran, Iraq and Syria), at minimum the U.S. could continue to keep the area in disarray and diminish (if not dismantle) any particular force from getting too much strength and threaten the oil supply chain that keeps the home fires burning.

To push this analysis a bit further, Obama has operated under an assumption that Iran is the natural leader of the Middle East. It is the only nation within the region he believes that has a chance to remain stable and bring that stability to the region. The U.S. must reinforce the borders established by Churchill while eliminating the old guard America presidents propped up in decades past, allowing Iran to bring the Middle East to order. That is why the Iranian nuclear technology deal inked on July 14, 2015,[52] was so crucial to U.S. strategy – and why the American public has never been allowed to see behind the curtains to appreciate the bigger, longer-term plans in play.

WHY OBAMA DID THE IRAN DEAL

Obama's perspective on "how to solve the Middle East" is well summarized by Herbert London in his November 25, 2015 article published on the web site of *Family Security Matters*. London is a Senior Fellow at the Manhattan Institute and the President of the London Center for Policy Research and thus, a highly qualified intellectual to advance this assessment.

> From a perspective that is coming into focus, President Obama and his colleagues see themselves as the Sykes and Picot of the Middle East. That is to say, like members of the British and French foreign offices in 1916 who drew lines in the sand creating states out of the dismembered Ottoman Empire, President Obama regards the nuclear deal with Iran as a way to redraft Middle East geography and, simultaneously, have the U.S. withdraw from the region.
>
> If Iran is in possession of nuclear weapons – a pathway created through the "deal" – it becomes the regional "strong horse," a

condition that justifies U.S. withdrawal. While there is the recognition Sunni nations will object to this hegemonic status for Iran, the Obama team contends that Iran will be a more reliable (Obama used the word "responsible") partner in stabilizing the Middle East than Egypt, Saudi Arabia, Kuwait, and Jordan. [53]

London asks why Democratic officials presume to imbue Iran with this much power. The answer appears to be multi-faceted. They believe:

- Persian Shia are better prepared and more stable that the Sunni-dominated nations in the region.

- President al Sisi of Egypt, while popular, remains a target of the Muslim Brotherhood.

- The House of Saud is considered to be in disarray with King Salman aging. Succession is not obvious nor automatic. A dramatic change is coming and no one can predict what change will mean to Saudi Arabia.

- London asserts that Jordan, led by the Hashemite family and its King Abdullah (although highly impressive to Westerners), could be running out of time and internal support. ISIS remains a big threat sitting on Jordan's border.

However, Iran is no oasis in the desert and therefore, many are right to criticize the guiding premise of Obama's Middle East policy.

> That there is instability in the three leading Sunni nations does not detract from the problems Iran faces as well. Twenty-percent of the population over 15 are drug addicts. Fertility levels have collapsed. Chlamydia infections rates, as David Goldman points out, are three times the worldwide average. By any objective measure Iran is a civilization in decline, one might even say one that is dying… While [his] calculus is probably wrong, it nonetheless offers President Obama his dream of extricating the United States from the Middle East. [54]

London believes that Obama sees Israel as a nuisance to his broader strategy. He speculates that the President would rather leave the Israel issue to the U.N. to debate in order to distance the U.S. from the "Israeli problem" and what has become a "tar baby" for U.S. foreign policy.

With this as a plan, the Iran deal from Obama's perspective makes sense even if it is entirely one-sided. The U.S. has justification for withdrawal; the president can concentrate on his plan to extend government influence at home and the U.S. can channel foreign policy through the United Nations. Yes, this is a different America and a very different world. [55]

OUR STRATEGIC PRIORITY WHICH GUIDES POLICY

However, the highest priority above all others in the Middle East remains for the United States to ensure that the economies of the Western world, and especially the U.S., are intact. This is an obvious, undisputed fact. There are other goals that may be in play, many which fall into the category of conspiratorial thinking. Such motives would include "fan the flames of conflict to keep the military-industrial complex humming along" or "control global politics to continue pushing toward the New World Order" and its implied one-world government. While these motives are speculations that many hold to be true (and I believe they comprise real aims of the power players whether they be corporate or financial), most secular sources and cynics sardonically castigate such thinking. Nevertheless, whether such motives have substance or not, the majority of experts concur with the overarching economic priority guiding U.S. policy: keep the oil flowing.

The popular maxim for several decades (specifically since Watergate) reminds us that to uncover the truth *you must follow the money*. In the Middle East, however, a more specific method to discern what matters most is to follow the pipelines – oil and gas pipelines that is. My friend Derek Gilbert, in a recent radio show in which I was his guest, pointed out to me a highly relevant fact that discloses another probable ulterior motive for the current conflict. Some Middle East leaders along with Russia envision a new gas pipeline to Europe, passing through Syria, then under the waters of the Mediterranean, bypassing Turkey (a NATO member). Russia's presence in Syria guarantees this revised pathway. Therefore, as I was quick to point out to Derek, we can see that the situation is much more "grey and not black and white." It is not that that the U.S. plays the bad guy and Russia the good guy. Both have their own self-serving goals. When cited by political leaders, moral issues become smoke screens for public consumption. The authentic dynamics affecting the geopolitics of our world (humanly speaking) are economic and political.

Russia's intrusion into the Syrian civil war changes the equation. One reporter in the region indicated that Putin's military has done more to decimate ISIS capability in three weeks than the U.S. had done in 3 years. How could that be? It isn't just because Putin wanted to strengthen his military base in Syria and keep his thumb on the pulse of the region. No, it must be much more than that.

Most analysts suggest Putin senses the "Arab Spring" now rages much too close to home for his comfort. He has grown strongly motivated to disperse the revolutions and the rebels in his Muslim provinces so they don't come calling upon Moscow. Putin rightly worries that Islamic revolution could spread not just onto his doorstep, but also inside his very own house. Terrorism comprises a proximate threat to Russia. He must deal with it within his own country far more than the United States does, despite the ongoing tensions terror causes here.

We can quickly surmise that Moscow's presence comprises a nationalist agenda. Russia wants to corner the market on oil and gas to control oil pricing. After all, over 52% of Russia's revenues (for its government) come from the sale of oil and gas. Driving prices upward could revive their economy, restore the Ruble to a solid currency, and put the West at an enormous disadvantage. To do business, metaphorically speaking, the West will have to kiss Putin's ring. Russia's move into Syria was obviously motivated for more reasons than to give the Russian military some firing practice (although pundits believe Putin wanted to put his military prowess on parade). It must be underscored that *both Washington and Moscow contend vehemently that they own the moral high ground in their respective actions in Syria. The reality is that neither does.* Moral arguments justifying policy are misleading, misguided, and ultimately immoral themselves because they are used to cloak the real reasons our leaders take the actions they do. Recalling the unembellished words of the rock group, *The Who*, the people, to whom these governments are accountable, "won't be fooled again."

A WATERSHED MOMENT "IN THE COURSE OF HUMAN EVENTS"

Given these new realities, Saudi Arabia should be feeling increased pressure because the Russian bear is breathing down their necks. Is the House of Saud, the monarchy so long an ally of the U.S., the next autocratic government to go? Is Saudi Arabia losing its grip on the world oil supply? To be sure, the Saudi princes must wonder just how soon Putin's military might come calling, eyeing their most prized possession: namely, their still oil-infused but otherwise worthless sands. Clearly, Russia's reemergence in the Middle East does not constitute just one of those little coincidences that the proverbial "man behind the curtains" sternly advises us to ignore. As Derek said when we spoke on his radio show, it may be time for the men in Mecca to pack and put the "for sale" sign out in their Kingdom's courtyard. In response, I said this development in the Middle East *constitutes the most important event in global politics since the Korean War*. It stands out more vital than Vietnam, more at the crux than the Cuban Missile crisis, and more far-reaching than any foreign intrigues in which America has played a part. *It is a watershed moment. The world has forever changed.*

The Petrodollar was based upon America securing the safety of the House of Saud through its military in exchange for Saudi Arabia's commitments to keep the oil flowing, insist that only the U.S. Dollar would be the currency to buy and sale oil on the world market, while also influencing OPEC to keep the price of oil within a range that the U.S. could tolerate. But with this U.S. administration's support for the overthrow of autocratic Middle Eastern regimes (of which Saudi Arabia is yet another), the House of Saud may have decided that they can no longer count on the U.S. The strong tie between Saudi Arabia and the United States appears more threatened day by day as 2015 comes to a close.

WHY LIBERALISM WILL BE OUR UNDOING

In summary, most Americans have missed the meaning of the carefully selected words within U.S. officials' public statements, indicating it has no intention of destroying ISIS, only "containing it." The most recent terror attacks in Paris could, in Obama's words, "change his calculus." But unless the political situation changes dramatically, Washington has no intention in either degrading or destroying ISIS as it once pledged. Presumably we selected our political and military approaches because we knew it would take boots on the ground to eliminate Assad and his army – and we didn't want to go down that path again. The "calculus" was understandable, but it was a giant failure to lead. The failure in the Iraq War reigns in the memory of Americans. And President Obama, fearing for his legacy, made politically calculated decisions that achieved too little, too late. The consequences of his choices will live with us for many years to come.

No doubt the U.S. does not have a stellar record lately in making good choices and picking the right dog in the fight. It would have helped if we had made the tough choices we needed to make three to four years ago, to keep a sizable contingent in Iraq to quell the inevitable uprisings surely destined to come. But we choose to abandon our post. We denied the wisdom of 370 years of geopolitics and forgot its core axiom known as the "balance of power." For some reason, we could see it in Korea where we continue to maintain 40,000 troops; but we couldn't see it in the Middle East. Now it's time we pay for our failure to learn history's lessons and our institutions' money-motivated approach to realpolitik. The unintended consequences are momentous with millions of refugees (many of them highly agitated Muslims) streaming into Europe and eventually to the United States seeking freedom and some measure of prosperity. We can't blame the vast majority who come looking for a better life for themselves and their children. But why are the Western "liberal" governments opening their doors so easily? Is it compassion? Perhaps. There is at least some smattering of humanitarian motivations, certainly not driven by Judeo-Christian principles, but by utopian notions – the classic characteristic of liberalism. However, in Germany's case, inviting the immigrants into their country likely hopes to fix a demographic problem of too few young people among an aging population in a socialist state committed to "social security" and benefits for the unfortunate. Of course, what frightens the cautious is the fact that Westerners have opened the doors for all manner of refugees, apparently with limited (or no) screening and background checks. The flood of humanity will not be easily abated. The United States, thanks to this administration's inability to enforce border controls and Congress' unwillingness to pass immigration reform, will also facilitate these movements whether legal or not.

"Give us your tired, your poor, your huddled masses yearning to be free." A wonderful guidepost, emblazoned on the Statue of Liberty, which characterizes what's best about our republic. Unfortunately, this maxim assumes a moral character no longer living in the hearts of many who come to live among us. The consequences are vast. The politicians fight over whether we can accept "three-year old orphans" when this cloaks the reality that ISIS terrorists lurk within the migrating masses as surely as they will say "Allahu Akbar" when they kill unsuspecting Americans.

Liberals seek to "guilt" Americans into accepting refugees who were made into unofficial exiles by massive failures in this administration's foreign policy in Syria since 2011. The public should resist this guilt trip. The terror of Paris on November 13, 2015 (which we will discuss next) will no doubt soon be repeated elsewhere in Europe and here in the States. Terrorists' slipping into Western countries through the torrent of refugees comprises an all too obvious strategy. Even House Democrats couldn't stomach the idea and rejected the President's plan in November 2015, to accept 100,000 Syrian émigrés.

Thus, our time for confronting Islamic terrorism "as a way of life" is almost here. It won't be pleasant and one day in the not-too-distant future we will wonder not only why we didn't see it coming. We will contemplate why we made it so easy for the "unassimilated masses" to enter our society with violent and rogue terrorists who hid in their midst.

In conclusion, the U.S. made the immoral decision to support Al-Qaeda to fight ISIS, and target ISIS before Assad, thus assuring that most Syrians would have little choice but to flee both. This wasn't making the best out of a bad situation. U.S. policy made a bad situation much worse. The barbaric deaths of hundreds of civilians, including many non-Muslim women and children, as well as the destruction of priceless historical artifacts in cherished ancient cities, have become the signature trademark of ISIS.

From a biblical perspective, ISIS will soon be judged for its gruesome murders. The U.S. (and Russia) will be judged one day for their respective complicity in allowing the disenfranchised and helpless to be annihilated so that their particular political ends could be achieved. Indeed, we know that *Babylon* (used here as a symbol of the world's economic system) trades in slaves and the souls of humankind (Revelation 18:13) and carries the blood of the saints on its hands (Revelation 17:8, 18:24). The day of reckoning will surely arise – and that day may only be months or weeks away. Judging by what happened in Paris on November 13, 2015, some of that reckoning may be underway already.

Figure 7 - Terror in Paris, November, Friday the 13th, 2015

5: WHAT LAY BEHIND THE PARIS TERROR ATTACKS

"The Gulf monarchies actually seem to believe that Iran's expansion
and stronger foothold are more dangerous than the success
of the self-proclaimed Islamic State."

Fyodor Lukyanov, Editor, Russia in Global Affairs

AMERICAN ARROGANCE AND THE TERRORIST CHALLENGE

THE TERRORIST ATTACKS IN PARIS ON FRIDAY, NOVEMBER 13, 2015, ARE NOT RANDOM. THERE IS A PRIMARY REASON WHY THEY HAPPENED. SPECIFICALLY, IT OWES TO THE "CONTAIN BUT NOT DEFEAT" strategy against ISIS. Western nations, led by the U.S., deserve considerable blame. We consciously decided not to destroy ISIS, but to merely "keep it under control." At the root of this strategy looms an arrogant, deeply held belief among the American political establishment that we are the only remaining superpower in the world. At first, this observation may seem to be a stretch. So how can this author connect the dots from the terrorism in Paris to Middle Eastern policies of the West?

From all the facts surfaced thus far, ISIS carried out the attacks and the blood of many stains their hands. This was no false flag operation. ISIS hates western culture and seeks *jihad* against the infidels. At this time, expert sources believe ISIS planned and carried out the highly organized attacks through immigrants entering France or Belgium some time ago and because of at least one Syrian jihadist hiding amidst the recent refugee flood into Europe. As a result, it is no surprise that western powers, especially France, have doubled-down in their fight against the ISIS caliphate and indirectly, Bashar al-Assad, the wobbly head of what's left of the Syria state. However, will Western powers alter their overall strategy for the Middle East? It seems unlikely because to do so would require a direct confrontation with Russia in the Fertile Crescent. There are many moving parts churning away in Syria right now. It isn't likely in the near-term however, that World War III will emerge from the tumult. Over the long haul, however, that may be exactly what happens.

The editor of *Russia in Global Affairs*, Fyodor Lukyanov, (posted on the Huffington Post), made a number of salient points in his article of November 24, 2015:

> Although it will take time to truly evaluate the consequences of the Nov. 13 massacre in Paris for the French, European and world politics, some conclusions can be made now.

> The attacks will almost inevitably lead to an escalation of war in Iraq and Syria, as well as to changes in the balance of forces in the Middle East as a whole. The French government has been challenged with such audacity that it does not have the right not to respond; Paris has found itself in the same position as Washington after the September 11, 2001 attacks.[56]

Lukyanov called on the U.S. to show support to its allies in the fight against ISIS as Europe, by itself, cannot carry the day. He also points out the likely changes coming in the Middle East and Europe as a result of the Paris terror attacks, and how the shift in U.S. policy in the region will affect Sunnis:

> The alignment of forces in the Middle East may change. The Gulf monarchies actually seem to believe that Iran's expansion and stronger foothold are more dangerous than the success of the self-proclaimed Islamic State. Until recently, the Syrian conflict largely revolved around the fate of Bashar al-Assad, which meant that his opponents were fixated on regime change in Syria, giving it priority above anything else. At a time when leading Western countries start seeing ISIS as an even more dangerous threat, Saudi Arabia and its allies might be growing increasingly at odds with this belief.

> Clearly a new round of the "big game" [sic, the "Great Game" is likely referenced here] in the Middle East is inevitable, and if France tried to avoid it, the country would simply lose its reputation in that critical part of the world, probably along with Europe losing its influence there altogether.

> As for Europe, it is likely to do a U-turn in its attitude to the refugees and further strengthen its commitment to a police-dominated handling of migration issues; a rise of right-wing sentiment can be expected there.

"ISIS IS CONTAINED" – OBAMA

Before Paris happened, President Obama had been seeking to reassure Americans and our allies that everything was copasetic. However, no sooner had President Obama proclaimed that ISIS was "contained" than terrorism exploded in Paris killing over 120 persons and leaving at least one hundred more in critical condition. CNN documented Obama's untimely remark during an interview with ABC's George Stephanopoulos:

> **Washington (CNN)** On Thursday, President Barack Obama declared in an interview that ISIS had been "contained," asserting that the terror cell had been stalled in Iraq and Syria.
>
> The next day, ISIS claimed responsibility for one of the worst terror attacks in European history, shattering what had been a growing sense of momentum in the global fight against extremists and driving home the frightening ability of ISIS to inspire and possibly coordinate attacks outside their power base in Iraq and in Syria.[57]

CNN elaborated:

> The stated goal of the U.S. had been to decapitate ISIS, but the group, claiming credit for the attacks in Paris, has shown that containment and decapitation clearly don't work against an organization that courts death and is atomized to the point individuals or small groups can act largely on their own. ISIS has quickly matured during the Obama administration from a group the President once called al Qaeda's "JV team" to a terrifying threat to the West. It's a threat the U.S. and Europe clearly do not yet fully understand. [58]

As I have written previously, what Obama promulgated on November 12, 2015 supplies transparency into what his primary directive concerning American strategy is. The U.S. may never have intended to destroy ISIS,[59] but merely to "contain it" in order to leave enough of its adherents in place to maintain pressure on Bashar al-Assad. The U.S. has stated without equivocation that it seeks regime change even though it is quite unclear who would ascend to Assad's place afterward.

Indeed, more pieces are in motion on the chessboard than just "taking out ISIS." The chess match involves the sparring between the U.S., NATO, and Russia. Consider the following: on the surface, the U.S. seeks to establish some semblance of democratic government in the Middle Eastern states. This effort may be sincere, but our will to accomplish this transformation has continued to be less than required. Since 1950, "nation building" on the heels of military action sanctioned by our foreign policy has not been one of our strong suits. Witness Libya where the CIA supplied the inspiration and the weaponry to take out Muammar Gadhafi. Likewise, look at Iraq where its crippled government cannot stand against ISIS without U.S. and Iranian support. What the U.S. leaves in its military's wake generally counts as little more than chaos.

DOES AMERICA COVERTLY INCITE "COLOR REVOLUTIONS?"

Russian President Vladimir Putin charges that this methodology of fomenting rebellion and "creating chaos" is intentional and stands as the underlying U.S. motive (rather than the U.S. typical moral argument that it seeks to nurture democracy). Putin alleges that U.S. objectives emanate from a conscious and sinister strategy thought out meticulously in the darkened corridors of power in Washington, i.e., the intelligence sectors (about one dozen at last count) within the American government. Putin asserts that the overarching U.S. plan seeks regime change but will settle for chaos through "color revolutions" – orchestrated domestic protests carried out by natives of foreign lands (but funded and supported by the CIA) against any government of consequence antagonistic to U.S. wishes. Little doubt remains that such covert operations constitute the classic signature of the CIA as has been well documented by Tim Weiner in his 700-page historical expose of CIA blunders, *Legacy of Ashes*. Other American critics such as F. William Engdahl in his book *A Century of War* asserts that the "rope" in this tug of war equates to *who controls the oil.* All U.S. action, according to Engdahl, is just as sinister as Putin says it is.

Others charge that the real motivation for Obama is his fondness with Islam and his connections to the Muslim Brotherhood. Former U.S. Representative Allen West contends that the "Brotherhood" even infiltrated Obama's administration.

> "[We] do have Muslim Brotherhood affiliated groups and individuals infiltrated into this current Obama administration," West wrote on his Facebook page. "This is serious." West slammed Obama's Middle East policies, criticizing his "very conciliatory speech" in Cairo in 2009[60] and his stance[61] on former Egyptian President Hosni Mubarak's resignation in 2011. "Many warned of the rise of the 'granddaddy of Islamic terrorism,' the Muslim Brotherhood, in Egypt as the only viable and organized political entity," West wrote. "We were castigated as alarmists and Islamophobes. The Muslim Brotherhood even lied about running a candidate for President. We are now witnessing the result of our blindness." [62]

However, given the record of President Obama, it stands to reason that incompetency and not just malfeasance constitutes a plausible fault in U.S. foreign policy. This administration has demonstrated an inability to discern its real enemies and allies as well as overlooking the consequences of its foreign policy throughout the Middle East.

Whether we can go so far as to declare that Obama is a closet Muslim or that a secret cabal of shadowy international bankers controls Obama, remains beside the point. What seems evident is that U.S. strategy builds on a perception that Russia continues to be a "regional power" and the U.S. can dominate Russia in virtually any sector in the world we chose. And for two months now, as I am completing this chapter on November 30, 2015, the skies above Syria have proven otherwise.

What I allege is that Obama's decision not to leave a residual force in Iraq and not to destroy ISIS outright underlies numerous horrific outcomes in recent events. Obama misunderstood the consequences of not forcing Sunnis, Kurds, and Shiites to build a unified government. Without U.S. presence after pulling out in 2011, Iraq deteriorated into chaos within two years. Al Qaeda soon transformed itself into ISIS. Disenfranchised Sunnis, former Baathist military leaders, and extremists responding to the call of a global caliphate, found an organizing principle by building an official "national" government (a caliphate) between Baghdad and Damascus from which it could influence the politics and create hysteria in both Iraq and Syria.

Obama failed to understand the critical balance of power in the Middle East between the Sunni and Shia. His decision to consummate a treaty with Iran will likely prove to be disaster, not just because of how it threatens Israel, but because of how it will exacerbate the conflict between Shia and Sunni in the Middle East. True, his seemingly indifference toward Israel's government springs from this assumption. However, it impacts other allies in the region as well. Saudi Arabia, which has been an ally for decades flowing hundreds of millions of barrels of oil to the U.S. (over a million barrels daily) and key to the support of the petrodollar, faces enemies that it may not be able to oppose. Jordan has been a moderating nation state and it lies in the path of ISIS designs. All of these issues demonstrate a serious inability to discern who are friends are and what could result from our failure to choose the right side to be on. At the end of November 2015, the news has come from Afghanistan that the government there has approached Russia for help as it fears the still existent Taliban and knows its days may be numbered with U.S. troops pulling out. We appear to be repeating the same mistake in Afghanistan that we made in Iraq (although it seems we are making it slower though no less surely).

> Obama's failed leadership has created a vacuum which is being filled by Russian President Vladimir Putin. President Ashraf Ghani asked Russia for artillery, small arms and Mi-35 helicopters to bolster Afghan Security Forces. Since Obama is hell bent on retreating from the world, Russia will gladly take on the lead role in fighting terrorism and selling weapons to Arab allies. Afghanistan sees that Obama is ready to abandon them both militarily and financially, which allows for the growth of its enemies, first the Taliban and now ISIS.[63]

THE DIREST CONSEQUENCES OF FAILED U.S. STRATEGY

It is not that difficult to go further and cite some of the direst consequences of failed U.S. strategy: (1) the Arab Spring demonstrably has run amok in every instance, (2) the flight of a million plus refugees into Europe is having a destabilizing effect on "domestic tranquility" there; and then (3) the instances of terrorism, already in Paris, soon elsewhere. We abandoned Iraq, left scores of weapons there, and virtually assured that either the Sunni radicals in ISIS or the extremist Shia in Iran would eventually gain the upper hand throughout the Fertile Crescent. These are all consequences of a shortsighted Middle East strategy. Furthermore, our approach to solve the turmoil there has horrendous implications over the longer term.

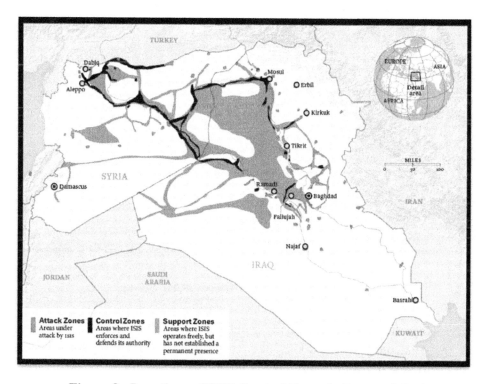

Figure 8 - Locations of ISIS Control Zones in Iraq and Syria
(Source: Business Insider)

The U.S. and its allies have been (and still are) willing to arm and train specific Syrian rebel groups with the stated objective of eliminating the threat posed by ISIS – despite the fact these groups have less-than-secret connections to Al-Qaeda (notably through Syria's Al Nusra). The U.S. aggressively demands Bashar al-Assad step down from office, but to no avail, especially given Russia's lending him an indispensable hand. Fur-

97

thermore, the American people should understand that our allies in the Middle East can also be our enemies. They play a "double-game" as stated in the following commentary from the *International Policy Digest*:

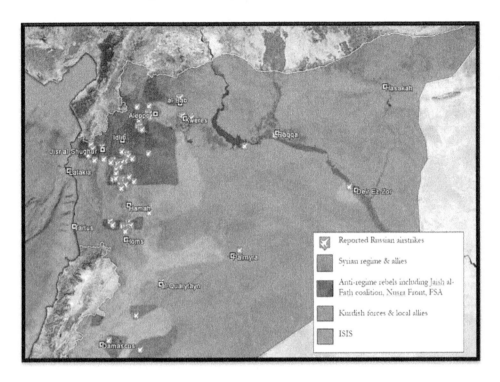

Figure 9 - Locations of Russian Air Strikes
(Source: VOX)

So what in the hell is really going on? Well, war of course. This is what modern war looks like. In particular this latest proxy war targets the multi-cultural, yet authoritarian regime of Syria's Bashar Al Assad. NATO dislikes Assad because he is an ally of Iran, Russia and Hezbollah in Lebanon. Oil and gas pipeline routes also factor in. Western powers and Gulf States that don't like Assad have, like a pack of wild jackals, been ripping at Syria since 2011. The primary supporter of ISIS and the Al Nusra Front is Turkey, which by any objective measure should be considered a state sponsor of international terrorism and isolated immediately.

Sometimes we are even provided short glimpses of the reality, by our own so-called leaders. Vice President of the United States

> Joe Biden said: "[Erdogan… the Saudis, the Emiratis, etc.]… poured hundreds of millions of dollars and tens of thousands of tons of weapons into anyone who would fight against Assad, except that the people who were being supplied were al-Nusra, and al Qaeda, and the extremist elements of jihadis coming from other parts of the world."
>
> Former Secretary of State Hillary Clinton said: "Still, donors in Saudi Arabia constitute the most significant source of funding to Sunni terrorist groups worldwide."
>
> Chairman of the Joint Chiefs of Staff General Martin Dempsey said: "I know major Arab allies who fund them [ISIS]." [64]

Throughout this effort, the U.S. has counted on Russia steering clear of the fray in Syria — which was a serious miscalculation. For decades Syria has been Russia's one certain ally in the region. Russia's port at Tartous on the Mediterranean remains vital to their national interests. And the issue of access to and the distribution of oil and natural gas is part and parcel of Putin's overall strategy to control the West by controlling access to this region's fossil fuels. (See Martin Katusa's timely study, *The Colder War: How the Global Energy Trade Slipped from America's Grasp*).

Consequently, Russia elected to enter the Syrian civil war and determined to destroy all rebel groups who threaten Assad — not just ISIS. On October 7, 2015, Zack Beauchamp documented this pertinent fact:

> When Russia started bombing in Syria last week, it said it was targeting ISIS — a claim it's stuck to pretty consistently in the past week. But this map [see above] of Russian airstrikes in Syria so far, put together by *the Levantine Group,* tells a very different story.
>
> The Levantine Group's analysts used a proprietary network of sources, cross-checked with open-source media and information released by the Russian Ministry of Defense, to determine the locations hit by Russian planes. This map shows those strikes overlaid on territory controlled by Bashar al-Assad's regime, by anti-Assad rebels, by ISIS, and by Kurdish forces.
>
> The results are striking — Russian strikes have overwhelmingly

targeted rebel-held territory in western Syria rather than the ISIS strongholds in the north and east:

> "The Russian air campaign is not geared toward the so-called Islamic State," Michael Horowitz, a Syria analyst at the Levantine Group, told me via email. "Russian airstrikes are focusing on opposition groups controlling northwestern Syria, including the al-Qaeda-linked al-Nusra Front, other Islamist groups such as Ahrar al-Sham, and 'moderate' groups including the Free Syrian Army (FSA)." [65]

THE "GREAT GAME" MAKES A COMEBACK

This vantage point allows us to zero in on what really is at stake in Syria. The United States continues to advance "the Great Game" of the nineteenth century, which was played between the Lion of Great Britain and the Bear of Russia. In the twenty-first century, the game continues. But now it is the United States primarily (with limited support from the U.K.) that seeks to offset the power of Russia, run through the "kleptocracy" of Mr. Putin and his cronies (aka oligarchy).

The United States is not the sole superpower anymore. The White House would like to think that is so because it's economically the world's superpower. But the economy alone "does not a superpower make." Because of advances in Russian military weapons, and because of its longer-term strategy, the U.S. stands in danger of attack from Russia through Russia's reinvigorated and highly capable nuclear arsenal. Russia's military can nullify the superior U.S. economy in less than one hour. Nuclear weapons are "the great equalizer." Likewise, U.S. superiority in the number of naval vessels, aircraft carrier groups, and nuclear submarines can all be marginalized by newly announced hypersonic weapons that both Russia and China have that make our carriers and submarines risky places to spend your days and nights when World War commences. (See *The New Tactics of Global War* by Benjamin Baruch and J.R. Nyquist, discussed earlier, for an elaborate discussion on the vulnerability of the U.S. and its military to advances in Russian military technology).

The response of both nations to terrorism drives them face-to-face in a search for long-term answers. Meanwhile, the only short-term answer is to bomb the perpetrators – and that they are doing with a vengeance – now side-by-side with the rest of the world hoping that they literally don't crash into one another and set off World War III in the process.

That is why the "chess match" underway today between Russia and the United States inextricably connects terrorist acts such as what we witnessed in Paris in November 2015 (and planned by ISIS at their headquarters in Raqqah, Syria) to the broader events in our world. The heat is on and it isn't likely to cool off anytime soon.

THE NEXT GREAT WAR
IN THE MIDDLE EAST

Part Two: Ezekiel's Prophecy of Gog

6: THE DARK FORCES BEHIND GOG

"Son of man, set your face toward Gog of the land of Magog, the prince of Rosh, Meschech and Tubal, and prophesy against him and say ... Behold, I am against you, O Gog, prince of Rosh, Meschech and Tubal."
(Ezekiel 38:1-3)

GOG FROM THE LAND OF MAGOG

THE IDENTITY OF THE GREAT ENEMY OF ISRAEL JUST BEFORE THE JEWISH MESSIAH COMES IN "THE LATTER DAYS" CONTINUES TO BE ONE OF THE MOST DEBATED SUBJECTS IN ESCHATOLOGY. BIBLE students know this enemy of Israel as "Gog from the land of Magog." While these names are familiar to students of Bible prophecy, the meaning behind "Gog and Magog" constitutes a *multi-layered reality* and stretches beyond the recognition of most everyone. Why would this be so? Because many teachers of Bible prophecy seek to place these names on a map *without acknowledging spiritual forces that act behind the scenes.*

While we are dealing with human personages and nations, we are also encountering *powers and principalities* actively influencing the affairs of humankind. To assert Gog and Magog represent *only* human personages or simply specific nation-states falls short of an informed biblical perspective. Yes, the identity of Gog and Magog rightly includes "persons and territories." Nevertheless, to plumb the meaning of scripture we must study more than people and places and look deeper to discern the puppet masters behind the marionettes.

The names, Gog and Magog, are mentioned in two distinct places in the Bible. *Magog* is a descendant of Noah's son Japheth. *"The sons of Japheth: Gomer, Magog, Madai, Javan, Tubal, Meshech and Tiras."* (Genesis 10:2) A different *Gog* is mentioned as a descendant of Rueben son of Jacob through the line of Shem, son of Noah (1 Chronicles 5:4). Consequently, no genealogical relationship exists between this "Gog and Magog."

Indeed, the tribes that descended from Noah's offspring and where they settled geographically comprises quite a different investigation than what we intend to concern ourselves in this chapter. [66] We will take it up in a subsequent chapter.

GOG AND MAGOG ARE NOT JUST ON A MAP

To understand the ultimate identity of Gog and Magog, we must recognize the "ultra-dimensional" nature of these entities. Recall the verse from Ephesians 6:12, *"For we wrestle not against flesh and blood, but against principalities, against powers, against the rulers of the darkness of this world, against spiritual wickedness in high places."* The New Testament teaches that the world is ruled by unseen powers although Jesus Christ, through his atoning death, has already defeated them. *"And having spoiled principalities and powers, he made a [show] of them openly, triumphing over them in it."* (Colossians 2:14, see also Colossians 1:6 and 1 Peter 3:22) While defeated, these powers continue to act through human agents, as men and women permit them and obtain power from them.

The Bible mentions Gog and Magog only seven times (in 1 Chronicles 5:4, five times in Ezekiel chapters 38-39, and once in Revelation 20:8). Most scholars doubt Gog to be a proper name at all, but rather a title akin to Pharaoh, Caesar, King or Czar. They associate the word *Gog* with a high mountain, implying "one with great authority." When Ezekiel references Gog, the Prince of Rosh, Meschech and Tubal, he may be speaking about *a supernatural power*, as well as a human agent.

FROM THE RECESSES OF THE NORTH

The five "I wills" of Isaiah 14 come into play here. This passage references the adversary of the Lord God, i.e., Lucifer or Satan. He delivers five self-seeking proclamations to the God of gods—an *apotheosis* demanding ascension to the throne where God dwells. We read:

> [12] *How art thou fallen from heaven, O Lucifer, son of the morning! How art thou cut down to the ground, which didst weaken the nations!*

*¹³ For thou hast said in thine heart, I will ascend into heaven, I will exalt my throne above the stars of God: I will sit also upon the mount of the congregation, **in the sides of the north:***

¹⁴ I will ascend above the heights of the clouds; I will be like the most High.

Two key Hebrew words in this passage must be considered in depth. The KJV reads "in the *sides* of the *north*" but their meaning surpasses this obscure phrase. The two words are *yĕrekah* (*Strong's* 3411) and *tsaphown* (*Strong's* H6828). *Yĕrekah* means the "extreme recesses or quarters," while *tsaphown* means "*north or northern.*" Thus, the more accurate translation of this phrase would be: "I also will sit upon the mount of the congregation, *in the extreme recesses of the northern most quarters (habitations)* "

Regarding this passage, the Vines Bible dictionary comments that the Hebrews saw the *north* as dark, gloomy, and opaque whereas they considered the *south* to be clear, bright and sunny. Additionally, the north was exceedingly far away, foreboding, and to be feared. The passage from Isaiah hints that it might have been customary to consider God dwelling in the north. Given so much folklore and mythology associating the dwelling of pagan gods with the far north, the belief that deities dwelt there seems universal. [67] However, while the ethereal hints at a distinct dimension where spiritual entities dwell, other biblical passages pull us back to locations where latitude and longitude apply. Indeed, Jeremiah uses the very same words:

*²² Thus saith the Lord, Behold, a people cometh from the **north country**, and a great nation shall be raised from **the sides of the earth.***

²³ They shall lay hold on bow and spear; they are cruel, and have no mercy; their voice roareth like the sea; and they ride upon horses, set in array as men for war against thee, O daughter of Zion.

According to Jeremiah the people that shall come are **from the north**, a great nation that shall arise from the **extreme recesses of the earth**. The judgment of Babylon prophesied in Jeremiah 25:9 uses the same language of Jeremiah 50-51 where *the daughter of Babylon* becomes the object of judgment. We read:

> *⁹ Behold, I will send and take all the families **of the north**, saith the Lord, and Nebuchadnezzar the king of Babylon, my servant, and will bring them against this land, and against the inhabitants thereof, and against all these nations round about, and will utterly destroy them, and make them an astonishment, and an hissing, and perpetual desolations.*

Jeremiah repeats these predictions in chapters 50 and 51:

> *For **out of the north** there cometh up a nation against her, which shall make her land desolate, and none shall dwell therein: they shall remove, they shall depart, both man and beast. (50:3)*

> *For, lo, I will raise and cause to come up against Babylon an assembly of great nations **from the north country:** and they shall set themselves in array against her; from thence she shall be taken: their arrows shall be as of a mighty expert man; none shall return in vain. (50:9)*

> *Behold, a people shall come **from the north**, and a great nation, and many kings shall be raised up from the coasts of the earth. (50:41)*

> *Then the heaven and the earth, and all that is therein, shall sing for Babylon: for the spoilers shall come unto her **from the north**, saith the LORD. (51:48)*

Likewise, the prophet Joel references the *northern army* that shall come against both Israel and Babylon. The prophet assures Israel of God's protection (unlike *the daughter of Babylon* that shall be utterly destroyed):

> *But I will remove far off from you **the northern army**, and will drive him into a land barren and desolate, with his face toward the east sea, and his hinder part toward the utmost sea, and his stink shall come up, and his ill savour shall come up, because he hath done great things. (Joel 2:20)*

To grasp the implications of these prophecies, we should note that the physical, historical Babylon exists in Iraq and lies almost directly east of Jerusalem, and *not from the north.* Secondly, Babylon is not located in the most extreme or remote parts of the earth. Israelites knew the world was not bounded by Babylon. They knew that the Persians lay further east. Babylon was *not from the extreme recesses of the east, let alone the north.*

Therefore, the prophets appear to be implying more than just lands lying to the north of Israel. They appear to link these events with powers and principalities that lie behind the scenes. Otherworldly entities are being factored into the prophetic events when God battles His archenemies. Earthly powers will rise and fall—but paranormal "partners" will persist.

DANIEL AND THE TRUE WORLD POWERS

Assuming Jeremiah's prophecies await fulfillment, the conclusion becomes apparent: the nations that come against Babylon *are future to Daniel and Jeremiah.* Babylon also must be a future incarnation reflecting its spirit (and by that I suggest the very same *principality* or *power likely lurks behind the scenes*).

Figure 10 - Fontaine's Daniel in the Lion's Den

If America is the daughter of Babylon today, our leaders could be unwitting puppets for the Prince of Babylon. [68]

In the Book of Daniel, we recall that Daniel talks with an angel about the Prince of Persia and the Prince of Grecia (Greece) that will come against Babylon. But the Prince of Babylon itself is not directly mentioned in Daniel's exchange with the angel. First in his vision in Daniel 8:20-22, we learn that the beasts that Daniel sees are associated with kingdoms yet future to Daniel. The angel conveys to Daniel, by reference to their "princes," the Persians as well as the Greeks. A future beast, an exceedingly great beast, is not named but will be the beast that the Messiah himself will defeat at the end of days. (See Daniel 8:25)

Later, we encounter Daniel once again talking with the angel who answers Daniel's prayer explains his vision. Through this conversation, we gain insight into what happens behind the curtain. In Chapter 10, Daniel relates his encounter this way:

> *[11] And he said unto me, O Daniel, a man greatly beloved, understand the words that I speak unto thee, and stand upright: for unto thee am I now sent. And when he had spoken this word unto me, I stood trembling.*
>
> *[12] Then said he unto me, Fear not, Daniel: for from the first day that thou didst set thine heart to understand, and to chasten thyself before thy God, thy words were heard, and I am come for thy words.*
>
> *[13] But the prince of the kingdom of Persia withstood me one and twenty days: but, lo, Michael, one of the chief princes, came to help me; and I remained there with the kings of Persia.*

To summarize: Jeremiah, Joel, as well as Ezekiel predict a future kingdom identified as the *daughter of Babylon. Just as with Israel,* this great empire will be opposed by a collection of nations from *the extreme northern recesses of the earth.* This "northern exposure" suggests a nation as far north as one can go AND principalities that may dwell there (at least figuratively, but I wouldn't rule out a literal location too). The prophecy of Ezekiel 38-39 references the very same set of nations, likely at the same time—despite the fact *that Ezekiel does not mention Babylon by name.* Gog "stirs up" the leaders of nations in the physical world, and leads these nations behind the scenes. Gog, like the Antichrist, becomes the instrument of a supernatural being. His mission is to attack and destroy the people of God.

The late scholar Donald Grey Barnhouse made the same point, writing:

> That, then, which has satisfied our minds in this matter, is that some of Satan's mighty angels, principalities, or powers which rule the darkness of this world (Eph. 6:12), TAKE HOLD OF EARTH DICTATORS, use them for their ends, and are defeated by God...

> The human instrumentalities are destroyed, but the demon forces live on, held back by the power of God until Satan is released after the thousand years. Whereupon they seize again some willing earthling and seek to lead the peoples against God in their final rebellion. (*Revelation Commentary*, pp. 387-8).

AN ISLAMIC ANTICHRIST AND AN ISLAMIC GOG?

Despite the supernatural forces behind Gog, we still must ask "Is Magog the land from which Gog arises? Is Gog just a Turk?"

Younger authors often assert, however, that the more sophisticated and educated position dismisses any region outside of the Middle East. From their perspective, Russian leadership of Gog's hordes is a Cold War anachronism or a simpleminded acceptance of the Scofield Bibles' dispensational footnotes. [69] Likewise, many teachers identify *Mystery Babylon* and the *Daughter of Babylon* with Islam. An ascendant empire in the Middle East (usually Turkey, Saudi Arabia, possibly Iran or now, ISIS) will become the power base of Antichrist, when he claims to be the Mahdi. Oftentimes they also propose that the physical, *historical city of Babylon* will be the Babylon of Revelation. Even though that town exists now as little more than a tourist attraction, they espouse Babylon and the country of Iraq will grow to become a leading commercial, political and even military power. Geopolitically speaking, that view is a real stretch.

In stark contrast, the conventional view has held for over a century that the "revived Roman Empire" (inferred from Daniel 9:24-27), from which Antichrist draws his earthly power, will arise from Western Europe (the "merchants of Tarshish") or its "young lions" (their colonies in the Western Hemisphere—See Ezekiel 38:13). Alongside this conclusion, the traditional view sees Russia leading the alliance of Islamic nations (featuring Iran, aka Persia, Cush and Put). While there are historical, geographical, and genealogical rationales supporting the conventional view, there are also important geopolitical, military, and economic reasons to substantiate the traditional perspective. Indeed, a scenario that sees Islam in the leading role of either Gog or Antichrist appears implausible for a wide variety of reasons. Allow me to enumerate for the reader:

- *The Middle East lacks unity.* Islam seems unlikely to rule the world since Islamic nations have such a poor record acting together in a coordinated manner to oppose Israel or the United States (OPEC has a most uneven record when it comes to unified action). Until the 1,300-year contest between Sunni and Shiite is settled, Islam will remain divided into two distinctive and highly disordered spheres with conflicting religious views and competing political confederations. The predicted appearance of the so-called Mahdi may make this conflict worse, rather than unifying these rival factions. When ISIS called itself a "caliphate" all Islam is then required to pledge allegiance to it and desert other nation states of which Muslims may be a part. However, based upon the fact that ISIS is predominantly Sunni, the Shi'ites in Iran, Iraq, and Syria are more than unwilling to fall in line. The fight continues to reach new heights day by day.

- *Other global powers must be decimated for Islam to become a domineering global power.* Today, Russia's Vladimir Putin dominates northern sections of this region, with the Iranian alliance now strengthened. To suppose he would implement a "hands off" approach that enables Turkey to assume leadership of the region overturns three centuries of Russian policy going all the way back to Catherine the Great. Likewise, the United States has exerted a dominating influence on the Middle East since WWII. There are vast oil reserves there, resources of which we can be certain the U.S. will not relinquish access.

- *Islamic nations do not possess global military capability able to project power.* There are no countries with nuclear weapons in the Middle East besides Israel, although the current U.S. administration unfortunately has opened a door for Iran to produce such weapons in the not-too-distant future. Pakistan remains the only official member of "the nuclear club" of eight nations that have formally admitted to having such capabilities. Turkey can share nuclear weapons with several other countries according to the rules worked out among the "nuclear club" inside NATO – but it cannot act unilaterally. Without autonomous nuclear capability, any nation or collection of nations cannot meaningfully assert its political will around the globe or in specific regions subject to global interest, such as the Middle East.

- *Islamic nations do not possess the economic means to dictate terms as does the U.S., the U.K., China, and even Russia.* Wall Street remains the economic center of the world. The City of London teamed with Wall Street appears irrepressible. The International Bank of Settlements, the International Monetary Fund (IMF), and the World Bank dictate globally almost all terms of debt and trade. And the United States dominates these institutions with secondary support from the U.K., Japan, France, Germany, and especially Saudi Arabia. Make note also that the Gross Domestic Product (GDP) of the United States remains double that of China, and over 50 times that of Saudi Arabia.

Still, despite what this author contends are irrefutable objections expressly identified here, the scenario that Muslims fulfill the mission of both the Antichrist and the lesser known figure, *Gog*, remains a scenario many continue to assert. This view, which sees Islam acting in the two leading roles against the people of God (both Jews and Christians), implicitly denies that America could be the incarnation of the daughter of Babylon as well as dismissing that the Russian Bear might fulfill the role of Gog. This view magnifies the power of Islam and relegates the U.S. and Russia to little more than "interested bystanders". By implication, this assumes the great wars of Bible prophecy are regional and not global wars. It has been a surprising development (from my perspective) that so many have adopted what is geopolitically a dubious point of view.

However, along with many others who have studied prophetic topics for over four decades, I contend this Islam-centric view will prove *incorrect* within a few short years. Islam plays no small part in the fulfilling Bible prophecy. Still, it is a subservient role to the bigger power players, the Daughter of Babylon (the U.S.) and Gog (Russia). Many will object, but I will continue to advance the much more conventional position that *Gog is not a Turk.* In a later chapter, we will consider a good deal of additional information regarding Turkey from a geopolitical standpoint and why it is not well positioned to ascend to a world dominating place of leadership.

7: WHERE IS THE LAND OF UNWALLED VILLAGES?

"Russia has pursued a clear policy of disruption, chaos and destabilization—in Ukraine and in the Middle East—in order to force the West to have to partner with Russia to "resolve" the crises it has created…"

Eerik-Niiles Kross, Former head of Estonian Intelligence

RUSSIA NOW IS THE DOMINANT PLAYER IN THE MIDDLE EAST

RUSSIA HAS GAINED A STRONG FOOTHOLD IN THE MIDDLE EAST. COMING TO THE AID OF BASHAR AL-ASSAD ON THE PRETEXT OF ELIMINATING THE THREAT POSED BY ISIS, RUSSIA HAS moved dozens of airplanes, gunships, tanks, as well as hundreds of operational personnel into Syria. In Early October, Mr. Putin and his military have warned the U.S. and the French (before the Paris terror attacks) to stay out of the way of Russian fighter-bombers as they target any and all groups

Figure 11 - Russia Parades its Weapons in Moscow

opposed to their barbaric ally, Assad, including both ISIS and the so-called moderate Free-Syrian army (half-heartedly supported by the U.S.).

The story occupies considerable airtime on mainline media. But the back-story is much more strategic, although no one will hear it discussed in much depth on FOX, CNN, or any other mainline media outlet. No one wants to alarm the American people to the point where the nation calls for a mean-ingful response to Russian aggression from this administration.

Figure 12 - A Frowning Obama Toasts Putin

What is that backstory? Russian intends to dominate the Middle East and push the U.S. out of the premier geopolitical position, especially in the so-called "fertile crescent" which begins in Syria, crosses the north-ern parts of Iraq, and includes much of Iran. As virtually everyone knows, because of the oil-rich lands spread across virtually the entire Middle East, this area comprises one of the most important expans-es impacting the entire global economy. Combined with the recent nu-clear technology deal made between Iran and five other nations in which Russia played a key part, Mr. Putin now stands tall throughout this re-gion. Writer Mark Langfan breaks through the clutter of opinion to nail exactly what the real story is:

> Russia intends to collect the Saudi Arabian part of the Black Gold Triangle and leave Mecca to Iran. The Black Gold Triangle is the topographic delta formed by the Tigris and Euphrates River in the Fertile Crescent that holds 56% of the world's oil supply. Iran's goal is to buy Russian military protection for its oil pipeline and hegemonic ground empire to the Eastern Mediterranean. Unlike the United States, Putin won't idiotically retreat and return the Sunni's oil riches to a power vacuum after he occupies them. He'll keep them for his Russian Mafiacracy. Unfortunately, the world can't wait for Russia and Iran to fight over the leftovers. [70]

Russia involvement in the region and its overall strategy appears clear to European experts familiar with Moscow. The former head of Estonian Intelligence and a member of Estonia's parliament, Eerik-Niiles Kross, points out that Russia has a grand plan involving its efforts in both Ukraine and Syria.

> Experts from the left and right alike warn that cooperation with Russia on Syria can have potentially disastrous consequences for the U.S., but too many Americans still don't understand how closely linked these two headline conflicts are, and American policy has yet to confront the reality that Syria and Ukraine are part of the same mission for Russia—the destruction of the post-WWII architecture of the West. To achieve this goal, Russia has pursued a clear policy of disruption, chaos and destabilization—in Ukraine and in the Middle East—in order to force the West to have to partner with Russia to "resolve" the crises it has created... The Kremlin has been opportunistic and decisive in grabbing a position of strength—in the Middle East and in Europe—while U.S. attention has waned and retracted. [71]

What Russia has really been up to, has escaped Western pundits. On the surface, Russia worked cooperatively with Western states to conclude the pact with Iran. Unlike other Western nations that celebrate the agreement, Russia like Iran, emerged from the negotiation in a much stronger position. Now Russia eagerly sells military weapons to Iran, (including the

117

anti-aircraft missile system, the S-300) and shows itself a friend to the Shia in Iran, Iraq, and Syria. As Russia exercises its military muscle, the rest of the region has awakened to the fact that the U.S. is not the quintessential player it once was. Mr. Putin will now be calling the shots. The request from Shi'ite Iraqi leadership in early October 2015 asking Russia to attack ISIS,[72] demonstrated that fact plainly enough. No wonder, all that President Obama could muster was a frown when meeting with Putin at the U.N. as he toasted Putin (at the end of September – see photo above).

Because of the significant events of the fall of 2015, students of the Bible must again reflect on the latter days' Battle of Gog and Magog and to reconsider the conventional view that Russia, not Turkey or Saudi Arabia, constitutes the leader of the pack of nations described in Ezekiel 38-39.

IS THE DAUGHTER OF BABYLON EXCLUDED FROM EZEKIEL'S PROPHECY OF GOG AND MAGOG?

I will take up in the next chapter the task of identifying the many nations Ezekiel chronicles when describing how Gog gathers an assembly of armies attacking Israel. Lest it be lost in reciting those issues, however, here I wish to introduce a different subject but one that has been discussed in my previous book, *Is Russia Destined to Attack the U.S.?* That subject: the presence of the daughter of Babylon which I believe lies implicit *within Ezekiel 38-39.* Moreover, I argue this passage pertains not just to the controversial view that Russia is Gog, *but that the United States comprises this "land of unwalled villages".*

It has been my contention (and many others, including my co-authors of *The Final Babylon,* Douglas W. Krieger and Dene McGriff, as well as friend John Price author of *The End of America*), that the U.S. constitutes the fulfillment of the daughter of Babylon (see Jeremiah 50-51, Isaiah 47, Zechariah 2, and Psalm 137). Given the vast importance of the Battle of Gog and Magog in the last days scenario, it is not unreasonable to suggest that there are a number of important aspects of prophecy encoded biblically in Ezekiel's passage that connect its prophecies to others in the Bible dealing with the identical, fateful times of the last days.

At the outset, we plainly see that Ezekiel 38-39 provides an intensive description of Gog's attack plan upon Israel. In the first eight verses of chapter 38, Ezekiel tells us that Gog shall assemble or "convoke" (Strong's H6950, *kä·hal*) the armies surrounding Israel. It will *kahal* or *gather together* (the same word used when Moses gathered together the assembly of Israel) numerous nations to come against the land of Israel. Ezekiel tells us that this land will have been restored from a waste, from violence, and will provide a safe habitation for the people of God.

> *After many days thou shalt be visited: in the latter years thou shalt come into the land that is brought back from the sword, and is gathered out of many people, against the mountains of Israel, which have been always waste: but it is brought forth out of the nations, and they shall dwell **safely** all of them.* (Ezekiel 38:8)

However, at this point it is crucial to ask, *"Exactly what does it mean that Israel shall dwell safely?"* The word *safely* (Strong's H983) is the word (transliterated) **betach** *(beh'takh).* The word connotes a *sense of ease,* being carefree, having no fear of being harmed. It is used 42 times in the KJV of the Old Testament, 26 of which are translated *safely* or *safety.*

Jeremiah also talks of the re-gathering of Israel in the latter days, using very similar language to Ezekiel.

> *Behold, I will gather them out of all countries, whither I have driven them in mine anger, and in my fury, and in great wrath; and I will bring them again unto this place, and I will cause them to **dwell safely**.* (Jeremiah 32:37)

Jeremiah assures Israel that the Lord intends only good for them:

> *Yea, I will rejoice over them **to do them good,** and I will plant them in this land assuredly with my whole heart and with my whole soul.* (Jeremiah 32:41)

It is in this passage that we see the God's covenantal promise explicitly stated once more: *"And they shall be my people, and I will be their God"* (verse 38). No mention is made that Israel should continue to fear attack, for *betach* promises deliverance from all the matters that have threatened the Jewish people through the ages.

However, just three verses later (verse 11), most respected commentators suggest a different meaning for *betach*:

> *And thou shalt say, I will go up to the **land of unwalled villages**; I will go to them that are at rest, that **dwell safely,** all of them dwelling without walls, and having neither bars nor gates.*

True scholar Gary Stearman indicated on his *Prophecy Watchers* television program (October 5, 2015), that the word in this specific verse references Israel and infers a "false sense of security" – a sense of safety Israelis possess based upon factors such as reliance upon the United States for its protection or confidence based upon the many prior successful operations of the Israel Defense Force (IDF). Stearman cites noted Hebraic-Christian scholars including the likes of noted prophecy expert Dr. Arnold Fruchtenbaum who, like Stearman, contends this particular translation to be its true meaning in this particular verse. Again, the conventional and respected view, which Stearman holds, contends that *the land of unwalled villages references Israel.* I might add, as Stearman points out rather colorfully, that Prime Minister Netanyahu used the two words *Shalom* and *Betach* (peace and safety) as his campaign slogan in his recent electoral campaign! Given this interpretation, Stearman and Dr. Fruchtenbaum assert that the use of "unwalled villages" in this case should *not be taken literally – but taken figuratively.* Concurring with the interpretation that *betach* is not always a "confidence derived from faith", the old standard – *Vines Bible Dictionary* – suggests it may on occasion convey a sense of *overconfidence.* We see this in Isaiah 47:8, where translators express the Prophet's rebuke against *the Daughter of Babylon* employing these words as if in an announcement over the "loud speaker"…

> *Therefore **hear now this**, thou that art given to pleasures, that dwellest **carelessly** (betach) that sayest in thine heart, "I am, and none else beside me; I shall not sit as a widow, neither shall I know the loss of children".*

In this instance, the context clearly demonstrates that *betach* conveys a sense of braggadocio or overconfidence.

But does this passage, Ezekiel 38:10-13 (specifically, verse 11), intend the same usage of *betach* as Isaiah 47? Is Ezekiel speaking about Israel in this passage, or are we encountering a prophecy pertaining to some other people (s) or land (s) as we are in Isaiah 47?

It should be noted that the King James Version translators back in the seventeenth century did translate the word *betach* as "carelessly" in several passages just as we cited in Isaiah 47:8. But they did not do so in Ezekiel 38:11. Certainly the translators knew the Hebrew word *betach* could mean overconfidence or a false sense of security, but in the instance of Ezekiel 38:11, they chose not to translate it this way. Their translation of *betach* was "dwell safely". Was their translation correct or incorrect? I argue that the translators of the King James *got it wrong*. That is, as Stearman and Fruchtenbaum contend, *betach* should have been translated in Ezekiel 38:11, "carelessly" implying a false sense of security. However as we are about to see (and what remains vital to recognize), Israel is *not* the subject of this passage. And that sets my point of view apart from the conventional view and why I differ from Stearman and Fruchtenbaum regarding "where" the land of unwalled villages lies.

My point is this: when *betach* is taken to mean "overconfidence" it never refers to Israel's confidence in God's provision for safety and security. Israel could be overconfident in themselves, in the IDF, or in its allies. But *Israel cannot be overconfident in God.* To assert that Israel is the "land of unwalled villages" in Ezekiel implies that Israel would be wrong to have confidence in God's promise. In no other passage in which the Lord promises Israel protection, does it infer or suggest that Israel would be overconfident or careless to trust in the Lord's promise. Does the Lord indicate that Israel will still be harassed or threatened after it has returned to its land? The answer is clearly *in the affirmative* due to the mere fact that the overall thrust of the passage indicates Gog will attack Israel with so many armies that it will be as if Gog's hordes seek to "cover the land." However, the thrust is also that Israel should be confident in God for God will deliver them even from Gog and his millions of minions! And not long thereafter, even from the Antichrist himself.

In verse eight of Ezekiel 38, we understand clearly God is promising that Israel will be secure.

> *After many days thou shalt be visited: in the latter years thou shalt come into the land that is brought back from the sword, and is gathered out of many people, against the mountains of Israel, which have been always waste: but it is brought forth out of the nations, and they shall dwell safely all of them.*

However, within the same passage the prophet is equally clear that Israel will not initially be free from threat or turmoil. So is the assurance in Ezekiel 38:8 insincere? Not at all. The promise remains true, even though *shalom veh betach* will not be immediately realized. We must always remember that from God's perspective time constitutes a transitory reality and *"a day is a thousand years to the LORD and a thousand years one day."* (2 Peter 3:8, paraphrased) Israel will be secure. That promise is true. But it is not necessarily at the very same time it is gathered together back to the land.

So yes, the prophets warn that Israel, even after returning to its land, will experience not just one, but two enormous threats making all other previous threats inconsequential. However, never does the Lord scold Israel for being overconfident in its trusting in Him. Indeed, Christian expositors suggest Israel will be the subject again of massive persecution *even after it has been delivered from Gog.* It will not be until the final battle, the *Battle of Armageddon,* when Israel finally and forever lives in complete *betach.* For in this last battle Israel will still suffer greatly, some going into "captivity" for a time and many others killed.

Scholars often refer to last battle as "the Battle of Jerusalem." We read of this battle in Zechariah: *"For I will gather all nations against Jerusalem to battle; and the city shall be taken, and the houses rifled, and the women ravished; and half of the city shall go forth into captivity, and the residue of the people shall not be cut off from the city.* (Zechariah 14:2)

The very final war, the Battle of Armageddon, will not just be Gog and the nations confederated with him, but the nations from all over the world allied with the Beast aka the Antichrist. It will be a concluding, no holds barred, all-out war against this single nation (and its Messiah) which almost everyone in the world will hold to be the mortal enemies of all humankind. Nevertheless, the end of this war will ultimately culminate in complete *betach* for Jerusalem: *"And men shall dwell in it, and there shall be no more utter destruction; but Jerusalem shall be **safely** inhabited"* (verse 11).

However, when looking at the passage in Ezekiel 38, there are reasons to distinguish between "dwelling safely" and "dwelling overconfidently" and to ascribe to that distinction an intentional differentiation in the subject of the prophet's comments. In other words, not all of the predictions about Gog's plans are directed toward Israel. To prove this to be the case, it requires we take into account all the scriptures in the Old Testament where the word *betach* is used. This is the key to decoding the meaning of Ezekiel 38:10-13 and exactly "where" the land of unwalled villages is.

WHAT *BETACH* USUALLY MEANS AND WHY IT MATTERS

First, the overwhelming majority of uses of the word can be cited to show that *overconfidence is **not** the typical sense of the term betach.* To underscore this point, allow me to share other verses where *betach* obviously does *not* mean overconfidence. For example, prior to chapter 38, Ezekiel frequently previews the use of the term in the context promising peace and safety to Israel,

> *And I will make with them a covenant of peace, and will cause the evil beasts to cease out of the land: and they shall dwell safely in the wilderness, and sleep in the woods.* (Ezekiel 34:25).

Likewise, we see further similar affirmations in the same passage:

> *And the tree of the field shall yield her fruit, and the earth shall yield her increase, and they shall be **safe** in their land, and shall know that I am the LORD, when I have broken the bands of their yoke, and delivered them out of the hand of those that served themselves of them. And they shall no more be a prey to the*

> *heathen, neither shall the beast of the land devour them; but they shall dwell **safely**, and none shall make them afraid.* (Ezekiel 34:27-28)

There are 33 other instances where *betach* simply means *safely* or *safety*. There are only a handful of verses where it means *carelessly*, implying a false sense of security. But looking at these verses that are the exception (and not the rule) *comprises the key to understanding why Ezekiel 38:11 does not reference Israel.*

As stated earlier, the Hebrew word *betach* occurs 42 times in the Old Testament. Here are the six instances in which it is translated as a *pejorative* (those cases where it disparages the subject's sense of overconfidence).

- Judges 8:7 and 18:7 conveys *overconfidence*. Judges 8:7 refers to the **enemies of Gideon**. Judges 18:7 speaks of a people of Laish put to the sword by the 600 Danites. Afterwards, the destroyed city was renamed *Dan* (it was here where Micah the son of Manasseh was installed as priest for an idolatrous perversion of Judaism).

- Ezekiel 30:9 also infers *carelessness* (referencing the **Ethiopians** in this instance), as does Isaiah 47:8 (referring to the **daughter of Babylon**). Ezekiel 39:6 refers to gentiles that dwell in Magog and nations far from Israel, who "dwell carelessly in the isles". *"And I will send a fire on Magog, and among them that **dwell carelessly in the isles**: and they shall know that I am the LORD."*

- Likewise, in Zephaniah 2:15, we read regarding the city of Nineveh, that the Lord would destroy this Assyrian city, *"This is the rejoicing city that **dwelt carelessly**, that said in her heart, 'I am, and there is none beside me:' how is she become a desolation, a place for beasts to lie down in! Every one that passeth by her shall hiss, and wag his hand."*

ISRAEL DOESN'T DWELL ARROGANTLY WHEN GOD RESCUES IT

In these six instances, *all of which deal with gentiles and the enemies of God, the KJV translates the word betach* as *carelessly*. However, in all 36 other verses, dealing with the righteous and with Israel, the translators used the words *safety* or *safely* and did not use *carelessly*. Therefore, to sharpen my point further:

124

- It appears highly improbable that Ezekiel 38:11 references Israel *dwelling carelessly* or overconfidently. *If it did, it would be the only place in scripture that uses the word betach disapprovingly when applied to Israel.*

- If in Ezekiel 38:11 *betach* is being used derogatively (and I believe it is so used although the KJV has in this instance translated it incorrectly), then *it must not reference Israel*. In all cases where the word *betach* is translated implying *a false sense of security,* it refers to gentiles or the enemies of God who are overconfident and careless.

Thus, the argument from the whole of Old Testament seems strong and clear: As it relates to *who* is dwelling safely, it is either Israel – and Israel will be secure in the promise of God (that they *will dwell safely*) – or it is *not Israel* because the people to whom Ezekiel makes his prediction are *overconfident and arrogant.* Therefore, if the people referenced in *Ezekiel 38:11 are overconfident and arrogant, then the people are NOT Israel.*

Consequently, we do not need to suppose that Gog cannot attack Israel now because Israel doesn't dwell in peace and safety. And this is indeed the reason why some scholars assert that Israel is not in peril from Gog's attack at this time. It is the overriding contention of otherwise highly capable teachers that suppose an intervening event must occur, such as the "Psalm 83 War", to bring a temporary peace to Jerusalem. *The Next Great War in the Middle East, in my opinion, is not the Psalm 83 War.*

My view contends the *Psalm 83 War,* those conflicts outlined there between Israel and her neighbors may in fact have been in play since the Jewish War of Independence beginning in 1948. No doubt that these disputes have been an ongoing reality leading to several wars and intifadas. Likewise, the Burden of Damascus spoken of by Isaiah the prophet (in Isaiah 17), may already be well underway at this time. It has probably not escaped notice to readers of this book that much of Damascus lays already in ruins. It is the Battle of Gog and Magog, not the Psalm 83 War, that current geopolitics strongly indicates is about to transpire and in short order. Israel does not comprise the nation of whom the prophet speaks when he asserts that *the nation of unwilled villages dwells overconfidently.* In other words, the attack of Gog can transpire when Israel has not yet been fully secured. It can happen at any time without conflicting with or contradicting the Bible. *The scripture does not convey that Israel will be in a paradisiacal state when Gog amasses its armies to attack it.* Obviously that will be the case whether walls exist there or not.

On the other hand, the attack of Gog against Israel will take place, almost simultaneously, when the nation that is the object of Ezekiel's condemnation *dwells overconfidently.* Who is that nation dwelling so carelessly?

Again, to reiterate, most scholars traditionally understand of verse 11 of Ezekiel 38 to *refer to Israel, because in the verses just prior, it definitely references Israel returning to its land. However, when the prophet speaks of the land of unwalled villages, he is not referencing Israel.* Ezekiel adds significant metaphors to amplify his castigation of the people living there:

- It is a land of unwalled villages,
- Its people dwell without walls around their city,
- These cities employ neither bars nor gates to keep invaders out.
- They dwell carelessly because they think they are invincible.

On the other hand, while the identity of the people in verse 11 may be debated, we know unquestionably, that the personage before verse 11 is **Gog**.

> *Thou shalt ascend and come like a storm, thou shalt be like a cloud to cover the land, thou, and all thy bands, and many people with thee. Thus saith the Lord GOD; It shall also come to pass, that at the same time shall things come into thy mind, and thou shalt think an evil thought.* (Ezekiel 38:9-10)

The many nations enumerated by Ezekiel such as Persia, Libya, Put, Meshech, Tubal, etc., come like a storm with Gog to "cover the land". Gog assembles a confederation that would be judged by almost anyone as *overkill* since they collectively drastically outnumber Israel. Israel wouldn't be that confident it would be able to withstand all of these nations, particularly if their leader is Russia. Their state of mind will be fear. They will be seeking faith and praying for deliverance. They will be fearful but hopeful – not arrogant. That will be the heart of Israel when Gog approaches.

126

ADDITIONAL REASONING TO INTERPRET THE PASSAGE

Since the usage of *betach* in other verses asserts the promise of peace and safety to Israel, why would verse 11 be a *pejorative* (a criticism) against Israel, and no longer a *promise?* What is it that makes Ezekiel 38:11 different from the other verses where *betach* is the fulfillment of God's covenant with Israel? Is it because the verse mentions a land of unwalled villages (which Jerusalem and Judea is not, possessing a 417-mile wall to protect its people from Palestinian terrorists)?

No, Israel is neither overconfident nor is it secure at this time. It believes in its military, the IDF. But it realizes that U.S. military support under President Obama can only be described as *shaky* at best.

Additionally, Israel knows it does not comprise a land of unwalled villages. We should not suppose that use the phrase "gates and bars" (or "neither gates nor bars") changes the interpretation. This phrase is used commonly in the KJV of the Old Testament to underscore that a village is either *walled and protected*, or *unwalled and unprotected* (for instance, see Deuteronomy 3:5, I Samuel 23:7, 2 Chronicles 8:5, 14:7, Jeremiah 49:31 among many others). It constitutes a common catchphrase used in the Hebrew Scriptures much like "signs and wonders" which is used throughout both the Old Testament and the New. The people referenced in verse 11 believe they live securely and do so overconfidently (in the same way the people depicted in in Isaiah 47:8), *living in unwalled villages without gates or bars.*

Thus, the word *betach* in Ezekiel 38:11, should have been translated "carelessly". If it had been as illustrated above, it would clearly indicate that the prophet is NOT condemning Israel. The criticism that should have been implied in verse 11 *references a different land altogether.* Therefore, could the "land of unwalled villages" be *the Daughter of Babylon?* After all, it has been so from its founding: America lives in a land of unwalled villages and has been generally overconfident regarding it military prowess, its assumption of being the "sole superpower", and its self-centered and self-serving approach to economics and politics.

Notice that Isaiah's use of *betach* is derogatory – the use of the word *be-*

tach seems cynical when saying to the effect, "You think you dwell safely, but you have a false sense of security". To cite this instance once again for the reader's convenience: *"Therefore hear now this, thou that art given to pleasures, that dwellest **carelessly**, (betach) that sayest in thine heart, 'I am, and none else beside me; I shall not sit as a widow, neither shall I know the loss of children'"*. (Isaiah 47:8) **The daughter of Babylon constitutes *overconfidence incarnate.*** This seems to be an essential element of its undoing as other passages mentioned above plainly express. It is an arrogant nation. Jeremiah says that *the daughter of Babylon is an arrogant land twice* prophesying in Jeremiah 50:31-32, *"O thou most proud."* While Israel has certainly sinned against its God and spoke arrogantly against him as the prophets lament so many times, in Ezekiel 38-39 there are no statements that castigate Israel for being "overconfident." Israel is ripe and ready to receive the biblical testimony that Jehovah is its God and comprises its sole source of salvation. As Douglas Berner, author of *The Silence is Broken* indicates, Jehovah is now ready to speak and will do so through the actions he will take on the daughter of Babylon and its rival Gog.

THE MANY HEBREW MEANINGS FOR *YOWM* ("DAY")

Indeed, another most striking element of the verse consists in the manner in which the original *King James Version* translated verse 10. Compare the words and the translation of the KJV with that of the *New American Standard Bible*.

- The KJV translates Ezekiel 38:10 in this way: *"Thus saith the Lord God; 'It shall also come to pass, that at the same time shall things come into thy mind and thou shalt think an evil thought...'"*

- The NASB translates Ezekiel 38:10 using these words: *"Thus says the Lord GOD, 'It will come about on that day, that thoughts will come into your mind and you will devise an evil plan...'"*

There are two key words used at the beginning of the verse: The word for day, *yowm* (*Strong's* H3117), and the word for "come to pass", *hayah* (*Strong's* H1961). The Hebrew word, *yow* or *yown*, translated typically *day* comprises an ambiguous term as the word *yowm* can literally mean so many different things, i.e., many different periods of time – from one day, two days, up to one year less-one-day; or an era, forever, continually, or just a period of a human being's life.

For those who argue that *yomn* ("day") never means anything other than a 24-hour period, consider these many uses according to the lexicon in the Blue Letter Bible:

> The Strong's H3117 (DAY) is translated in the following <u>manner:</u>
> day (2,008x), time (64x), chronicles (with H1697) (37x),
> daily (44x), ever (18x), year (14x), continually (10x),
> when (10x), as (10x), while (8x),
> always (4x), whole (4x), alway (4x), *miscellaneous* (44x).

When one argues that the **day** *of the Lord* must be a 24-hour period, which many do, the extensive uses of **day** argues quite to the contrary – the period may consist of a wide-variety of durations.

In contrast, *hayah*, is quite specific. It means an emphatic occurrence such as "it shall surely happen" or "it will most certainly come to pass". Thus, the translation that virtually all versions employ conveys something to the effect that "on that day" or "at that time" it will "come to pass". But it should be *emphatically* stated as "on that day, it will *most certainly* come to pass". The closest English synonyms would be *inexorably* or *inevitably*. In other words, it would impossible for it not to happen. This gives us a true sense of how providential the event is.

For our purposes here, the point is that the Hebrew word for day, *yowm*, is not necessarily a single day, but likely expresses a compressed period of time – perhaps a matter of weeks or several months. "At the same time" could mean within the same 24-hour period, but it might also mean "during this same period of time." However, its emphatic usage suggests the Prophet wanted to stress how *two* events were tied together and occurred within a definite and limited span of time. The two events were inexorably or inevitably connected. History would record these events to be dependent upon one another.

What is different about the KJV translation, which is generally missed perhaps because the other translations do not include the word, is the insertion of the small adverb ***also***. We know that ***also*** is used to link a series of items or events. *Also* is not necessary unless it is specifying something distinct from what the speaker was previously discussing. To express this more clearly, one could use these words, "In addition, it shall *also* be the case..." meaning that in addition to what I just told you, let me tell you something else which is not the same thing as what I just told you." In this instance, the KJV suggests that what is about to be shared in the verses that follow amounts to something different than what has been said previously.

Perhaps we could consider this prophecy in Ezekiel 38:10-13 to be *a parenthetical comment*. It is an "aside" as we now say. However we term it, the inference is that we are not dealing in these verses with the land of Israel. We are dealing with a different land or several other lands. *For at the same time that Gog is thinking about attacking Israel he also has yet another evil thought.* He will go up against "the land of unwalled villages" where those that dwell securely do so carelessly, overconfidently.

It is most intriguing that the translators of the King James Bible, when examining this passage, *judged Gog to be about two things, not just one*. While Gog is planning to come up against Israel along with what the consensus agrees comprise Islamic hordes, Gog thinks up another evil action. "At the same time, you Gog will also think of attacking a land of unwalled villages." I contend this use of *also* was not accidental or careless (no pun intended). The translators here believed the Hebrew was conveying that Gog has two plans in mind, not just one. If so, then the obvious question becomes, "Where is this land?" And that leads to asking follow-up questions attempting to pin down what has happened to that land, that it deserves the scorn of God through the prophet Ezekiel? What is going on there? Why is it being attacked?

This land constitutes a land that seems to be at rest. It comprises a wealthy land; it has cattle and goods. Its people, like Israel, have been gathered from many nations. Unlike Israel, its cities lie without walls. Because of their dwelling so peaceably, Gog will think to himself...

> *I will go up to the land of unwalled villages; I will go to them that
> are at rest, that dwell safely, all of them dwelling without walls,
> and having neither bars nor gates, To take a spoil, and to take a
> prey; to turn thine hand upon the desolate places that are
> now inhabited, and upon the people that are gathered out of the
> nations, which have gotten cattle and goods, that dwell in the
> midst of the land.* (Ezekiel 38:11-12)

What we see are contrasting situations. One is a land promised safety but
has not yet achieved it and will thus be threatened by Gog – so much so
that when it is delivered, only God can be given credit for its salvation.
This land is Israel. God will be glorified by Israel's deliverance (Ezekiel
38:23, 39:22, 27). The other land is not promised safety at all, but judgment. And it is stunned when it is attacked. We can see this by considering its comments upon being attacked as described in Ezekiel 38:13.

EZEKIEL 38:13 – A NATION ATTACKED, OR JUST A PROTEST?

Indeed, verse 13 buttresses the argument for this land and its peoples being the *daughter of Babylon.* The standard view is that in this verse we
read about Sheba and Dedan, the Merchants of Tarshish, and its "young
lions." Almost every author and scholar from Hal Lindsey and John
Walvoord in 1970, to Chuck Missler and Bill Salus today, propose these
peoples are easy to identify. Sheba and Dedan refer to those that live on
the Arabian peninsula, the Merchants of Tarshish are Europeans (most
likely England, but also Spain and Portugal), and the young lions are the
"offspring" – the colonies – of these European nations which include the
countries of the Americas, but most importantly, the United
States. Those that have written about this verse interpret the meaning of
the words Ezekiel uses to suggest that these peoples *protest* about the
invasion of Gog as it comes against Israel, *but do nothing.* As author and
teacher Ron Rhodes says in his book, *Northern Storm Rising,* the verse
smacks of a "lame protest". But it is this author's contention that there is
much more to the statement in verse 13 than just a protest, an expressed
astonishment that Gog would have the nerve to attack Israel.

Indeed, verse 13 could just as easily convey a shock or surprise as if these nations are in fact *the recipients of Gog's attack.* In other words, these nations are not protesting what Gog is planning for Israel; they are expressing their astonishment that Gog is attacking them! But "being astounded" is not the main point of the statement. Some conjecture these nations look upon Gog as taking possession of what they (the nations) had coveted. However, that is not the point of this statement. What is most surprising to them: *they are under assault.* Read verse 13 from this perspective:

> *Sheba, and Dedan, and the merchants of Tarshish, with all the young lions thereof, shall say unto thee, Art thou come to take a spoil? Hast thou gathered thy company to take a prey? to carry away silver and gold, to take away cattle and goods, to take a great spoil?*

If America were the subject of the attack, we would ask ourselves "why are we being attacked Gog?" We would wonder (rather quickly I would suppose as there would be little time to conjecture), why Gog's missiles are heading toward us, "Are you planning after you attack our major cities to take away our cattle and goods, our silver and gold, to take our people away as captives? Gog, what's up?"

The subjects of verse 13, the nations (peoples) called out, are not as concerned with Israel being attacked as much as they are concerned that *they are being attacked.* However, does this square with other verses within Ezekiel 38-39? It absolutely does. These nations that are the "third parties" (Israel being the first and Gog the second), provide clear insight into the mindset of those *villagers living without walls.*

THOSE THAT LIVE IN THE ISLES

Ezekiel 39 supplies the details of how Gog is judged on the mountains of Israel. The prophecy says that five-sixths (83%) of his armies will be destroyed. (Ezekiel 39:2) They that shall dwell carelessly (*betach*) are those that dwell in the *isles*: *"And I will send a fire on Magog, and among them that dwell carelessly in the isles: and they shall know that I am the LORD." Ezekiel 39:6)*

The land of *Gog – Magog* – will be the recipient of God's judgment. But Magog is not the only land receiving judgment. Those that "dwell in the isles" are subjected to the assault of fire as well. *So who are these people?*

The scripture paints a picture of these "island people" typically as merchants, as Canaanites (Canaan means merchant), as the people of the Canaanite (Phoenician) city of Tyre and Sidon (aka Zidon), and the merchants of Tarshish. We already encountered the Merchants of Tarshish in Ezekiel 38:13. The reference here to this same people, however, seems quite clear when one considers the use of the little Hebrew word for *isle*, the small word **iy** (pronounced "e", *Strong's* H339). The word *iy*, appears 36 times in the Old Testament – 30 times it is translated as *isle*. Its usage, however, seems idiomatic for Old Testament writings which connote those lands extending *"far from the center of the world"* – that center being, of course, *Jerusalem*. A good example of its usage is seen in Isaiah 23. And guess who the subject of this passage is?

- *Be still, ye inhabitants of the **isle**; thou whom the merchants of Zidon (Sidon), that pass over the sea, have replenished.* (Isaiah 23:2)

- *Pass ye over to Tarshish; howl, ye inhabitants of the isle.* (Isaiah 23:6)

In the one instance where the translators of the KJV employ the word "country" instead of *isle*, we see the same people identified once more: *"Because of the day that cometh to spoil all the Philistines, and to cut off from **Tyrus and Zidon** every helper that remaineth: for the LORD will spoil the Philistines, the remnant of the **country** (Strong's H339) of Caphtor."* (Jeremiah 47:4) [73]

At the very beginning, the Old Testament tells us that the sons of Japheth will inhabit the *isles* (the countries far away). This testimony is supplied in Genesis 10:2-5. *"By these were the **isles** [iy] of the Gentiles divided in their lands; every one after his tongue, after their families, in their nations."* (Genesis 10:5) It should be apparent that the Bible does not often use the term *iy* explicitly to convey an "island" although it can mean that. Instead, the biblical meaning relates to lands that are distantly outside the realm of the Levant, *far from the shores of Israel.*

Figure 13 - The Minoan Civilization, Contemporary to Ancient Egypt, 2,500 years before Christ

Likewise, in Isaiah 11:11, we see the term *iy* used in regard to the second re-gathering of Israel:

> *And it shall come to pass in that day, that the Lord shall set his hand again the second time to recover the remnant of his people, which shall be left, from Assyria, and from Egypt, and from Pathros, and from Cush, and from Elam, and from Shinar, and from Hamath, and from the **islands** of the sea."*

In fact, Isaiah uses the word *iy* 17 times. His last usage reinforces the same theme underscored throughout this chapter:

> *And I will set a sign among them, and I will send those that escape of them unto the nations, to Tarshish, Pul, and Lud, that draw the bow, to Tubal, and Javan, to the **isles [iy]** afar off, that have not heard my fame, neither have seen my glory; and they shall declare my glory among the Gentiles.* (Isaiah 66:19)

There are many cases, as the instances above demonstrate, in which Isaiah relates the *isles* to Tyre, Sidon, and Tarshish. Indeed, yet another reference that connect *iy* to these specific peoples can be found in Jeremiah 25:22: *"And all the kings of Tyrus, and all the kings of Zidon, and the kings of the isles which are beyond the sea."* As my co-authors and I put forth in *The Final Babylon,* these names reference the lands of the New World, lands discovered and exploited by ancient peoples (the Phoenicians) dating at least as far back as Solomon (1000 BC) and possibly all the way back to the time of the Minoans (2000 BC). When Ezekiel declares that God will send fire on Magog and those that *dwell carelessly in the isles,* he is most likely conveying that the lands explored and settled by the Sidonians (aka the Canaanites or Phoenicians), will be judged with fire as well as Magog.

For these many biblical reasons, America comprises the daughter of Babylon; and God through Ezekiel has encoded it within this grand prophecy. (See Appendix B for a more detailed review of why America is Babylon).

Even Sir Halford MacKender in his pivotal strategy known as the *Heartland Theory* (first published for the Geographic Society of England in 1904, and which serves as the basis for geopolitical theory today – see Zbigniew Brzezinski – *The Grand Chessboard*), considers the *heartland* to be the contiguous continents of Europe and Asia (nowadays called Eurasia), with the rest of the world as the "islands" that are disadvantaged by being outside the world's core landmass. In this sense, MacKender used biblical terminology. MacKender's theory laid the groundwork for understanding how those who lie beyond the *heartland* (like England and America), must play what the British called *The Great Game* in the nineteenth century, predominantly with Russia (as the Ottoman Empire of the Turks was crumbling). The Crimean War (1853-56), where Britain and France allied themselves with the Turks against Russia, was the last vestige of life for the old Ottoman Empire. World War I ended what was already a tired and decimated kingdom. Thereafter, only Russia and China would contend with England and be future rivals to the Anglo-American world of the twentieth (and the twenty-first century).

Consequently, to understand the current situation in the Middle East, one must understand the notion of *heartland* and the *isles* that exist outside Eurasia, and therefore, how *the geopolitical game must be played.* Arguably, the current U.S. administration does not fully grasp MacKender and does not play *the Game Great* which much skill. It has moved away from the notion that America, like England, should consider itself any sort of empire, and thus should make no claims on the Middle East. The other core geopolitical strategy, the "balance of power" discussed earlier (referencing the Treaty of Westphalia), would demand the U.S. maintain a strong presence in every region it considers strategic (and which it cannot afford to cede to Russia), and is now overturned or "superseded". Some say the U.S. has a new strategy. I would argue that it has *no strategy at all.*

CONCLUSION

The standard bearers of biblical prophecy from Hal Lindsey and Tim LaHaye in the 1970s to Chuck Missler and Bill Salus today, uniformly agree that the reference *in Ezekiel 39* to those that "dwell carelessly in the isles" *likely means the Americas.* My conviction in this regard: they are exactly right. To quote an old standard, the isles are those "far away places with strange sounding names" (especially if you speak Hebrew and reside at the center of the world!) Whether we are reading the Bible or evaluating current world geopolitics, we should draw the same conclusion. When we dig deeply into the prophetic mindset of the prophets like Isaiah, Jeremiah, Zechariah, and especially Ezekiel, we understand that the world in the last days will consist of the lands and people of (1) Gog from Magog supported by the nations like Iran (and possibly Syria and Turkey) in striking distance of Israel; (2) those that dwell in *isles* far away across the seas, notably the Merchants of Tarshish and its young lions; and (3) most importantly, the apple of God's eye, Israel. Additionally, in the final analysis, *Israel will stand alone* with only its God, Jehovah, to protect it in the latter days before the coming of its Messiah, the Lord Jesus Christ.

To make the point even more concise: the Daughter of Babylon will be destroyed by Gog, Gog will be destroyed by God, and then only the "little horn" of Daniel, the Antichrist, will remain to gather up what's left of the pieces of the world to bring these resources, weapons, and soldiers to bear against tiny Israel, God's people. But that is getting ahead of the story.

Returning then to the context of what's happening today in Syria, which is where we began, we must point out that the U.S. appears destined to fail in its efforts to remove Bashar al-Assad. It likely will not position troops or continue any meaningful presence in the Levant, while Russia appears destined to install itself as the prime mover and shaker not only in Syria but in all the lands just to the north of Israel. It is there from whence the prophets of the Bible uniformly assert the powers seeking to destroy Israel will originate. Gog will follow the same approach – attack from the north.

Author Taimoor Khan says as much in his analysis published October 9, 2015, in *ValueWalk*:

> The prime mission in the region is to eliminate ISIS, but for that very purpose, the U.S. and Russia have adopted different approaches. The U.S. believes that defeating ISIS will not be possible without removing Assad, while Russia sees Assad as a heroic fighter against terrorism, as recently characterized by Putin in a 90-minute meeting with Obama.
>
> American intentions are clear in the region, as they not only want to end terrorism but also the long regime of Bashar al-Assad to introduce democracy and ensure that peace ensues through this ideology. However, it appears to be an interesting waiting game considering that Washington is once again pursuing the same approach *that has **never worked** in such a volatile region and is a mission that is already set for failure.* [74] *[Emphasis added]*

As Ezekiel prophesies, this colossal failure in geopolitical strategy will have disastrous consequences for the nation whom the Bible calls the *Daughter of Babylon* – and for the mighty Gog from the land of Magog as well.

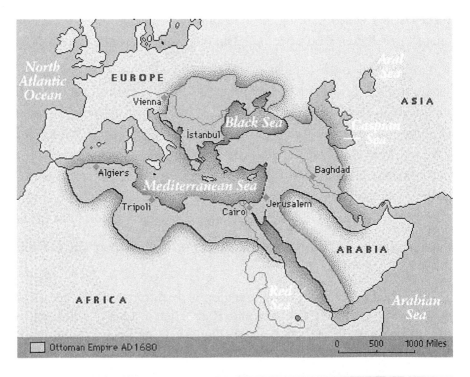

Figure 14 - The Dissolution of the Sultanate 17 November 1922

8: The Ottoman Empire Revived – A Mortal Head Wound Healed?

"The Turkish Empire was the seat of the Islamic caliphate. It was not until 1923
that the Islamic caliphate was officially abolished.
Today the Islamic world awaits the restoration of that caliphate."

Joel Richardson, author, **The Islamic Antichrist**

A QUICK HISTORY OF THE OTTOMAN EMPIRE

DEPENDING UPON WHAT CONSTITUTES AN EMPIRE, THE OTTOMAN EMPIRE OF THE TURKS LASTED BETWEEN 700 TO 1,000 YEARS. MORE COMMONLY, SCHOLARS STATE ITS BEGINNING COMMENCES with Osman 1 (1259 1326, from which the name *Ottoman* was derived), when it gained control of the region known as Anatolia (today's Turkey). Its story actually began two hundred years earlier while the group only a small tribe in the Asian steppes. This then unremarkable tribe originated as a shamanistic-oriented people (pagan/occultist), eventually converting to Islam. The Seljuk, a powerful Islamic tribe that had "settled down" instead of remaining nomadic (as most other tribes in this region were in the year 1070), pushed the Ottomans out of their original location in the Asian steppes and drove them toward Byzantium, specifically into Anatolia. After Osman ascended to power, he would soon dominate Anatolia. Under his son, the Empire would extend its reign into the Balkans and the Eastern Mediterranean.

The Ottomans advanced toward Europe but were pushed back in 1444 at the Battle of Varna. In 1453, the Ottomans finally captured Constantinople, the capital of the Byzantine Empire, and changed its name to Istanbul. The threat of the Ottomans and Islam led many Orthodox (the "Eastern Church") intellectuals and great works of classical times to retreat to Europe. As has been taught, the wealth of Byzantium stimulated the Renaissance and would eventually lead to great advances in many of the sciences. Also of note, the Ottoman Empire controlled what is today South Africa locking up trade routes to India and Asia. In 1488, the Portuguese discovered *The Cape of Good Hope* at the tip of Africa. It was during this time when Columbus sought to prove a Western route to India, no doubt in part to avoid the Ottomans he would have to pass by in South Africa.

Beginning in 1566, however, the Empire began to stagnate and fell behind in technology to the Europeans. The failed Battle for Vienna in 1683 marked another key date in the decline of the Ottoman Empire as Europe was spared from Islamic control. (Of particular note, in 1517 the Ottoman Empire conquered Jerusalem. The Ottomans were dispossessed of it in 1917 – 400 years later – with Major Allenby took Jerusalem for the British.)

The abolition of the Ottoman sultanate occurred on 17 November 1922. By then, the modern Turkish leadership was hated by the Arabs, had murdered 1.5 million Armenians (beginning in 1915 and continuing until its dissolution), and had been soundly defeated in World War I having joined with "the Huns" (the Germans) in a last gasp attempt to strengthen its faltering empire. The caliphate was officially declared ended on 3 March 1924. Until ISIS declared itself a caliphate in 2014 from the territories of Syria and Iraq, few Muslims recognized any caliphate for 90 years.[75]

In summary, Ottoman Empire grew into a powerful force dominating the Middle East, the Balkans, Northern Africa, the tip of Africa, and selected other territories for several centuries. It was not, however, by any means uniformly Islamic. By the nineteenth century, Christians were thriving within the empire, creating resentment among their fellow Islamic citizens.[76] Long before this time, certainly by the time of the Crimean War (1853-1856), the Ottoman Empire struggled to remain in control of its territories. It assumed five million pounds sterling in debt from the British in 1854. According to Eugene Rogan in his 2011 history on the Arabs, the threat of European banks was far greater than outside armies! The Ottoman government declared bankruptcy by 1875 and gave over financial control to the British and the French through the Ottoman Public Debt Administration. Nevertheless, the empire suffered ignominious military defeats to the Russians in 1877-78 and in the Balkans War of 1912-13, involving several countries (Bulgaria, Serbia, Greece) preceding World War I.

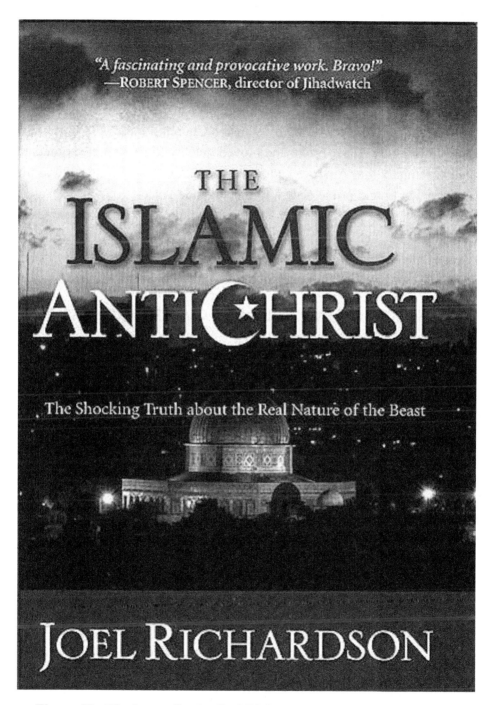

Figure 15 - The best seller by Joel Richardson, *The Islamic Antichrist*

The Sykes-Picot Treaty between the English and the French took what was left of the Ottoman Empire and paved the way to create new nation states after World War I, states that had little to do with ethnicities and logical tribal groups. The insanity in the Middle East today owes itself in part to the dissection of the Ottoman Empire and its partitioning among the victors of World War I, led by Winston Churchill in the 1920s. (Britain as an empire was nearly broke and moved quickly to resolve the borders in Mesopotamia before America came into the picture to claim its stake in the post-war world and prime access to the strategic "black gold" so prevalent in the region). In conclusion: the world continues to pay a heavy price for the British and French colonialism during this era (along with a growing threat of the American Empire entering the mix in the 1920s). (See Appendix A: "The Climax of Colonialism and the Roots of Jihad").

WILL THE TURKISH EMPIRE LEAD ISLAM AGAINST ISRAEL?

Joel Richardson and Walid Shoebat have become popular authors writing on the topic of Bible prophecy over the past decade. Shoebat's history is most colorful (to say the least, declaring himself a converted Islamic terrorist – although some like the *Jerusalem Post* in 2008 disputed his testimony[77]). Richardson's background remains less certain to this author. His published biographical comments do not include any clarity about his history other than he lives in the United States with his wife and five children. Although I cannot confirm any details, it seems reasonable that Richardson, like Shoebat, has a Middle Eastern heritage especially given the number of Muslim friends he mentions in his books. Both authors have written extensively on the "Turkey thesis" that the Antichrist will be a Muslim and that his powerbase will be the modern state of Turkey. [78]

Joel Richardson asserts that Muslims look forward to the day when Turkey will once again be the caliphate of the Islamic world:

> The Turkish Empire was the seat of the Islamic caliphate. It was not until 1923 that the Islamic caliphate was officially abolished. Today the Islamic world awaits the restoration of that caliphate. The Bible teaches that someday soon the Turkish empire will be revived: The inhabitants of the earth whose names have not been

written in the Book of Life from the creation of the world will be astonished when they see the beast, because he once was, then he was not, and yet came again. (Revelation 17:8) At that time, we may expect to see the Islamic caliphate restored. Eventually a man might rise to this position whom the Muslim world would refer to as the Mahdi, but people of understanding will identify him as the man known biblically as the Antichrist. [79]

Shoebat writes with considerable passion concerning Turkey as the nation that will lead Islam, reinstating a caliphate. In one article, he advances seven scriptural arguments asserting together they testify Turkey will lead Islam and give rise to the Antichrist. *Shoebat, like Richardson, conflates the Antichrist with the personage of Gog from Ezekiel 38.* Since Ezekiel identifies the various tribes from Genesis 10 (the table of nations) that comprise Gog, for Shoebat, this proves that Turkey constitutes the home for Satan and from which the Antichrist arises.

> The first requirement the head nation of the Antichrist Empire must fulfill is the political capital to fill the role of mediator and guarantor of a comprehensive peace treaty between Israel and the surrounding nations that represent a threat to her: *'He will confirm a covenant with many for one 'seven''* (Daniel 9:26).

> In order to mediate such a covenant or treaty, this nation needs to have the reputation for being moderate and must possess the trust of the Israelis and the world. The Bible says that Israel will rely on this nation and will feel secure through the promises and terms established in the peace treaty. The Bible says that after Christ returns, *"In that day the remnant of Israel, the survivors of the house of Jacob, will no longer rely on him who struck them down but will truly rely on Jehovah, the Holy One of Israel."* (Isaiah 10:20) [80]

For Richardson, like Shoebat, *Antichrist is Gog and Gog is Antichrist.* In stark contrast, conventional scholarship draws a solid line distinguishing the two which both of these authors reject. Richardson believes it is inconceivable they could be distinct for numerous reasons. He also draws upon Ezekiel 38. And he recognizes that if this assertion is true, "this absolutely changes everything." His pronouncement, if true, would indeed comprise a most iconoclastic claim among teachers of Bible prophecy.

For years, students of Bible prophecy have been taught that "Gog," spoken of in Ezekiel 38 and 39, cannot be the same as the Antichrist/Beast spoken of in the New Testament. Among the reasons set forth to argue that the two cannot be the same, none carry any weight. [In Richardson's opinion]

In fact, any examination of the text will establish *that the two are, in fact, one and the same individual.* If this is the case, however, this changes everything within the world of popular biblical prophecy. If it can be shown *that Gog is the Antichrist/Beast, then it is also clear that the Antichrist and his armies are from the Middle East and not Europe, as is popularly taught.* But more importantly, it means that until Jesus returns, Islam is not going away. Instead of being a system of belief that is about to be "eliminated," as so many actually claim, Islam represents the single greatest challenge that the church will ever face. [81] *[Comment and emphasis mine].*

For Shoebat, Turkey will declare jihad once it has pronounced itself an official caliphate (again). When this happens, it will be no small matter. Shoebat sees the Western world threatened to the greatest possible extent:

The Caliphate confers legitimacy to jihad. According to Islamic law, without a Caliphate, it is not possible to declare a genuinely sanctioned pan-Islamic Jihad. Similar to the need for the President of the United States to declare a state of war, it is also necessary for a Caliph to be in office for any official pan-Islamic Jihad to be declared. But once a Caliph is in office, it is actually law for him to engage the non-Muslim world in war in order to spread Islam. This is not to say that Muslims have not conducted jihad against non-Muslims, but these have largely been the acts of small groups or individuals. In other words, jihad under a Caliph would be genuine 'old school' jihad – not a bombing here on an attack there. It would become the modern world's first true full-scale global religious war. It would involve everything that the Islamic world could throw out, from economic jihad to withholding oil to cyber jihad to multi-front military conflicts.

From my vantage point, Shoebat and Richardson strive to reconcile certain challenges they see in the conventional view. First, Islam truly is an enormous challenge for the Christian Church. But beyond this, they hope to reconcile inconsistencies related to Israel's restoration. "How could Israel be restored to its Holy Land, be attacked by Gog, be rescued from Gog, and then still face an even greater adversary in the Antichrist?" That is, "How could Israel be promised safety in their land, then rescued, and still face an even greater terror than Gog, perhaps 3.5 to 7 years later?" Of course, the conventional view argues this is exactly what happens. And there is some tension here. The LORD God miraculously saves Israel from Gog, (no indication that Israel suffers any losses then) and yet Israel still does not appreciate that the God of the Bible is the only true God and He seeks their devotion. Afterwards, Antichrist arrives on the scene, confirms a covenant with Israel for seven years, and then breaks that covenant halfway through its term (Daniel 9:24-27). This initiates another holocaust in which Jerusalem will be attacked and many Jews are killed and taken captive.

> *7 Awake, O sword, against my shepherd, and against the man that is my fellow, saith the LORD of hosts: smite the shepherd, and the sheep shall be scattered: and I will turn mine hand upon the little ones. 8 And it shall come to pass, that in all the land, saith the LORD,* **two parts therein shall be cut off and die; but the third shall be left therein.** *9 And I will bring the third part through the fire, and will re-fine them as silver is refined, and will try them as gold is tried: they shall call on my name, and I will hear them: I will say, It is my peo-ple: and they shall say, The LORD is my God. (Zechariah 13:7-9)*

At this time, the whole world moves against Israel (not just Islam). Finally, all of the true Israel repents and believes in the LORD and in His Christ:

> *And it shall come to pass in that day that I will seek to destroy all the nations that come against Jerusalem. And I will pour upon the house of David, and upon the inhabitants of Jerusalem, the spirit of grace and of supplications: and they shall look upon me whom they have pierced, and they shall mourn for him, as one mourneth for his only son, and shall be in bitterness for him, as one that is in bitterness for his firstborn. (Zechariah 12:9-10)*

Toward the end of the seven-year covenant, the Kings of the East move against the armies of Antichrist and come through Mesopotamia (the River

145

	Battle of Gog and Magog	Battle of Armageddon
1	Occurs before or at the beginning of the Great Tribulation	Occurs at the end of the Great Tribulation.
2	Specific nations are identified immediately surrounding Israel	Nations from all over the world come together to fight Israel
3	The enemies of Israel attack Israel from the northern quarters mustering in Israel's mountains	The enemies of Israel gather at Megiddo but may attack from multiple directions
4	The person Gog leads the attack	The Antichrist leads the attack
5	The dead are left on the ground becoming food for birds – it takes 7 months to bury the dead and 7 years to burn the weapons.	The dead are annihilated and do not litter the ground – the earth is soon renovated. No time is specified for weapons or bodies.
6	The nature of the destruction could be nuclear – described as fire and brimstone and plague	The destruction of the enemies is the Word of the LORD. The armies appear to be swept away.
7	The enemies are destroyed on the mountains of Israel.	The enemies are destroyed on the plains of Megiddo.
8	There is no indication that Israel loses land or population due to the war against Gog	Two-thirds of Israel's population is destroyed and Israel is occupied by the Antichrist
9	There are no specific instructions for Jews to flee Israel	The Jews are warned to flee to Bozrah (Petra) to be protected
10	Gog comes against Israel for God's glory through their defeat – no judgment against Israel	Antichrist attacks Israel as judgment for Israel's rejection of its Messiah

Euphrates is dried up to prepare their way – Revelation 9:11 – 14), on their way to the Battle of Armageddon in which not just Islamic armies, but all the armies of the world come to face the Christ of the Jews in a final battle to kill the Jews and attack their Messiah. This war is NOT the Battle of Gog and Magog. The two are distinct in many ways. Let's consider ten essential differences between the two battles according to conventional scholarship (in contrast to Shoebat/Richardson et al) – which I believe comprises what the Bible *expressly* says (not what is inferred or left out of its prophetic accounts). [The table is presented on the preceding page].

As the table highlights, the battles appear to transpire at different times. The parties involved in the fight are different. The scope of the attack is not the same. The Bible does not expressly identify the attacking leader. What happens to the dead bodies from the battles are distinct. How the destruction happens seems to be different. Precisely where the battle is fought differs. The warning and directions the LORD gives to Israel are not the same. The purpose of God does not constitute the same rationale. And lastly, the impact on Israel is entirely different. To conclude the battles are "the very same fights with the very same fighters" is quite a stretch.

OTHERS LESSER KNOWN AUTHORS FOLLOW SUIT

On June 7, 2015, Craig C. White published on his blog warnings about the Turkish President Recep Tayyip Erdogan. Asking, "What is Erdogan Up To?" White suggests Erdogan seeks to complete a palace as prelude to announcing his highly esteemed role as Sultan of a new caliphate.

> A Sultan is the political and religious ruler of a Turkish empire. Every past Sultan of the Turkish ruled Ottoman Empire had his own Mosque built that was dedicated to himself. Guess what? Turkish President Erdogan has commissioned the building of a mega Mosque in Istanbul with a capacity to seat 30,000 worshipers. The Mosque is being built on top of the highest hill in the Asian part of the city overlooking the Bosporus towards Europe. The Mosque property covers the area of more than 2,000 soccer fields. This will be the largest Mosque in Turkey with the tallest Minarets in the world. The name of the Mosque suggests that it will

be dedicated to the Sultan of the Turkish Empire. Wait for just one minute! There is no Turkish Empire today. For that matter there isn't a Sultan either. What is Erdogan up to? All parties involved suspect that Turkish President Erdogan wants to be the new Sultan of a revived Turkish ruled Ottoman Empire.

This new palace is called the "White Palace" signifying its cleanliness and purity. It is to be built in a preserved area dedicated to Suleiman Shah, the grandfather of the Ottoman Empire. In so doing, Erdogan ignored two court rulings to stop his plans to build the palace in Ankara, Turkey's capital city. According to White, to build there is illegal. Additionally, and more to the political point, Erdogan hoped that with the

Figure 16 – Is there Room for Two Caliphates? ISIS and Turkey.

election of June 7, 2015 he could establish a mandate allowing Turkey to rewrite its constitution and move toward a Presidential system, with greater authority for the executive office. Perhaps it follows, so White says, that there is a move in Turkey to proclaim Erdogan God, including changing the wording in the national anthem to make a special note that Erdogan gets his power from Allah himself. Why is he going so far? White, like Shoebat and Richardson, believes Turkish destiny leads to it becoming home base to the Antichrist. For these authors, all eyes hold fast upon Erdogan:

> Turkish President Erdogan intends to revive the Turkish ruled Ottoman Empire with himself at its head. He intends to bring many other nations under Turkish control beginning with Syria. The bi-

ble tells us that the Antichrist will invade Syria and then invade Israel just like the ancient Assyrian kings did. [Note: This is the interpretation that White and Richardson assert; I assume Shoebat does as well] I hope you are listening. Erdogan is the Antichrist. [White's contention] He has already claimed to be god. He will soon invade Syria and then lead the forces that are already fighting in Syria today into Israel! [82] [Of course, now we know Russia might disagree since it has 4,000 personnel, 34 fighter-bombers, and many artillery pieces, antiaircraft guns, and armored vehicles there.]

So what happened? Breitbart News Network supplies the details of what became one of the bloodiest times in modern Turkey history. I summarize the facts below:

- The June 7, 2015 election went well but did not give Erdogan a true majority. "One reason that the Kurdish party HDP did so well on June 7 was that they promised the voters that they would disarm the Kurdistan Workers' Party (PKK), which is considered a terrorist group by Turkey, Europe and the United States. However, once the election ended, they reversed that promise."

- Another election held in November 2015 did get a majority but not a "super majority" – meaning that Erdogan's political party still did not win as many seats as needed in order to rewrite the constitution.

- During the interim, terrorism began to manifest. There was a July 20, 2015 terrorist attack in the city of Suruc that "killed 33 people, mostly young pro-Kurdish activists." Shortly thereafter, a two-year old ceasefire between the PKK and the government fell apart. Erdogan declared war on the PKK.

- According to the reporter, "But that was not the worst of it. On October 12, Turkey went into a state of shock after a massive terrorist attack at a 'peace rally' in the capital city Ankara that killed 97 people and injured hundreds more. It is considered the worst terrorist massacre in Turkey's history, sometimes even called "Turkey's 9/11.""

- In this atmosphere of increasing chaos in Turkey, millions of Turkish voters decided that they really preferred a strongman to be in charge, and so they voted for Erdogan's AKP party.[83]

Weeks later, Turkey now seems destined to institute a "fascist regime" (as so many Western countries seems to be flirting with these days). If Erdogan appears ready to step into the shoes of the Antichrist – the Beast of Revelation – the news finding its way out of Turkey leaves something to be desired. Nevertheless, the revival of the Turkish Empire is *the wound that is healed* (according to these Islamic antichrist proponents).

> *The Right Scoop*, a conservative Christian blog, reinforces the same contentions as the previous authors: Erdogan is striving to become President, this will turn into a caliphate, and then he will become the Antichrist (Gog who attacks Israel is the same personage as Antichrist): "So let's cut to the chase. If Erdogan is indeed the caliph of the coming Turkish caliphate, then that makes him…. the ANTICHRIST. No, I'm not kidding."

> The beast with 7 heads and 10 horns, mentioned in the book of Revelation is the coming Turkish caliphate. The wound that it suffered in 1924 will be healed and it will rise again. And the leader of that caliphate is indeed the Antichrist (Gog) who will eventually lead the invasion into Jerusalem (Ezekiel 38). [84]

As I am completing this book, speculation runs rampant regarding what action Russia may take against Turkey for shooting down its aircraft over Syria on November 24, 2015. However, Russia appears to be taking a diplomatic point of view, although Putin has indicated that Erdogan and his son are making money trading with ISIS and facilitating ISIS oil sales through Turkey. Revenues are millions daily. This could potentially isolate Turkey from NATO and is no small matter.

ERDOGAN IS THE ASSYRIAN – THE ASSYRIAN IS ANTICHRIST

Another theme prominent within this prophetic teaching is the contention that the label "The Assyrian" is not just a reference to Sennacherib in eighth century B.C. or to Nimrod from a 1,200 years before. The Assyrian (who came to judge the Northern Kingdom, circa 706 B.C.), is seen as yet another moniker for the future Antichrist. Amy Van Gerpen, from *Tracking Bible Prophecy*, states this explicitly in one of her more meaty blogs. The antichrist will rule a region north of Israel in the first part of the Tribulation, as Daniel calls him the "king of the north" and Isaiah and Micah call him the "Assyrian." Ms. Van Gerpen first points out that oppressors of Israel have been Assyrians before, and this has implications in the future redemption of Israel. To begin with, the Pharaoh who first oppressed Israel was an Assyrian:

> *Isaiah 52:2-4 - Shake yourself from the dust, arise; sit down, O Jerusalem! Loose yourself from the bonds of your neck, O captive daughter of Zion! For thus says the LORD: "You have sold yourselves for nothing, and you shall be redeemed without money." For thus says the Lord GOD: "My people went down at first Into Egypt to dwell there; then the Assyrian oppressed them without cause.*

Likewise, Sennacherib the second to oppress Israel was also Assyrian:

> *2 Kings 18:11-13 - Then the king of Assyria carried Israel away captive to Assyria, and put them in Halah and by the Habor, the River of Gozan, and in the cities of the Medes, because they did not obey the voice of the LORD their God, but transgressed His covenant and all that Moses the servant of the LORD had commanded; and they would neither hear nor do them. And in the fourteenth year of King Hezekiah, Sennacherib king of Assyria came up against all the fortified cities of Judah and took them.*

Van Gerpen points out that a third Assyrian, Antiochus IV Epiphanes, best fits the bill from the standpoint of illustrating the nature and person of the Antichrist. Antiochus was king of Assyria from 175-164 BC. When Antiochus defiled the Jewish temple, his act was considered an "abomination of desolation" which futurists believe will happen again in the last days. For Gerpen, "While there are other foreshadows of the antichrist in Scripture who were not Assyrian, Isaiah and Micah call the antichrist "the Assyrian." She then cites the following prophetic passages:

> *Isaiah 10:24-25 - Therefore thus says the Lord GOD of hosts: "O My people, who dwell in Zion, do not be afraid **of the Assyrian**. He shall strike you with a rod and lift up his staff against you, in the manner of Egypt. For yet a very little while and the indignation will cease, as will My anger in their destruction."*

> *Isaiah 14:25-26 - That I will break **the Assyrian** in My land, and*

151

on My mountains tread him underfoot. Then his yoke shall be re-moved from them, and his burden removed from their shoulders. This is the purpose that is purposed against the whole earth, and this is the hand that is stretched out over all the nations.

Micah 5:3-6 - *Therefore He shall give them up, until the time that she who is in labor has given birth; then the remnant of His brethren shall return to the children of Israel. And He shall stand and feed His flock in the strength of the LORD, in the majesty of the name of the LORD His God; and they shall abide, for now He shall be great to the ends of the earth; and this One shall be peace. When* **the Assyrian** *comes into our land, and when he treads in our palaces, then we will raise against him seven shepherds and eight princely men. They shall waste with the sword the land of Assyria, and the land of Nimrod at its entrances; thus He shall deliver us from* **the Assyrian**, *when he comes into our land and when he treads within our borders.*

Van Gerpen points out that "the head of gold represents the Babylonian Empire, the chest and arms of silver represent the Medo-Persian Empire, the belly and thighs of bronze represent the Greek Empire, and the legs of iron represent the Roman Empire." She also makes an interesting point with potentially significant prophetic implications:

The historic Roman Empire became divided because it became too large to govern effectively. The western leg eventually fell, but the eastern leg continued as the Byzantine Empire for almost 1000 more years, with the kingdom centered in Turkey. The Ottomans conquered the Byzantine Empire near the turn of the 14th century, and ruled until the 1920s. Therefore, the two legs of iron in Nebuchadnezzar's dream represent the divided empire... (Daniel 2:33): [85]

That the Roman Empire is the empire identified by John the Revelator (and the empire from which Antichrist arises), comprises the essence of the conventional view. However, the supposed breakthrough that the esteemed Chuck Missler proposed a number of years before was that the Antichrist might come from the "eastern leg" of the Roman Empire (western Asia), and not the "western leg" (Europe) as Van Gerpen indicates. As mentioned earlier, this supposition has buttressed the premise that *the Antichrist originates from Turkey.* When combined with the supposition that "the Assyrian" is a veiled reference to a future personage from Anatolia (Turkey), the argument certainly appears to be a strong one. However, all is not necessarily what it seems at first glance. We must raise several questions: "Is *the Assyrian* a reference to a future Turk? Should the translation of *the Assyrian* actually imply a person? Does it name a person or a place? Does it relate to a present day personage? Or does it merely prefigure an antichrist "type"? Furthermore, could it be a case of reincarnation (the only place the Bible seems to sanction this possibility), where a previous person possessed by the spirit of Antichrist returns to live again?

THE SECOND COMING OF THE ANTICHRIST

My friend Peter Goodgame wrote extensively on this topic in his book, *The Second Coming of Antichrist.* From an abbreviated study Peter did for Tom Horn's *Raiders News* site several years ago, Peter provides a careful study of "the Assyrian" that merits mention here.[86]

Peter crafts an intriguing presentation on what could be the most unusual yet compelling proposal for the meaning of the Assyrian concluding with the identification of the Antichrist. He begins by explaining that the word translated Assyrian should be translated as a name of a person, not a designation. The word is *Asshur.* It first appears in the Old Testament in Genesis 10 (as mentioned before, the "Table of Nations" so-called)...

> *And Cush begat Nimrod: he began to be a mighty one in the earth. He was a mighty hunter before the Lord: wherefore it is said, Even as Nimrod the mighty hunter before the Lord. And the beginning of his kingdom was Babel, and Erech, and Accad, and Culneh, in the land of Shinar. Out of that land went forth Asshur, and builded Nineveh, and the city Rehoboth, and Calah, and Resen between Nineveh and Calah: the same is a great city.* (Genesis 10:8-12, KJV)

"The conclusion that I have arrived at is that *Asshur* is simply another name for Nimrod." Peter then asks,

Will the Antichrist come from Iraq?" and the answer is, "Yes! The Antichrist *founded* Iraq!" Nimrod's kingdom began in southern Mesopotamia with the cities of Babel and Erech (Uruk/Iraq), but then he invaded north and built Ninevah and the other cities that became the foundation of the kingdom of Asshur (Assyria). This view that Asshur is Nimrod is rather straightforward but there are several arguments against it that must be addressed."

Peter explains that both the King James Version and the Septuagint (LXX) translate the word *Asshur* as an individual while modern versions translate it as *Assyria*, a place. *Genesis indicates that Asshur built both Babylon and Ninevah.* It was *Asshur* (aka Nimrod) who built the cities from which invasions of Israel were launched and Israel and Judea conquered.

> The KJV and Septuagint (LXX) translations of Genesis 10:11 give the impression that "Asshur" is an *individual*, but in most modern Bible versions "Asshur" is translated as "Assyria"—*a place*. They generally read, *"From that land he* (Nimrod) *went to Assyria, where he built Ninevah..."* The fact is that "Asshur" can be read either as an individual or as the region of Assyria— we just don't know for sure and the text alone does not prove either case. However, because the name "Asshur" is not modified by the preposition *el* or the directional *heh* (thus giving either *"el Asshur"* or *"Asshurah"*), which would confirm "Asshur" as a *place*, it remains a distinct possibility that Asshur is meant to be understood as an *individual* and as *another name for Nimrod.* [87]

Consequently, Peter associates the assertion most expert writers and teachers sustain that the Antichrist will be resurrected from the Abyss:

> *The beast that thou sawest was, and is not; and shall ascend out of the bottomless pit, and go into perdition: and they that dwell on the earth shall wonder, whose names were not written in the book of life from the foundation of the world, when they behold the beast that was, and is not, and yet is.* (Revelation 17:8)

Peter's conclusion is that the Antichrist is a reincarnated Nimrod. He was the first antichrist figure of Scripture. Antichrist is not just the "spirit" of Apollyon or Abaddon (as referenced in Revelation 9:11 – *"And they had a king over them, which is the angel of the bottomless pit, whose name in the Hebrew tongue is Abaddon, but in the Greek tongue hath his name Apollyon"*), but will literally be *a resurrected Nimrod.*[88] Peter's conclusion builds upon excavations at the Great Pyramid and the possible discovery of the Tomb of Osiris there. Others have speculated that Nimrod's tomb may have been maintained in Iraq, at Babylon, or in the antiquities museum in Bagdad that some speculate wildly might have been the target of American forces for reasons not fully made clear by the speculators. While this conjecture goes beyond the scope of this book (see Goodgames's *The Second Coming of the Antichrist* to pursue this further), the point here: there are a number of possible explanations for the meaning of *the Assyrian.* The speculation that it relates to the Ottoman Empire, to a revived Ottoman Empire in the guise of modern-day Turkey, and identifying antichrist with the Erdogan of Turkey's existing government, seems to be a case of "special pleadings" (pressing for a verdict that either intentionally or unknowingly ignores logical if not obvious counter-arguments). In the case of arguing for the Ottoman Empire and Turkey as the "Gog" of Ezekiel (and denying Gog is a distinct figure from the Antichrist of Daniel and Revelation), builds upon a suspect premise that Islam is the antichrist religion of the last days. It explains away contradictory elements of Bible prophecy that don't fit the Islamic scenario. And it ignores other possible empires that are equally if not more logical fulfillments of the biblical prophecy that antichrist will come from an empire that opposes the LORD.

WHICH EMPIRE? WHICH ANTICHRIST?

The pivotal question, especially as it relates to the Ottoman Empire Shoebat and Richardson promote is whether this particular empire constitutes the Bible prophetically identifies as most significant and whether it qualifies as the one from which Antichrist will come. Could the empire be the Ottoman Empire? Could it be the English Empire that figures so prominently in the real powers of today, Europe and the United States? Better yet, why not the Holy Roman Empire that lasted from 800 A.D. at the coronation of Charlemagne on Christmas Day, to the defeat of Napoleon on June 18, 1815? The reader may not know the curious fact that Otto I of Germany (emperor of the Holy Roman Empire, from 962 to his death 973) exhumed the body of Charlemagne fearing that Karl would be revived at the end of the Millennium (1000 AD approached!) and become John's Antichrist! It seems that Otto wanted to keep an eye on Karl the Great's body! Also, the sixteenth century prophet Nostradamus regarded Napoleon as the first Antichrist who would be followed by two others. Nostradamus saw the next antichrist coming from Europe as well. Nostradamus' students believe the prophet made a precise prediction of Adolf Hitler's rise to power. Recall that Charlemagne represented the First Reich, The German Kaiser (Caesar) Wilhelm the Second Reich from 1871 to 1919 (and the defeat of Napoleon III in the Franco-Prussian War), and then Hitler would become the antichrist of the Third Reich, a short-lived span of time too, from 1933 to 1945. Many propose that there will be a Fourth Reich, also with ties to the royal families of Europe. This notion seems much more historically viable than does the notion that the empire of Antichrist would arise from the old Ottoman Empire. It fits with the legacy of "the kings of the earth", the "illuminated ones", the 13 leading occult families of the world, and other members of a shadow government commanding a final and ultimate world government.

But to return to the Bible's specific prediction, citing Revelation 17:10-11: *"And there are seven kings: five are fallen, and one is, and the other is not yet come; and when he cometh, he must continue a short space. And the beast that was, and is not, even he is the eighth, and is of the seven, and goeth into perdition."* There are seven kingdoms or empires that the Bible recognizes as concurrent with its scope of revelation. Most scholars recognize these kingdoms below as those which the Bible regards pertinent through the prophecies of Daniel and John:

1. Egypt (Pharaoh)	"FALLEN"
2. Assyria (Sennacharib)	"FALLEN"
3. Babylon (Nebuchadnezzar)	"FALLEN"
4. Media-Persia (Cyrus)	"FALLEN"
5. Greece (Alexander)	"FALLEN"
6. Rome	"IS" (when Revelation was written)
7. The Mystery Empire	"NOT YET COME"
8. The Beast	"REALLY OF THE SEVEN"

Shoebat and Richardson contend that the seventh empire is not a revival of the Roman Empire, western leg, but a revived Roman Empire, eastern leg. They incorporate the "Assyrian" scriptures to reinforce their position. But what other empire might comprise the seventh to which John refers? Could it be the Ottoman Empire? Perhaps. But might it be Babylon, the iconic symbol of the Kingdom that opposes the Kingdom of God? Could the Mystery Empire be Mystery Babylon? Could it be the Daughter of Babylon? This author has written extensively on the topic of the United States as the fulfillment of the prophecy regarding the daughter of Babylon, and has been joined by, among others, John Price author of *The End of America*, and Benjamin Baruch and J.R. Nyquist in their book, *The New Tactics of Global War,* asserting that the United States will likely be neutralized by a nuclear first strike by Russia. Regardless, the Antichrist *may combine elements of all the empires* ("be of the seven"). The visions of Daniel and John suggest this amalgamation. See Daniel 2:37-45, Daniel 7:1-11, Revelation 13:1-6.) A true mystery.

COULD GERMANY BECOME THE FOURTH REICH?

Could it be a rebirth of Germany as the dominant power? Today, Germany has already become the leader of Europe once more. It is the world's fourth largest economy. In 2014, it recorded the largest trade surplus in the world ($285 billion). In 2015, *Time Magazine* named German Prime Minister Angela Merkel "Person of the Year". Merkel has established positive relationships with Vladimir Putin, Putin having served with the Russian KGB in East Germany for many years. And if any empire were to have a mortal head wound healed causing the entire world to wonder after it, surely it would be Germany. If there were to be a Fourth Reich to become the powerbase of the Antichrist, would any single country seem more logical than Germany? I am not saying Germany will be the nation from which the antichrist arises, but I am saying it is more logical and historically than Turkey. Geopolitically, in today's world, Germany bears watching very closely.

Joseph P. Farrell, in his recent book, *The Third Way: The Nazi International, the European Union, and Corporate Fascism*, hypothesizes that

Germany is quietly, but steadily, moving itself back into the status of a world power – not just economically, but politically and even militarily:

> While Germany is not categorized officially as a nuclear power, it produces nuclear warheads for the French Navy. It stockpiles nuclear warheads (made in America) and it has the capabilities of delivering nuclear weapons. Moreover, The European Aeronautic Defense and Space Company— EADS, a Franco-German-Spanish joint venture, controlled by Deutsche Aerospace and the powerful Daimler Group is Europe's second largest military producer, supplying France's M51 nuclear missile. Germany imports and deploys nuclear weapons from the US. It also produces nuclear warheads which are exported to France. Yet it is classified as a non-nuclear state. [89]

One wonders, should the prospective war disclosed in Ezekiel involve a nuclear exchange between Gog and the Merchants of Tarshish (England) and its young lions (the United States), how the political landscape of the world would appear. It would not require fanciful speculation to suppose Germany could emerge as the Western World's powerhouse, uniting Europe and the adopting the antiquated if not totally anachronistic moniker "Leader of the Free World." A post-U.S./Russian world would leave Germany and the "kings of the East" (China, Japan, perhaps India) as the "last men standing". Going further in this scenario, the covenant to protect Israel from its remaining enemies commencing the seven-year covenant of Daniel's Seventieth Week would be none other than Germany! "Poetic justice" perhaps, but ultimately the greatest of deception, eventually becoming *the treaty of death and hell* (Isaiah 28:15) when the antichrist, having first confirmed the covenant with many, breaks the covenant, mounting an attack on the Jews to annihilate them once and for all!

Douglas Berner, whose research on the Battle of Gog and Magog we will consider carefully in the chapters following, cites the venerable John F. Walvoord (1910 – 2002), late President of Dallas Theological Seminary and noted prophecy author, who asserted that the United States and Russia would not be party to the treaty between Antichrist and Israel. Walvoord's *argumentum e silentio* (argument from silence) doesn't share the same exact rationale; nevertheless, Berner recaps Walvoord's worthy assessment:

> I agree with Walvoord that there is no direct scriptural evidence pointing to the involvement of either Russia or the U.S. in the "final" peace covenant that Israel will enter – a peace covenant with the Antichrist which will initiate the end-time period of Daniel's 70th Week. I also believe that the strength and ambitions of both Russia and the U.S. serve as obstacles, hindering the emergence of the world leader who will ultimately initiate the "final" covenant of peace with Israel. But, if neither of these two large nations is to be involved in the "final" peace covenant, then something must happen to take them out of the picture – out of their present positions of power and influence. Some event must neutralize the massive military capabilities of both nations. The most likely candidate for that event is Ezekiel's War of Gog and Magog.[90]

And specifically, as this author has previously asserted, Berner proposes the cause is nuclear war between the two countries. Berner confirms he shares this author's conviction on this topic in numerous other passages. In the first, Berner dismisses the supposition that Ezekiel's use of language referencing ancient weapons ("bows and arrows") suggests that modern weapons will not be used in Gog's attack on Israel:

> [That] is an inconsistent and very unrealistic view. Conventional military disarmament will not even be imaginable to the world prior to a massive global catastrophe, which probably involves large-scale nuclear warfare. Ironically, we see the very potential for that nuclear war accompanied by a global catastrophe of unprecedented proportions in Ezekiel's prophecy of Gog and Magog. [91]

Berner contends,

> As long as the U.S. and Russia maintain their military capabilities, and as long as Islam promotes a violent holy war or jihad against the nations of the West for control of the Middle East and the direction of the world, a single leader or nation will never gain control of a one-world government and the world will not see large-scale disarmament.[92]

And then later, Berner acknowledges that many people throughout the world look for the dominating presence of a powerful leader that could solve the world's problems, but "it will take the shock of a massive global catastrophe to give a potential one-world leader his mandate for power." More to the point:

> The most likely catastrophe that could produce this global effect is a massive nuclear war. The use of nuclear weapons by one or more nations against other nations is not that unforeseeable: Israel against Syria or Iran; Russia against the U.S.' North Korea against South Korea or the U.S.' Pakistan against India, or India against Pakistan; China against any perceived threat or as a tactic to gain total control over Taiwan; a nuclear terrorist strike against the U.S. or another Western nation, Iran's present quest for nuclear weapons, supported by Russian technology and political backing, presents an extreme threat to the safety and stability of the Middle East and the entire world. The prospect for nuclear war is a very real threat.[93]

In regards to the correlation of the War of Gog and Magog with the Sixth Seal of Revelation, Berner examines considerable material. In this context, Berner states:

> It is very interesting that the specific descriptions of the sixth seal judgment, the destruction caused by God in conjunction with the invasion of Gog and Magog, and the first four trumpet judgments are so descriptive of thermonuclear warfare. If the invasion of Israel by Gog and Magog is accompanied by the release of nuclear weapons, possibly through the exchange of nuclear missiles between the armies and navies of Russia and the United States, then the resulting destruction may well be responsible for the decimation of one fourth of the population of the world as depicted by the opening of the fourth seal judgment by Christ (Revelation 6:7-8). That will make the survival of Israel even more miraculous. [94]

THE TWO ENEMIES OF ISRAEL ARE NOT THE SAME

The War of Gog and Magog must become a geopolitical necessity if the Antichrist and his one-world government are to come to fruition. The greatest obstacles to this world government and its singular leader are these:

160

- Russia's drive to restore its empire (its nationalist agenda), which opposes globalism as currently led by the United States;

- Islam's goal of a global caliphate, along with the implicit destruction of all other religions and governments opposing Islam.

- The voice of the American people who oppose globalism, the abrogation of the U.S. constitution, and stand for individual liberty and freedom that those seeking a one-world government will never allow.

The Battle of Gog and Magog will eliminate all three of these obstacles:

- The lands of Sheba and Dedan (Saudi Arabia), the Merchants of Tarshish (England), and its young lions (the United States and perhaps Canada) will be attacked by a great power from the north. Unless an unexpected and unforeseen transformation occurs, the U.S. and perhaps England as well awaits a destiny likened to "Sodom and Gomorrah".

- The principal powers of Islam that team with Russia, (primarily Iran, but perhaps Turkey even though at this moment it is on the outs with Russia due to its downing of a Russian fighter plan on November 24, 2015) would all likely share Gog's fate. If they join the confederation, they will be destroyed on the mountains of Israel along with Gog's military mustered for battle.

- And then God will judge Russia (Gog) for its attack on Israel and upon the daughter of Babylon. *"And I will send a fire on Magog, and among them that dwell carelessly in the isles: and they shall know that I am the LORD."* (Ezekiel 39:6).

The timing of the scenario will be detailed in the final chapter of this book.

So to recap: in this chapter we have examined the possibility that an Islamic Antichrist might be the predicted final enemy of Israel. We have noted that the advocates of this view not only reject the conventional view of a "Western Antichrist" *but also reject two other major apocalyptic axioms:*

- *Axiom One:* the Battle of Gog and Magog are separate and distinct end time's battles. In contrast, I argue the first battle must precede the second for the second cannot happen geopolitically until the first battle has taken place.

	ATTRIBUTES OF GOG	ATTRIBUTES OF ANTICHRIST
1	His motivation: seize plunder from the "land of unwalled villages" and destroy Israel.	His motivation: annihilate the people of God in Israel and from any and all lands of the world.
2	No indication Gog ever seeks to protect Israel.	He presents himself as a covenant protector of Israel for 3.5 years.
3	He has no authority to rule over Israel for any period.	He is granted authority to rule over Israel and dominate it.
4	Gog is killed in the invasion of Israel and buried with his troops (Ezekiel 39:11) – he has no memorial, no tomb. He is buried at Hamongog.	Jesus Christ disposes of the Antichrist and he is seen by the world as a spectacle. He is cast alive into the lake of fire along with the False Prophet forever and ever.
5	It is not specified that Satan empowers Gog.	It is evident that Satan empowers the Antichrist.
6	God hooks Gog and drags him to Israel – God controls Gog.	Satan empowers and motivates Antichrist, not God.
7	No indication that Gog revers or worships Satan. But Gog may be empowered by "a principality or power".	It is extremely clear that Antichrist exalts Satan. It is also expressly stated that he is the son of perdition and seed of Satan.
8	Gog is the sole leader of many armies pitted against God.	Antichrist leads with an associate – the False Prophet.
9	After Gog is killed, the dead are buried for seven months and weapons burned by Israel for seven years.	After Antichrist and False Prophet are thrown into the Lake of Fire, no mention is made of the dead; the Kingdom of God commences.
10	Gog seeks to conquer only the region of the Middle East through the War of Gog and Magog.	Antichrist seeks to conquer the entire world through the elimination of God's people and the Battle of Armageddon.

- *Axiom Two:* Gog and Antichrist are entirely different persons. Allow me to conclude this chapter presenting a table that underscores why Gog and Antichrist are, as the conventional view states, two distinct personages. (Previous page). If we attempt to conflate the two, we twist other prophetic truths that scholars have taught for centuries.

WILL ERDOGAN SURVIVE THE ISIS/SYRIA/RUSSIA SITUATION?

Will Turkey's President Erdogan even be able to survive 2016 and the dangerous situation he has put himself in as 2015 comes to a close? Far for being the leading candidate for the Antichrist (a world leader ready to head a global government), Erdogan may become a victim of regime change. Erdogan has facilitated ISIS oil sales through Turkey, irresponsibly downed a Russian fighter on 24 November 2015, and continued his attacks on the most effective fighters against ISIS (the Kurds) in Turkey's border regions of Syria and Iraq (under the "political cover" of purportedly attacking ISIS). Erdogan has alienated just about everyone.

Stuart Rolio posted an engaging article for the Wall Street Journal on December 29, 2015, entitled, "Turkey's Dangerous Game in Syria." [95] Rolio points out that in 2011, Turkey was a primary mover in the plan to oust Assad and place a Sunni leader in Damascus (Rolio jibes: "probably a member of the local Muslim Brotherhood!") Erdogan has sought to curb the prominence of Iran in the region. But his actions over the past year (as outlined above) have placed Turkey at odds with NATO members as well as Russia. The Shi'ites already hate him. Putin labeled his government "accomplices of terrorists". So Rolio offers this assessment:

> Turkey has figured that its important position in NATO as a bulwark against Russian power would shield it from criticism by its Western allies, and buy it enough time to shape the Syrian conflict in its favor. But Russia has effectively turned the international sympathy over the downing of... its jets into increased sway in Syria.
>
> Mr. Putin has promised to "immediately destroy" anything that threatens Russian forces in the country. He also upgraded the local Russian arsenal to show that he can make good on his promise.

It remains to be seen what will happen to Erdogan and how effective he can be in helping to resolve the Syrian issue, the fight against ISIS, and whether he can fashion a productive relationship with Moscow. But until he accomplishes these things, any speculation about his capacity to become a world leader borders on the absurd. Could he be the Antichrist? Think again.

9: The Sons of Japheth

And the word of the Lord came to me saying, "Son of man, set your face toward Gog of the land of Magog, the prince of Rosh, Meshech and Tubal, and prophesy against him and say, 'Thus says the Lord God, "Behold, I am against you, O Gog, prince of Rosh, Meshech and Tubal. I will turn you about and put hooks into your jaws, and I will bring you out, and all your army, horses and horsemen, all of them splendidly attired, a great company with buckler and shield, all of them wielding swords; Persia, Ethiopia and Put with them, all of them with shield and helmet; Gomer with all its troops; Beth-togarmah from the remote parts of the north with all its troops—many peoples with you.
Ezekiel 38:1-6

THE TABLE OF NATIONS

WHEN WE READ EZEKIEL'S LIST OF NATIONS THAT CONFEDERATE WITH GOG, WE ARE CONFRONTED WITH NAMES UNFAMILIAR TO MOST OF US. HOWEVER, THE NAMES ARE NOT UNFAMILIAR WITH those that have studied the history of peoples and places around the world (demographers). These names refer back to the sons, grandsons, and great grandsons of Noah. Place names for regions, mountains, and cities often harken back to these biblical names. Indeed, the Bible teaches that the entire world population today traces its lineage back to Noah and through his three sons, Ham, Shem, and Japheth.

At the most general level, we can state that Ham was father to the Hamites the predominant peoples of Africa; Shem the father of the Shemites or Semites settling for the most part in the Middle East and Southwest Asia; while the third son Japheth was father of the Japhethites (by now you get the idea), peoples that spread to the North, far east, and far west of the place where Noah's Ark came to rest at Mount Ararat. While disputed as to which country accurately lays claim to Mount Ararat, most scholars identify Turkey as the launch pad for the reprised human race, thoroughly cleansed by the judgment of the Great Flood. Only Noah who was "perfect in all his generations" (Genesis 6:9) and his three sons were eligible to replenish the earth. [96]

The tribal names cited in Ezekiel 38-39 are listed in Genesis 10, the so-called *Table of Nations*. Indeed, we don't have to wade very far into the list before we encounter almost all of them. The sons of Japheth sit right up top:

> *Now these are the generations of the sons of Noah, Shem, Ham, and Japheth: and unto them were sons born after the flood. The sons of Japheth; Gomer, and Magog, and Madai, and Javan, and Tubal, and Meshech, and Tiras. And the sons of Gomer; Ashkenaz, and Riphath, and Togarmah. And the sons of Javan; Elishah, and Tarshish, Kittim, and Dodanim. By these were the isles of the Gentiles divided in their lands; every one after his tongue, after their families, in their nations.* (Genesis 10:1-5)

Tim Osterholm has done an amazing amount of work, studying no less than three-dozen books tracing these lineages, graciously providing his research without copyright at his web site, *sounchristian.com*. Among the books in his bibliography are titles authored by John Walvoord, Lambert Dolphin, Paul F. Taylor, Ken Ham, J. Talmadge Wood, Ray Stedman, Henry M. Morris, John C. Whitcomb, and Arthur C. Custance and ancient historians like Flavius Josephus. His work is a treasure trove for those interested in pursuing the ancestry of the human race. Regarding the tribal history and etymology of the names in Ezekiel, it brings exemplary credibility.

As a secondary source for the information contained in this chapter, I will also refer to Douglas Berner's extensive work, *The Silence is Broken*, which compiles the many commentaries and analyses of perhaps two dozen scholars, some modern and some dating back centuries before Christ, to locate the origins of the various peoples and places where they reigned. Also referenced, Ken Johnson's *Ancient Post-Flood History*. My summarization here relies heavily on their earlier outstanding research.

THE FAMILY TREE OF JAPHETH

According to Osterholm, the proper anthropology terminology would specify that Japheth was the father of the Caucasoid/Indo-Europoid, Indo-European, Indo-Germanic, or Indo-Aryan people groups. When we speak of Gog and Magog, we are speaking about the Caucasians. The most notorious reference would be the Caucus Mountains in Russia. According to Mark Hitchcock, *caucus* literally means "Gog's Fort". We don't have to safari very far from the place of the Ark's landing to ferret out where Japheth headed after getting his feet back on dry land. Specifically, we know that Magog was a land sitting between and above the Black and Caspian Seas. (See map below) Meschech and Tubal are also locations on the quasi-peninsula that comprises Anatolia, stretching across modern day Turkey. Each of the names requires some additional study with scholars differing on precisely when and where the peoples known by these names and forebears came to reside. My notations here are intentionally generalized.

The table adjacent is derived from Osterholm's research to show the connections between descendants, the "handing down" of names (their transitional forms through time), and especially *the dispersion of the names across broad geographic regions.* Why is this important? Because the argument that Gog and Magog implies only the natives of Anatolia owes in no small part to Japheth's sons settling first in Anatolia. What is downplayed: *their descendants scattered across Eurasia, from the Asian steppes to the lands of Baltics, to the islands of the United Kingdom.*

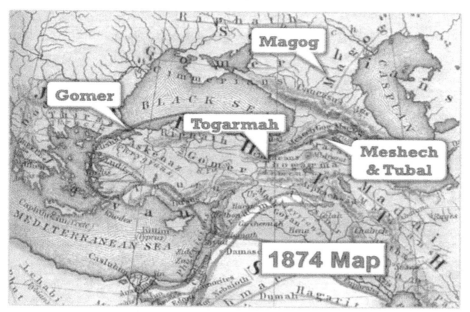

Figure 17 - A Map from 1874 Locating Tribal Names in Turkey

NAME OF SON	MEANING OF NAME	NAMES OF GRANDSONS	SELECTED NAMES AND NATIONS OF DESCENDANTS
Gomer	Complete	Ashkenaz Riphath Togarmah	Gallic, Gaul, Galacia, Celt, Gimmer, Cimmer, Crimea, Cimmerians, Armenians, Phyrgians, Ostrogoths, Goths, Germans, Belgians, Saxons, Britons, Welsh, Scots, French
Magog	Land of Gog	Elichanaf Lubal Baath Jobhath Fathochta	Cog, Gogh, Gogarene, Jagog, Agag, Magug, Magogue, Gugu, Magogian, Scyth, Scythia, Slovan, Slavs, Ishkuzai, Rosichi, Rhossi, Rus, Ruska, Russian, Ukrainians, Chechens, Czechs, Laps, Croatians, Bosnians, Serbians, Slovenians, Avars, Tartars, Turks
Madai	Middle Land	Achon Zeelo, Chazoni Lotalso	Mada, Amada, Madaean, Megala, Medes, Aryans, Persians, Parsa, Parsees, Caspians, Kassites, Iranians, Kurds, Romani, Afghanistan, Pakistan, Azerbaijan, Turkmenistan, Tajikistan
Javan	Miry	Elishah Tarshish Kittim Dodanim	Jevanim, Iawon, Ellas, Ellines, Hellas, Hellenese, Yavan, Yuban, Xuthus, Grecians, Greeks, Elysians, Spartans, Dorians, Tartessians, Britons, Aeolians, Myceneans, Macedonians, Albanians, Carthaginians, Cyprians, Cypriots, Cretans, Latins, Romans, Sicilians, Italians, Spaniards, Portuguese
Tubal	Brought	Ariphi Kesed Taari	Tabal, Tubalu, Thobal, Tbilisi, Tibor, Sahir, Sapir, Subar, Subartu, Tobol, Tobolsk, Cossacks, Samoyeds, Siberians
Meschech	Drawing Out	Dedon Zaron Shebashinialso	Me'sheck, Mes'ek, Meskhi, Mushch, Muschki, Mushki, Mishi, Mushku, Muska, Moskhi, Moshch, Moschis, Moskva,Moscow, Muscovites, Latvians, Lithuanians, Romanians
Tiras	Desire	Benib Gera Lupirion Gilak	Tiracian, Thracian, Thiras, Typitae, Thrasus, Thrace, Trecae, Troas, Trojae, Troyes, Troi, Troy, Trajan, Tyras, Tyre, Taurus, Tyrrhena, Illium, Tursha, Tusci, Tuscany, Etruria, Etruschi, Truscan, Euskara (Basque), Danir, Daner, Aesar, Asir, Svear, Urmane, Norge (Carians, Pelasgians, Scandinavians, Urmane, Vikings, Swedes, Norwegians, Danes, Icelandics, Baltics

THE EURASIAN MIGRATION OF THE FAMILY OF JAPHETH

In this section I narrate the more fascinating aspects of the research of the previously mentioned authors. Quotations are from Osterholm. Note throughout this discussion how Gog and Magog and the names of their children lend their appellations to literally hundreds of place names *far beyond Anatolia.* We are not restricting the pertinent location of Gog and Magog to Turkey. Instead we see how their offspring settled throughout widely divergent regions (named in Ezekiel 38-39), indeed *across all of Asia and Europe. The supposition is clear:* When Ezekiel references these peoples, no biblical principle exists that demands we limit our scope of their residence *to where they resided when Moses listed the earliest genealogy in Genesis 10.* By the time of Ezekiel, the migration of the sons of Japheth had been underway for almost 1,500 years. However, the locations and patterns of settlement are still highly relevant today. People travel all over the world. Families move from place to place. But large people-groups generally stay in the same region and tend to stay put. To establish the peoples listed by Ezekiel and where they call home, we are wise to consider the demography scholars have developed over the centuries which I summarize here.

The Celts and the Scythians

"The whole Celtic race has been regarded as descended from Gomer, though history suggests modern Celts are descended from both Gomer and Magog." Scholars concur that the Celts and Scythians were mingled cultures with the Celts dominating the south and west, the Scythians to the north. The Irish claim to be descendants of Magog and the Welsh, Gomer. Archeological evidence demonstrates the Irish were descended from the *Magogians.* The Greeks referred to these peoples as the Celto-Scythae. The Romans called them the *Galli* (the Gauls) associated with France (the Franks). Galatians, the city to whom the Apostle Paul wrote, were Gauls. "In the third century before Christ (about 280 B.C.), the Gauls invaded Rome and were ultimately repelled into Greece, where they migrated into the north-central part of Asia Minor (Anatolia). They conquered the indigenous peoples of that region and established their own independent kingdom. The land became known as Galatia (Gaulatia)." Osterholm indicates the Welsh claim their ancestors landed on the isle of Britain about 300 years *after* the Great Flood. The Gaelic language derives from Celtic, although the Welsh call their language *Gomeraeg*. The Scythians "roots" are traced from many of the different demographic groups we will discuss.

The Germans

The Germans are usually associated with Gomer. History suggests that the descendants of Gomer settled in northern Europe and comprise the Germans and Scandinavians. Gomer's descendants included the Goths, Ostrogoths, Visigoths and the Teutons. Osterholm comments:

> The Askaeni were descendants of Ashkenaz, son of Gomer, son of Japheth. When the Askaeni arrived in northern Europe, they named the land Ascania after themselves, which later translated Scandia, then Scandinavia. Later in history, we find the Askaeni being referred to as Sakasenoi, which became Sachsen, and finally Saxon.

Semitic peoples, descendants of Shem, also migrated to central Europe. These were descendants of *Assur*, the father of the Assyrians (as noted in the previous chapter). Osterholm shows how the names were transformed from *Teiw* to *Ziu* to *Diu* and then *Diutisc*, which became Dietsch and then later Deutsch or Duetsche (German). The Romans called the *Deutschen* the *Teutons* although they wiped out this tribe in the second century B.C. We refer to Germanic attributes as Teutonic today. The term German comes from Roman sources, specifically a city on the lower Tigris River, "Kir" which held Assyrian captives or Kir-men. (See 2 Kings 16:9, Isaiah 22:5-6, Amos 1:5, 9:7). In 610 B.C. the *Kirmen* were driven from their land, migrating to central Europe where they became known as the *Germanni* – a general name used by the Romans to reference all Assyrian tribes. (Note: if "the Assyrian" indeed refers prophetically to a specific person and to the tribe from which he descends, it would refer to the Germans, not the Turks!) Osterholm provides this additional fascinating insight:

> The known Assyrian tribes were the Khatti (also, Chatti, Hatti and Hessian)—Chatti is still the Hebrew term for German, and Khatti was also used by the Romans to represent various Ger-

manic tribes; the Akkadians (Latins called them Quadians); the Kassites (or Cossaei); and the Almani (or Halmani, Allemani was the Latin name). Almani or Almain were historical terms for Germans living in southern Germany. Without question, these *Assyrian Germans* assimilated with the previously established tribes of Askaeni (descendants of Gomer) and adopted their Indo-European language [Aryan], becoming one people. [Emphasis mine – note the German connection to the Assyrians.]

The Gargarians and Gogarenes

In the ninth century B.C. there existed an Assyrian inscription, "Mat Gugi" which means "Country of the Gugu". Hesiod, the father of Greek literature, connected *Magog with the Scythians and southern Russia in the seventh century B.C., written about a century before Ezekiel.* He may have derived this from the Colchi people (a Thracian tribe, Osterholm relates) where in Chaldaic language, Russia's southern region is called Gogchasan" or "Gog-hasan" which translates to Gog's fort. Some scholars (Hitchcock) speculate that *Gog-chasan* is the origin of the name Caucasus.

Herodotus, the father of history writing in the fifth century B.C., identified the people of this area as the *Gargarians*, or more specifically the Gorgons. He wrote about the descendants of Magog by their Greek name, Scythians. He states that they were already terrorizing the territory north of the Black Sea in the tenth century B.C. Flavius Josephus confirms this as well noting that the Greeks knew the *Magogians* as the Scythians. Philo likewise identifies Magog with southern Russia. Additionally, another ancient source, Strabo (who wrote a mere 17-volume work called *Geographica)*, mentions the *Gogarene* as a region in Armenia and Georgia (in Asia that is, not the southern U.S.). Osterholm cites numerous connections but culminates this discussion with this interesting point:

> In the 6th century A.D., geographer Stephanus of Byzantium referred to the region as *Gogarene*, and in the 7th century the region was known as *Gougarq*. Today it still exists as Gugark, a historical region in Armenia. As noted earlier, commentators suggest Georgia also derived its name from Gogarene, and today the Turkish name for Georgia is *Gurgistan*. In recent history, certain Georgians referred to themselves as "Gogi."

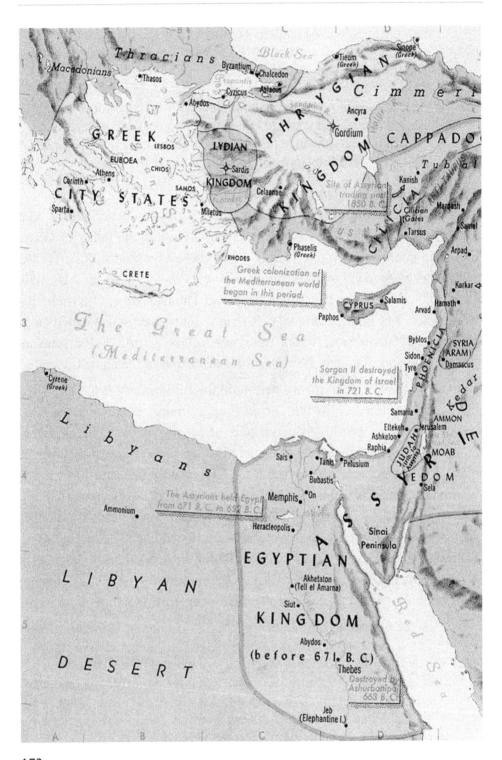

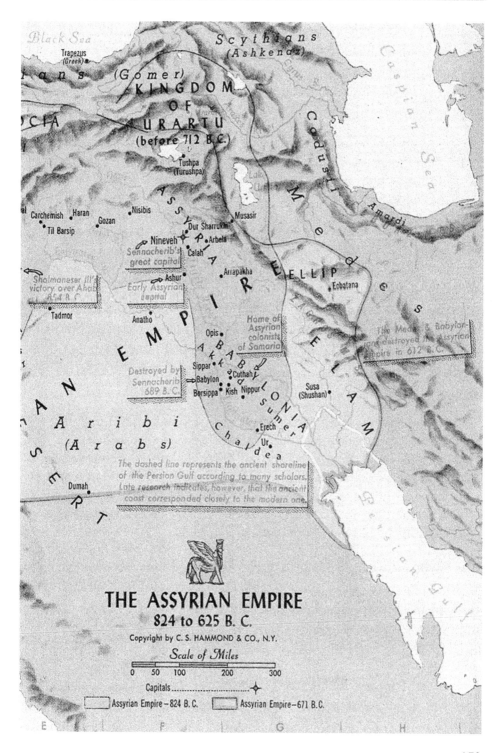

Black Sea

Trapezus
(Greek)

Scythians
(Ashkenaz)

Caspian Sea

(G o m e r)

KINGDOM
OF
URARTU
(before 712 B.C.)

Tushpa
(Turushpa)

Lake
Urmia

Coduschi

Amardi

Carchemish   Haran
Til Barsip   Gozan

Nisibis

Musasir

Dur Sharrukin
Nineveh   Arbela
Sennacherib's   Calah
great capital

M e d e s

ELLIP

Ecbatana

Shalmaneser III's
victory over Ahab
854 B.C.

Ashur
Early Assyrian
capital

E M P I R E

Arrapakha

Tadmor

Anatho

Home of
Assyrian
colonists
of Samaria

The Medes & Babylon-
ians destroyed the Assyrian
Empire in 612 B.C.

Opis

E L A M

Destroyed by
Sennacherib
689 B.C.

Sippar
Babylon
Borsippa   Kish

Cuthah
Nippur

Susa
(Shushan)

A k k a d

B A B Y L O N I A

A r i b i
(A r a b s)

Sumer

Erech

Chaldea

Ur

D E S E R T

Dumah

The dashed line represents the ancient shoreline
of the Persian Gulf according to many scholars.
Late research indicates, however, that the ancient
coast corresponded closely to the modern one.

Persian Gulf

THE ASSYRIAN EMPIRE
824 to 625 B. C.

Copyright by C. S. HAMMOND & CO., N.Y.

Scale of Miles

0   50   100   200   300

Capitals..............⬦

Assyrian Empire—824 B.C.   Assyrian Empire—671 B.C.

E   F   G   H

173

Osterholm comments that *Jerome*, famous for translating the Greek Bible into the Latin Vulgate in the fourth and fifth century AD (official Bible of the Catholic Church), noted that the Jews understood Magog as the vast nations of Scythia, about Mount Caucasus "stretching from the Caspian Sea to India." From Osterholm's research we learn:

> Many of the mountains peaks in the Caucasian mountains and land areas there retained the place name "Gog" in medieval European and Armenian maps. Scholars also regard Gog and Magog as the wild tribes of Central Asia, including the Scythians, Alans, Parthians, Turks, Tartars, Mongols, and Huns, who had been making incursions on various kingdoms and empires from very ancient times.

The Russians

As stated earlier, the Scythians descend from Ashkenaz, son of Gomer, son of Japheth and grandson of Noah. (Many Jews today are known as Ashkenazi Jews, meaning that they do not descend from Shem, but from a Japheth, and racially, if true, would be Gentile and not Semite as far as ancient origins are concerned). Osterholm clarifies:

> The Scythians are descended from Ashkenaz, son of Gomer, son of Japheth, and first appear in Assyrian records as "Askuza" or "Ishkuzai." The Assyrians tell of the Askuza as being involved in a revolt and pouring in from the north sometime around the beginning of the seventh century B.C., which is also mentioned in the Old Testament (Jeremiah 51:27). The Askuza later became the Skythai (Scythians) of Herodotus.

The Scythians were also known as *Rukhsas*, the *Rashu*, the *Rasapu*, *Rhossi*, Rosh, *Ros* and Rus. There is no debate, according to Osterholm, that these peoples were inhabitants of southern Russia, related to the existence of the River Rus. Russia means "land of the Rus."

The Aryans

History asserts that the Aryans existed over 1,000 years before Christ. They invaded India and threatened Babylonia, led by a chief name Cyazeres. He was also known as the king of the Medes and Persians (today's Iranians), although known to the Jews as *Elam* or *Elamites*. Oster-holm indicates that the Aryans, Medes and Persians, were descended from Elam, the son of Shem, and Madai, the son of Japheth. He states:

> The Medo-Persian people groups are divided into hundreds of clans, some sedentary and others nomadic. All speak Indo-European languages, and some groups have pronounced Mongoloid physical characteristics and cultural traits, derived from Mongolian invasions and subsequent cultural integration. An example today would be the Uzbeks of Uzbekistan, and remnant groups living in Afghanistan and parts of Central Asia.

The British, Welsh, and Scots

The British descended from Javan (through his sons Elishah and Tarshish) as well as Gomer and Magog. It is suggested that it was the Welsh, from Gomer, who created Stonehenge. Tarshish may be referenced in Genesis 10:4 as the "isles of the Gentiles". The *Phoenicians* (also known by their principal cities of Tyre and Sidon whose ruins exist in today's Lebanon), traded precious metals with them. Herodotus calls the islands the "Tin Isles" and designates them "far to the north and west". Britain and Spain were both rich with tin. When combined with copper (perhaps from North America near the Great Lakes!) we get bronze, obviously the defining metal of the Bronze Age. Solomon's navies possibly worked in conjunction with the Canaanites to his north (aka the Phoenicians), creating what may have been a sea bridge to the New World. Osterholm doesn't quite go that far; however, the linkage of Tarshish to Britain is relatively certain:

> King Solomon acquired precious metals from *Tarshish* (1 Kings 10:22). English historians assert that British mines mainly supplied the glorious adornment of Solomon's Temple, and in those days the mines of southwestern Britain were the source of the world's supply of tin.

According to Osterholm, the name Briton (aka Brythons) (descendant of Elishah) derives from Brutus, the first king of Britain (Popeye's arch foe would be his namesake). Kamber and Albanactus, referenced in Britain's pre-history, were sons of Brutus. Cambaria and Cambrians derive from

Kamber, while Albanactus supply the name for Albans while Albion is their land. These peoples would integrate with the Celts. The Scythians also joined the party invading the Isles as well and were known as the Skoths which would eventually become the Scots.

> The name for the Celts or Cymru was "Weahlas," from Anglo-Saxon origins, meaning "land of foreigners"—Wales. The Welsh still call themselves Cymru, pronounced "Coomry." Later the Romans referred to the land as *Britannia*, invading there about 50 years before the birth of Christ. By the third century A.D., Jutes, Franks, Picts, Moors, Angles, Saxons and other groups were invading from surrounding Europe. In the sixth century A.D., Saxons called the land Kemr (Cymru), and the language *Brithenig* (Breton). The Angles eventually conquered Britannia, renaming the territory *Angleland*, which became *England*.

The Romans and Italians

The great people we know as the Romans were initially known as the *Italics* (note the connection to Italy and to the font type we use so often). They were an agrarian people but war-like and settled in the mountains of Northern Italy. They become known as the Sabines, Umbrians, and Latins. Rome was founded in part by these people living south of the Tiber River. The exact time of its founding cannot be known for certain, but some point to the year 753 B.C. According to Osterholm, they imitated their neighbors the Etruscans (formerly known as the Trojans). The Roman legend contends Aeneas, a prince of Troy who fled the city after the infamous Trojan War fought against Greece, founded the city, although a descendant of Aeneas, specifically Romulus (twin of Remus) was the person after which the city was named. The people from Troy, the Etruscans, purportedly settled in the region as far back as 1260 B.C. [97] From Osterholm's narrative: we pick up several other interesting insights into the peoples of Italy:

> The Etruscans were greatly influenced by the Greeks, and the Etruscans brought that influence to the city of Rome. The Romans called Etruscans the *Tusci*, and Tuscany still bears the name. The Etruscan language, once thought lost, is still spoken by the Basques, called *Euskara*... The Romans were first a subject

people of the Etruscans, but the Romans would later be their con-
querors. After many battles with the Etruscans, the city of Rome
identified itself as Latin, eventually integrating the Etruscans...

We also learn from Osterholm that the Basques' language has commonali-
ties to the language of the Georgians in southern Russia. This link suggests that the Etruscans were originally Trojans who fled Troy after the
famous mythologized war there, sailing across the Black Sea to the Caucasus region in southern Russia as well as to northern Italy. DNA markers in
these two peoples also support their ancient connection. The Basques
would eventually migrate to southeast France and northeast Spain.

The Scandinavians

As noted in the discussion of the Germans, the Scandinavian peoples
(Danes, Norwegians, and Swedes) hail from Germanic people groups in-
cluding the Goths, Visigoths, Teutons, and Burgundians (from which the
French province and its famous wines derives its name, i.e., Burgundy).

Latin and Greek writers called the land *Scandza* or *Scandia* (now Scandinavia). Roman records from 350 A.D. reference a mountain chain, the As-
canimians, the region *Sakasene* (derived from Ashkenaz), and a large city
on the south side of the Caspian Sea. The dwellers of the city were known
as the *Saki*. The Saki called themselves the Sakasenoi, from which Sach-
sens or Saxons comes. This group migrated further and further north.

> Around 280 A.D. the Romans tell of the employment of Saxons
> to guard the eastern British coasts against barbarians. About 565
> A.D., the Saxons battled over territory in the Baltic region with
> another powerful people, the *Svear*. Historical records indicate
> that descendants of Tiras also settled in Scandinavia, a people
> called the Svear. The Svear are descendants of the first inhabit-
> ants of the ancient city of Troy, a people then known as the Tira-
> cians (also Thracians, Trajans or Trojans). They were described
> as a "ruddy and blue-eyed people."

These people were also known as the *Aes*, meaning "iron" for their superi-
or weaponry. The Black Sea was also known as the Sea of *Aesov* or Iron
Sea and is today still named the Sea of Azov. The Aes or *Aesir* journeyed

from the Baltic Sea to Scandinavia about 100 years before Christ. Scholars, archeology, and DNA studies support this migration. The Aesir came to be known as the Svear a forerunner to the Swedes and the *Vanir* or *Danir*, i.e., the Danes. The Svear and Daner people groups were known to be fairer (blond) and taller than other peoples in the Baltic. The Romans documented that the Svear along with the Goths were seafarers and already ravaging the Black Sea and the Mediterranean supposedly using similar weapons to their Trojan ancestors. Osterholm provides considerable additional information about the history and origins of the Scandinavian peoples:

> The Svear and Goths dominated the Russian waterways, and by 739 A.D. together they were called *Varyagans* or *Varangians* (from the Swedish *Vaeringar*), according to written records of the Slavs near the Sea of Azov. Like their ancestors, Scandinavians lived in large communities where their chieftains would send out maritime warriors to trade and plunder. Those fierce warriors were called the *Vaeringar*, which literally meant "men who offer their service to another master." We later know them by their popularized name, the *Vikings*.

Osterholm concludes his study pointing out the major splitting of the Japhethites was into two groups, one of which settled in present-day India and Central Asia while the other group settled on the European continent. Together the Japhethites are known as the Indo-European people group and the contraction of this designation is known by the infamous name "Aryan". Early Aryans referred to Japheth as *Diapatischta* (the chief of the race), while Greeks called Japheth *Iapetos* or *Japetos*. East Indians refer to him as *Jyapeti* or *PraJapati*. The Romans used the name *Ju-Pater* or the much more recognizable, *Jupiter*. The Saxons knew him as *Iafeth*, subsequently *Sceaf* (pronounced "Sheef" or "Shaif") and their earliest genealogies referenced him as the son of Noah. As Osterholm concludes concerning the importance of the identification of ancestry: "All of these peoples, we must remember, were pagans whose knowledge or even awareness of the book of Genesis had been lost, or was non-existent."

IS THE BIBLE JUST A REGIONAL BOOK?

Ezekiel's identification of the descendants of Japheth to the first and second generation and the immediate lands where they initially resided was not meant to imply that these initial generations were passive "homebodies" – bound strictly to the land they first staked out. And yet some writers in our day assume that listing only the names of the first generation or two of Japheth's sons, means restricting the scope of their domiciles, such that Ezekiel's prophecy refers only to the locations where these initial generations lived. *This is highly unlikely for a number of reasons, as we will investigate here.* Ezekiel intended to disclose to future generations which peoples would attack Israel in the last days and from whence they would come. The mindset of the prophet, his understanding of geography and demography, was far more advanced than what we, looking back 2,500 years assume (we moderns wrongly presume to know most everything and the ancients next to nothing).

History teaches us that migration was a constant reality of our forebears. Since the descendants didn't remain only in the region where they first settled, where do we draw the line and declare, "this far and no further" in terms of peoples and their final "resting" place? As mentioned earlier, if we accept biblical chronology dating the flood of Noah to about 2350 B.C., by the time Ezekiel penned his prophecy circa 550 B.C., 1,800 years had already elapsed. How many human beings were contemporaries to Ezekiel? How dispersed were they? Where were the Sons of Japheth living by the time that Ezekiel wrote his book? We cannot assume they were still tightly clustered within a thousand mile diameter of Noah's Ark. They weren't. Most had left the confines of Anatolia for new horizons over 1,500 years before (the "grass was greener" even back then).

The reality is that the various groups comprising Japheth's family had already spread from England to Indochina, from the Nile to the North Pole (almost). While significant migrations would continue to occur for yet another 1,500 years after Ezekiel, (mostly in the New World were "settlers" were sparser) there was considerable stability as to where various groups lived in Europe, Asia, and Africa. In other words, by Ezekiel's day dramatic migrations in Eurasia and Africa were already slowing. When the prophet spoke about peoples and regions, he didn't just "talk Turkey". The Egyptians were in Egypt, the Greeks in Greece, the Romans in Rome, the Persians in Persia, and the Magogians far east of the Caspian Sea. And, as we will discuss soon, the *Rus were already living in Russia.*

It is reasonable to assume that Gog, Meschech, Tubal, and the other cast of characters had separate domiciles approaching tens of thousands of square miles. By 550 B.C., Gomer's descendants were already in Germany, Scandinavia, and England. Gog and Magog's offspring already lived throughout the Asian steppes. Aeneas' sons and grandsons were in Rome, having left Troy seven hundred years prior. The Greeks were verging on creating an empire to rival the Median/Persian Empire. In other words, limiting these various family groups to just the immediate surroundings where Noah's Ark landed would have seemed ignorant to the Hebrews of Ezekiel's day. The Magogians, the Gogarenes, the Scythians, (you pick the name) were known to have dispersed throughout the better part of Asia. Ezekiel wasn't thinking only of Anatolia when he used the names of Meschech, Tubal, Gomer, Tarshish and so on. To assume that these ancients were ignorant of how vast the domain of humanity already was and the regions where they lived in 550 B.C., would be a profound case of patronizing the Hebrew prophets, minimizing the wisdom of God spoken by those prophets – and concocting abhorrent scholarship to boot.

We know Jonah sought to elude God's command to travel to Ninevah to preach repentance by heading as far away as possible from Assyria (it was only a 3 day walk from where Jonah lived). When the whale swallowed him, he had been a passenger on a slow boat to *Tarshish* (likely England). This was 200 years before Ezekiel talked about Tarshish and its colonies.

> *Now the word of the Lord came unto Jonah the son of Amittai, saying, "Arise, go to Nineveh, that great city, and cry against it; for their wickedness is come up before me." But Jonah rose up to flee unto **Tarshish** from the presence of the Lord, and went down to Joppa; and he found a ship going to **Tarshish**: so he paid the fare thereof, and went down into it, to go with them unto **Tarshish** from the presence of the Lord.* (Jonah 1:1-3)

Solomon had been trading with "Angleland" (recall the earlier discussion) for almost 500 years. Jewish history credits Solomon…

> With having been successful in diplomacy and trade with the majority of his neighbors. A prime example of this diplomacy was mentioned in 1 Kings Chapter 5 [which] relates his alliance with the ruler of Tyre, which was the chief seaport of the Phoenicians at that time. It was these key alliances in trade, diplomacy and the ability to keep the peace that [led] to the apparent success of his administration. Other trading alliances credited to Solomon were with, Chittim, Ophir and Tarshish. Add to this list a list of countries from which Solomon took wives and he can truly be said to have been be a figure of international reputation.[98]

The Phoenicians (Tyre and Sidon) dominated trade and likely had already discovered the New World. It is even possible that refugees from Joshua's conquest of "Canaan-land" had fled to the Americas 1,000 years before Ezekiel prophesied about Gog and Magog attacking Israel in the last days.[99] Great peoples, where they lived, and what they were able to accomplish were common knowledge. The prophet Ezekiel was well-schooled and would have known all these things.

Another factor to take into account: just how many persons were living in the world leading up to Ezekiel's day? We could ask in jest, "How much pressure was there in his day to move far away from one's in-laws?" Since some things don't change, we can be assured that wanderlust as well as needing "wide open spaces" motivated human beings too, even in 550 B.C. Fear of warring peoples led peaceable tribes to seek other lands. The ascendancy of Assyria in the eighth century B.C. likely led the Phoenicians of Tyre and Sidon to close shop and move to Tunisia, where Pygmalion founded the city of Carthage in 800 B.C., "no mean city" from which Hannibal would spring 400 years later (his exploits would drive Rome to distraction and nearly defeat their empire).

According to the *Atlas of World Population History* (McEvedy and Jones, 1978), there were about 27 million humans alive in the year 2,000 B.C., and 50 million at the time of Ezekiel. Of course, these secular scholars did not assume the earth's population was reset to less than two-dozen persons (Noah and his family) in 2350 B.C. Their estimates are virtually useless in light of biblical history. Factors regarding fertility, desired family size, length of life and what was the acceptable "child bearing age", as well as infant mortality, all such factors are challenging to fathom if we judge the past by the present. And it is important to recognize that population growth exceeds our imagination. According to these same sources (which are reliable regarding the past half-millennia, but not so much 2,500 years prior), humanity numbered barely *one billion* only 150 years ago, in 1850. 150 years later, in the year 2000, there were over *seven billion* persons. Exponential growth explodes faster than we can contemplate. Not to beat the point to death, but the reality is that humanity spread out far faster than we presume today. Now there are no new frontiers and no available territory. That was not the case 4,300 years ago. "Go west young man!" (and north, south, and east) was an adage persons heeded well before the time of the American frontier. Opportunity lay just beyond the hills "overthar".

THE POPULAR "MINORITY REPORT" IS NOT WELL SUPPORTED

The number of scholars favoring a limited scope for Ezekiel's identification of Gog (restricted to Turkey and directly south from Syria to Iran) constitutes a *minority*. It is important to note the context of the "minority report" since it appears to be popularly supported at this moment in time. In reality, *conventional teaching refutes it and marshals a stunning number of scholars against it*. To recap some of the major elements of the issue:

1. The list of teachers and authorities holding to this position comprises a much smaller assembly than those who identify Gog and Magog as constituting a far broader geographical "sphere of settlement" with references pertinent to global locations in our day.

2. The two most popular authors favoring Turkey as the fulfillment of Gog (and not Russia), namely Walid Shoebat and Joel Richardson, follow "the minority report" and not the vast number of conventional scholars who believe Gog and Magog refer to much greater territory (and peoples) than just the area of the Black and Caspian Seas.

3. This minority view limits the application of Bible prophecy principally to a Middle East focus and not a global perspective. According to this point of view, the Bible is *just* a Mediterranean book of Semitic peoples.

Therefore, the majority report rejects this position. Listing those who disagree with the "limited" scope of Ezekiel's (to Turkey, aka Anatolia) includes: Arnold Fruchtenbaum, Rabbi Moshe Eisemann, Mark Hitchcock, Thomas Ice, Grant Jeffrey, Jack Kelley, Hal Lindsey, Thomas McCall, Zola Levitt, J. Dwight Pentecost, Jon Mark Ruthven, John F. Walvoord, Bill Salus, Gary Stearman, J.R Church, and yours truly.

However, Douglas Berner discusses perhaps one of the most noteworthy and appreciated evangelical scholars of our day, Dr. Michael Heiser, who advocates the "minority report" – the limited scope of Ezekiel's prophecy seeing Turkey at the center. Berner states,

> Michael Heiser observes that the descendants of Japheth, one of Noah's three sons, are "associated with locations throughout Anatolia and south of the Black Sea: Gomer, Magog, Javan, Tubal, Meschech, Tiras, and Togarmah (a son of Gomer)." Heiser then concludes that the invasion of Gog and Magog comes from the territory of Anatolia and not Russia. [100]

Heiser asserts this view because the Bible, he contends, is a book of the Middle East and therefore, should be understood in this context alone. For Heiser, to assert "Gog refers to Russia" amounts to a relic of Cold War thinking. Berner summarizes Heiser's position with these words:

> Michael Heiser promotes this perspective and further attests that prophecy needs to be interpreted based on a "Mediterranean-centered" biblical world. Heiser claims, "The Bible is a Mediterranean-centered document, and so is not concerned with countries and people groups unconnected to these regions." He later propounds "there is no need to rip a geographic name out of the text and, through various intellectual machinations, somehow arrive as the conclusion that a modern non-Middle eastern country was really in view." [101]

Expanding why Heiser says this is so, Berner quotes Heiser's premises:

1. The issue in prophecy is what happens to God's people, God's prom-ises to those people, and the nations caught up with those people and pledges.

2. Prophecy revolves around divine goals and how God sees fit to bring this most ancient play to its climax.

3. Biblical prophecies were given to biblical people in biblical lands, and so their meaning is dictated by the circumstances into which God interjected them through the mouths of the prophets. [102]

Berner provides, however, an excellent rebuttal to what, on the surface, seems to be an intelligent and biblically-centered rationale substantiating Heiser's point of view. In essence, Berner says that while Heiser has rightly stated crucial and strategic biblical principles, nonetheless, he has missed the even more strategic point that the dynamic of the Bible changed when Jesus created His church and commissioned it to go out into the entire world – and Jesus understood that the Bible's prophecies were global in nature and in scope, no longer limited to events pertinent only to the people of Israel in their land. The Jews and virtually all other Middle Eastern peoples are intermarried into other peoples (at least in part) and live throughout the world. The core hermeneutic changed along with the issuance of the Great Commission (Matthew 28:19-20). Likewise, the threats that exist should not be understood to be literal, i.e., are not just "bows and arrows with riders on horseback" as described by Ezekiel, but include weapons of mass destruction beyond anything that the Bible's prophets could contemplate, but not beyond what God could foresee.

Additionally, God's chosen people of the Old Testament, the Jews have not only survived, but have thrived in many ways, particularly dominating the world economy in many quarters. Nor is God surprised by the world-wide travel and communications unimaginable millennia ago. His revela-tions delivered through His prophets, even while cast in symbolic lan-guage in many cases, nevertheless anticipated this amazing state of affairs. And despite these incredible advances and unforeseen circumstances (by those who did not have the advantage of biblical prophetic insight), the Jewish people and their land would once again become the center of the world's attention at the end of days… all despite the fact the plan of God remains *globally* and not just regionally relevant.

> When God breaks His longsuffering silence and refocuses His divine attention on Israel again. He will maneuver events which will result in a worldwide exodus of the Jewish people back to the Promised Land. One of God's purposes will be to concentrate His people in Israel so that He can focus on them as He did during Old Testament times. [103]

And then Berner stresses once again a key premise to his study and an important conclusion to mine:

> One of the ways He [God] will accomplish [His] will through the *invasion of Gog and Magog* and the simultaneous *destruction of Russia and the United States as world powers.*[104]

So are Russians sons of Japheth? Is Russia explicitly named in Ezekiel's prophecy, or are we "reading into" the text from a "Cold War" mindset?

ON NOT RUSHING TO JUDGMENT ON RÔ'SH AND RUSSIA

*"Son of man, set your face toward Gog of the land of Magog, the prince of **Rosh**, Meshech and Tubal, and prophesy against him.* (Ezekiel 38:2)

If only one word were selected that comprises the greatest controversy in the passage of Ezekiel 38-39, it would be the word transliterated rô'sh. This discussion in this section becomes a bit technical, but the implications are so significant that we must take the time (and muster our concentration) to dig into the original language, sentence construction, and use of adjectives and nouns.

For instance, the New American Standard Bible (NASB) uses *rô'sh* as a name, but notes that *rô'sh* could be translated "*chief* Prince of Meschech." The King James instead uses "chief" as in "O Gog, the chief prince of Meshech and Tubal" in all three verses where rô'sh pops up, Ezekiel 38:2, 38:3 and 39:1. And we must admit the term *rô'sh* is used many times as an adjective in the Old Testament where it means *chief, leader,* or *head.*

185

The compilers of the King James Version, however, added a marginal note pertaining to this phrase implying that "the chief prince of" could be rendered "prince of the chief" and according to Douglas Berner, ultimately acknowledge the potential legitimacy of the rendering "prince of Rô'sh."

The issue is whether *in this special instance* where in the text it is combined with another Hebrew word transliterated, *nâsî'*, it should be seen as a *proper noun or name*, lest we have two adjectives placed together that are needlessly redundant or uncharacteristic of Hebrew. In other words, is the Hebrew *"nâsî' rô'sh"* properly translated "prince of Rô'sh" or "chief prince of Meschech" as in "high priest of Meschech" (which is the Old Testament similarity that opponents to rô'sh as a noun, readily cite, seeing it as a parallel convention to the designate the "head honcho" of the Temple priesthood, aka the Chief Priest.) [Note that *head honcho* would be a similar construction!]

The Septuagint Bible (abbreviated LXX, aka the Greek version of the Old Testament which was most used in the New Testament when citing Old Testament scriptures), was written about two hundred years before Christ. LXX inserted the name *Rô'sh* instead of a synonym such as "chief" (which is how Jerome translated *rô'sh* in his Latin version of the Bible, the Vulgate). Thus, the Septuagint would be translated, the "ruler of Rosh". The early German versions employed the same approach as the LXX. Rô'sh was considered a noun of a *place* or a *people*. In 1885, the Revised Version in England used "Prince of Rosh" – again, meaning that rô'sh referred to a *place* or a *people* (or both). Thus, while controversial, there is a longstanding tradition of using *Rô'sh* as a proper name long before the Scofield Bible was published in 1909. This chronology matters because Joel Richardson, among several others, alleges that the reason evangelicals misunderstand *rosh to be Russia* is due to the fact that the Scofield Bible said it was so and the undereducated masses in America took Scofield's word for it. Remember, Richardson wants to identify *Gog with Islam* and **not** with Russia. Hence, ruling out Russia by "dissing" the translation of Rô'sh as *Ros* for Russia comprises an important aspect of his argument. And yet, to be fair to Richardson, there are other champions for his cause that are worth noting. A quick comment on two such points of view.

Opponents to using rô'sh as a proper noun find support in the New International Version (NIV), which also made a big issue of the choice of words, and even asserts it likely means "commander-in-chief" in the way we Americans use the phrase.[105] NIV scholars go even further to make sure that no one can think Ezekiel meant *any nation or people existent in modern day.* "The NIV text note gives the possible translation 'prince of Rosh' and if this is correct, Rosh is probably the name of an unknown people or place. Identification with Russia is unlikely, and in any case cannot be proven." [106]

Michael Heiser rises to the challenge to reinforce the unlikelihood that the prophecy of Ezekiel could be looking forward to a contemporary nation. Following in the line of Richardson (although preceding him chronologically), Heiser states, "it has been fashionable among premillennialists to argue that 'Rosh' is a reference to the country of Russia..." He continues most sardonically, "In my view, the entire premise underlying this speculated reconstruction, that rô'sh is the name of a place, is without exegetical foundation, and connecting this grammatically misguided assertion with Russia seems based on some type of Cold War hermeneutic." [107] Of course, given our discussion in the first half of this book, a reference to Cold War Russia might not be an anachronism at which we should scoff.

In his comprehensive study, Berner follows Heiser down the rabbit hole on linguistic permutations and vowel markings of ancient Hebrew. The study of the word rô'sh as used in the Old Testament indeed is a rich one to say the least, but it is much too much detail for our purposes. On this aspect of the discussion, a summary of Berner's position must suffice: Heiser's polemic does not cinch the argument. Others like Jon Mark Ruthven assert rô'sh is the name of a place and states unequivocally "It is clear that the LXX [Septuagint] knew of a nation called Ρως (ROS)" [108]

Mark Hitchcock and Thomas Ice, who are proponents for Ezekiel's usage of *rô'sh* as the name of a location and not a title, provide perhaps the best summary to satisfy our study. I will further abbreviate Berner's recap. [109]

- Eminent Hebrew scholars C.F. Keil and Wilhelm Gesenius both hold that the better translation of *rô'sh* in Ezekiel 38-39 is a proper name referring to a specific location, region, or country.

187

- The Septuagint (LXX), translated only three centuries from Ezekiel's writings, translates rô'sh as the proper name *Ros*. Jerome's Vulgate (the Catholic Bible) mistranslates rô'sh and many modern versions follow his lead down a mismarked path, making it an adjective instead of a proper noun.

- There are many Bible dictionaries and encyclopedias in their articles on *rô'sh* take the position that Ezekiel uses it as a proper name. Examples include *New Bible Dictionary*, *Wycliffe Bible Dictionary*, and *International Standard Bible Encyclopedia.*

- *Rô'sh* is mentioned three times in Ezekiel 38-39. According to Hitchcock and Ice, it is uncharacteristic of Hebrew to continue to repeat the full title of a leader multiple times in adjacent passages. In other words, repeating "Chief Prince of Meschech" in each of the three places would be abbreviated to Prince of Meschech and the word, rô'sh or chief, would have been dropped – unless Ezekiel was wanting to emphasize the name of the guilty party, which seems highly *likely*, if we understand prophecy as the serious business it is – predicting the future to prove the providence of God.

- Finally, Hitchcock and Ice cite G. A. Cooke, a Hebrew scholar who translated Ezekiel 38:2, "the chief of Rosh, Meschech and Tubal." Cooke indicates that this is "the most natural way of rendering the Hebrew." For Hitchcock, Ice, and Berner, the matter is just that simple.

However, I especially appreciate Berner's testimony to why the translation of rô'sh as *Ros*, aka Russia, rings so true to Ezekiel's intent. Berner writes a glowing passage with a particular kind of passion that I share:

> I believe God intended this prophecy to be specific enough that its fulfillment will be very clear to Israel and the world when God's preordained tie for Gog and Magog comes. However, considering the extreme length of time between Ezekiel's pronouncement of this prophecy and its ultimate fulfillment, it does serve a purpose for the identity of the leader, Gog, and the nation which he represents, to be somewhat enigmatic. God's prophecies are directed at an ultimate audience and a time of ultimate fulfillment, but they have to speak to and be meaningful to all of the generations of people throughout the ages between Ezekiel and a specific point in the End Times. When we consider the vast changes in the empires of the Gentiles through-

out history, it is not surprising that the is prophecy was written with a series [of] internal cryptic enigmas which allow for this vast amount of change but still point to the identity of the ultimate enemies that will be involved in this invasion.[110]

When Berner wrote his book in 2006, Russia looked like it might grow to be a partner to the United States. But Berner didn't trust that the transformation was real. He stated most presciently:

> Russia, the land of Magog, has attempted a political and economic reversal of direction by adopting some measures of democracy and capitalism. How much of this change is for real and how much is a charade to lull the U.S. and the West into complacency and provide economic assistance remains to be seen. *However, it may be that God has plans for Russia to do another about face, and revert back to its former leadership system under a strong totalitarian Gog.* [Emphasis added]

Indeed, as outlined in Part One of this book, the *about face* is complete. Perhaps it is best to close this chapter with a passage from the late and great Grant Jeffrey who made the following equally prophetic statement:

> It is important for us to realize that the Bible's prophecy in Ezekiel about the coming War of Gog and Magog is not influenced by the temporary maneuvering now going on in Moscow. The prophet Ezekiel does not declare that 'Communist' Russia will come down against the mountains of Israel; rather he says that "Magog," which is Russia will lead an alliance of nations against the Jewish state. Even if Russia should genuinely repudiate communism it would not change the fact that God has declared that Russia's appointment with destiny will not be postponed.

Jeffrey's prosaic insight provides an apt segue to our next chapter in which we will delve into a more precise consideration of the timing of that appointment with destiny awaiting Gog, Israel, the U.K. and the United States of America.

Figure 18 - Archenemies Make Good Antichrists

10: When the Next Great War Happens

"The attack by Russia will be a desperate attempt to recoup her position as a world power with influence over the Middle East."

John F. Walvoord, *Armageddon, Oil, and the Middle East Crisis*, 1974

AMERICA'S ENEMY ALWAYS MAKES FOR A GOOD ANTICHRIST

AMERICANS WHO BELIEVE IN BIBLE PROPHECY, FUTURISTS THAT IS, HAVE A NATURAL TENDENCY TO VILIFY THE NATION'S CURRENT ENEMY AND ASSOCIATE THAT ENEMY WITH THE ANTICHRIST, OR IN the case of Russia, with the personage of Gog. In World War II, many American evangelicals believed that the Italian fascist leader Benito Mussolini was the Antichrist and the Pope, the False Prophet. Later, Adolf Hitler became the obvious stronger of the two Allied enemies. It didn't take long for opinions to shift to Hitler as the "man of sin", the "son of perdition", and the "little horn of Daniel". Later, after Hitler was no more, and with the advent of the Cold War, the Soviet Union was easily assigned "most-hated-nation status" by Americans. Whoever was the then *Premier* (Prime Minister) of the Soviet Union, whether Nikita Khrushchev, Leonid Brezhnev, or Mikhail Gorbachev, was assigned the role of Antichrist, or more in line with Ezekiel, Gog from the land of Magog. Because Gorbachev had a distinctive birthmark on his forehead, some speculated that this birthmark was the "mark of the beast" and he was surely to turn out to be the archenemy of Christendom. However, when the Soviet Union disintegrated in 1991, many supposed that the biblical scenario, as put forth popularly by Hal Lindsey and Tim LaHaye, was not likely to happen – not anytime soon at least.

In 1979, Iran had come onto the scene and it was the Ayatollah Khomeini that gave rise to speculation. As Islam became much more threatening during the 1980s, and by the time the Soviet Union vanished in 1991, the cast of characters had shifted. America was still supportive of Israel but also had a strategic alliance with Saudi Arabia to make oil the principle commodity backing the global currency – the Petrodollar. Gold was just too hard to come by. For the most part, Saudi Arabia helped keep the OPEC nations in line and manipulated the price of oil to make Arab and American oil companies filthy rich, while the world moved into a new alignment of nations.

However, Bible prophecy teachers like John F. Walvoord, continued to point to Russia as the evil empire and the "power quest to corner the petroleum market" as the principal factor that would one day lead the world into a major war. Boris Yeltsin seemed pro-American and after the collapse of the Soviet Union, Mr. Gorbachev and his lovely wife Raisa, seemed quite Western and even likable. Vladimir Putin also seemed like a reasonable person. Not long after Putin took the reins in Russia, George W. Bush looked into his eyes and saw his soul… or so Bush said, and assured Americans we had nothing to worry about. We could work with Russia.

During the past decade, however (from about 2005 forward), Putin wasn't such a sure bet to befriend the West and embrace America's version of global cooperation aka *The New World Order*. Russia participated in the "Quartet" of entities working on Middle East Peace Plan (consisting of the United States, Russia, the United Nations, and the European Union). But the plan for George H.W. Bush's New World Order, proclaimed possible with the fall of the Soviet Union, begin to get mired in the mud. Russia, was building up its petroleum business and Putin was either sending the so-called Russian "oligarchs" (who "raped and pillaged" Mother Russia during Yeltsin's term) to Siberia or having them assassinated. Russia, through Putin's leadership, had designs on becoming the Old Empire once more. "Step aside *Katherine the Great*. Rest in peace *Peter the Great*. There is a new Czar in town, KGB-trained, and the surprising champion of the Russian Orthodox Church." One day this man might even be known as "Putin the Great" who also happened to hail from St. Petersburg. Not since *Vlad the Impaler* (the authentic Dracula dating back to the fifteenth century) had a Vladimir portended such bad tidings for the Eastern Hemisphere. Stepping on U.S. foreign policy seemed to become Putin's favorite pastime. Just look at Crimea. Might Russia become the "heavy" once more? Yes, but not just yet. Meanwhile, the undisputed archenemy of America became Islam. Despite the fact that the current president of these United States assured Muslims that America was not and had never been at war with Islam, most of the American populace wasn't so sure. We recall his words:

> "I've come here, to Cairo, to seek a new beginning between the United States and Muslims around the world. One based on mutual interest and mutual respect. And one based upon the truth that America and Islam are not exclusive and need not be in competition. In Ankara, I made clear that America is not and will never be at war with Islam." (Barack H. Obama, 2009)

Still, with the destruction of the Twin Towers on 9-11-2001, *Osama* had become Public Enemy Number One and *Obama* wasn't going to change that. The Bin Laden's, his Saudi family, were best friends with the Bushes. This made the average "Joe the Plumber" weary of all Arabs and ties between American and Muslims elites. What's up with that? How is it that a member of this Saudi family of not one but two American Presidents could be the ringleader for the archenemy of the United States, *Al Qaeda*? Terrorists always turned up Muslim, from the "Shoe Bomber" (2001) to the "Underwear Bomber" (2009) to the 2015 San Bernardino couple killing 14 American citizens (while someone babysat with their kids). Americans had valid reasons to think that although we might not be at war with Islam, Islam was obviously at war with us. There was no glossing over that fact.

It is against this backdrop that Islam replaced Russia as the villain of our day. It is not accidental that this is the societal context in which some apocalyptic teachers have supposed that the Antichrist will be Islamic, the land of Magog will be Muslim, and the next great war in the Middle East must be a nuclear war between the Jews and the Muslims (an anticipated Israeli nuclear bombing of Iran that has not yet to take place). The best way to reconcile fifty years of divergent apocalyptic teaching would be to see *one bad guy instead of two* (Gog and Antichrist were one and the same) and *one war instead of two* (The War of Gog and Magog was just another name for the War of Armageddon). If Islam is the real enemy, isn't there biblical support to prove this scenario true?

PSALM 83: A CURRENT OR FUTURE WAR?

For quite some time, Bible teachers have proffered that a war between Arab states and Israel might be a necessary precursor to the War of Gog and Magog. This idea is not new. Back in 1979, the late Noah Hutchings and his partner David Webber proposed that such a war could take place. In their book, *Is this the Last Century?* these great teachers explained:

> We may divide the Arab nations in the Third-World bloc into two categories, based on their relationship to Israel. The inner six – Syria, Jordan, Lebanon, Iraq, Egypt, and Saudi Arabia – are not mentioned in the accounts of war recorded in Ezekiel 38. We cannot be certain why these nations will not be involved in that great war. It may be that they will have been either conquered or destroyed in a smaller, regional war. In fact, such a war might provide Russia with the very excuse it needs to launch a full-scale invasion… When Russia unleashes her fury on Israel, she will be joined by the outer four Arab nations – Turkey (biblical Togarmah), Libya, Ethiopia, and Iran (biblical Persia).

The two nations mentioned in Ezekiel 38, subject to considerable discussion and debate, have to do with lesser states (not endowed with great military strength), notably "Put" and "Cush". Scholars differ on whether these references are to North Africa nations west of the Nile (such as Libya and Tunisia) or to its south (e.g., the Sudan and today's Ethiopia); or whether *Cush* actually references the geographical area adjacent to the Persian Gulf near the Tigris and Euphrates Rivers. Ancient sources seem to indicate that might be the case. This discussion, however, would appear to be of little consequence given that the primary question marks are (1) whether *Turkey* is the primary leader (or not at all involved) in these wars opposing Israel, (2) whether *Egypt* is included in any future war with Israel (as it seems to be entirely missing in the accounts), and (3) why Syria, the traditional enemy to Israel is not more prominent (the "King of the North" aka home of *the Assyrian* – unless you assume his home was Anatolia and not Iraq, as proposed by Walid Shoebat and Joel Richardson. Just for the record: the location of ancient Nineveh, the capital of Assyria, is Iraq's city of Mosul.)

PSALM 83

¹ Keep not thou silence, O God: hold not thy peace, and be not still, O God.

² For, lo, thine enemies make a tumult: and they that hate thee have lifted up the head.

³ They have taken crafty counsel against thy people, and consulted against thy hidden ones.

⁴ They have said, Come, and let us cut them off from being a nation; that the name of Israel may be no more in remembrance.

⁵ For they have consulted together with one consent: they are confederate against thee:

*⁶ The tabernacles of **Edom**, and the **Ishmaelites**; of **Moab**, and the **Hagarenes**;*

*⁷ **Gebal**, and **Ammon**, and **Amalek**; the **Philistines** with the inhabitants of **Tyre**;*

*⁸ **Assur** also is joined with them: they have holpen **the children of Lot**. Selah.*

*⁹ Do unto them as unto the **Midianites**; as to Sisera, as to Jabin, at the brook of Kison:*

¹⁰ Which perished at Endor: they became as dung for the earth.

¹¹ Make their nobles like Oreb, and like Zeeb: yea, all their princes as Zebah, and as Zalmunna:

¹² Who said, Let us take to ourselves the houses of God in possession.

¹³ O my God, make them like a wheel; as the stubble before the wind.

¹⁴ As the fire burneth a wood, and as the flame setteth the mountains on fire;

¹⁵ So persecute them with thy tempest, and make them afraid with thy storm.

¹⁶ Fill their faces with shame; that they may seek thy name, O Lord.

¹⁷ Let them be confounded and troubled forever; yea, let them be put to shame, and perish:

*¹⁸ That men may know that thou, whose name alone is **Jehovah**, art the most high over all the earth.*

Ironically, the key assumptions that the teachers make who emphasize Psalm 83 as the "next great war" are not contained in Psalm 83. As elaborated earlier, these premises are based on Ezekiel 38:10-13; namely, that (1) Israel must be gathered again from among the nations; (2) Israel *must be living in safety and security* – i.e., *betach*, and (2) Israel must possess great wealth (*living in luxury*), presumably by capturing the spoils of its Arab neighbors. Recall the verses from Ezekiel 38:11-12:

> *And thou shalt say, I will go up to the land of unwalled villages; I will go to them **that are at rest, that dwell safely**, all of them dwelling without walls, and having neither bars nor gates, **To take a spoil**, and to take a prey; to turn thine hand upon the desolate places that are now inhabited, and upon the people that are gathered out of the nations, **which have gotten cattle and goods**, that dwell in the midst of the land.*

Within its verses, Psalm 83 does not supply these details and provides no clue regarding the time of its fulfillment. To reiterate: proponents for the "Psalm 83 future war theory" establish its timing primarily based upon interpreting details derived from the passage in Ezekiel. And, as I pointed out in the Chapter 7: "Where is the Land of Unwalled Villages?" these conclusions are nullified if we consider the possibility that the peoples/nations addressed in this very specific passage (Ezekiel 38:10-13) are those listed in verse 13; namely, *Sheba and Dedan, the Merchants of Tarshish, and their "young lions"*. As stated in my Introduction, these nations comprise the wealth of today's world. If you want to rob great wealth, you want to rob it from them. And the easiest way to do that is to rain weapons down upon them, destroying their economy and banks, and *to free yourself from the trillion dollars in debt you owe to them.*

The psalmist who wrote Psalm 83, Asaph, identifies the enemies of Israel, then contemporary to Israel in ninth century B.C. Those enemies existed then just as the psalmist testifies. His imprecatory prayer was straightforward: he implored the LORD God to avenge Israel's defeats at the hands of its enemies. But he does not identify the characteristics of Israel's living conditions before, during, or after this prayer. We assume these enemies were threats when he wrote. Regardless, the most intriguing element of the Psalm, as today's most prominent and respected "Psalm 83 war theory" proponent Bill Salus notes, is the rationale for the war: *that the enemies learn God's name is JEHOVAH.* The implication we are led to conclude: God's name is NOT Allah. The argument for why Psalm 83 could suggest a current day war builds upon the supposition *that the enemies then are still Israel's enemies now.* With some analysis performed by both those in favor of the PSALM 83 war theory, and those not so much, this naming game is not that hard to play.

The list of peoples and the connections to modern day nations are:

TRIBAL NAME IN PSALM 83	MODERN REGION OR NATION
THE TENTS OF EDOM	JORDAN
THE ISHMAELITES	SAUDI ARABIA AND PORTIONS OF JORDAN
MOAB	JORDAN
THE HAGRITES / HAGARENES	JORDAN
GEBAL	LEBANON
AMMON	NORTHWEST JORDAN
PHILISTIA	GAZA
AMALEK	SOUTHERN ISRAEL
TYRE	LEBANON
ASSYRIA	NORTHERN SYRIA EASTERN IRAQ
THE CHILDREN OF LOT (AMMON AND EDOM)	JORDAN

Figure 19 - The Enemies of Israel in Psalm 83

Among those who do NOT support "the Psalm 83 war theory" is Joel Richardson. Given his obvious concern about Islam and its potential to fulfill Bible prophecy as the power base of Gog/Antichrist, it is somewhat surprising that he does not believe that Psalm 83 is a prophecy waiting to be fulfilled. Why is that? He dismisses it because of its premise that Israel will enjoy the spoils of war by defeating the surrounding Arab countries, and in the process kill millions of Muslims. He considers this outcome to be most unrealistic and uncharacteristic of the nation of Israel. I agree. Richardson relates that there are several different versions of what supposedly happens when the Psalm 83 war transpires (some even employ the ghastly label "The War of Extermination"). However, he suggests all fall short when it comes to believability:

> The idea that Israel, a single nation with approximately 6 million Jews, will either subdue and concurrently occupy, or worse yet, "annihilate" several nations with a total population of approximately 170 million Arabs is quite a claim, making Israel responsible for the equivalent of 30 Holocausts. In my opinion, not only is this view difficult to believe, but it also casts the people of Israel in a murderous and imperialistic light far worse than what even the most obsessed anti-Semitic conspiracy theorists, so common throughout the Islamic world, would ever claim.[111]

Richardson argues, perhaps correctly, that the death of millions of inhabitants to these lands occurs during *the Day of the Lord*, a special period of judgment in which Jesus Christ himself delivers wrath upon the enemies of the people of God, (God's people who have been hidden away in the land of Edom, in the area of Bozrah, and in the now well-known city of Petra – thanks to the concluding scenes of *Indiana Jones and the Last Crusade*). Richardson recites a series of passages from Isaiah, Obadiah, Amos, and Zephaniah, calling attention to the teachings there that indicates that the Messiah will conquer the enemies of Israel upon His return.

> Again we must ask; If Edom and Moab are utterly conquered, "annihilated", or even "exterminated" by the Israeli Defense Forces several years prior to the return of Jesus, how is it that the Messiah is consistently and repeatedly portrayed over and over again, throughout the prophets, as carrying out these things personally when He returns? But it is not merely Edom and Moab

that this can be said of. This same pattern occurs with every name or place mentioned in Psalm 83. In Zephaniah 2, for example, we find the Day of the Lord judgment of the Philistines and Assyria. In Joel 3, Philistia, as well as Lebanon (Tyre and Gebal) are judged at the Day of the Lord. In Ezekiel 30, several nations, including Arabia are specified as being judged in the Day of the Lord. In the end, every last people, nation or region listed in Psalm 83 are described, often in great detail, within the prophets as being judged in the Day of the Lord, at the return of Jesus. Any effort to argue that these peoples, nations or regions are going to be utterly annihilated before the return of Jesus will result in a view which stands in stark conflict with the Biblical prophets. [112]

Richardson points out an understanding of the return of Christ that is generally neglected; that being, Christ returns during a "campaign" and not just a single event, known as the Armageddon Campaign or as Dwight J. Pentecost called it, "The Battle for Jerusalem". The war is not just a single battle at Armageddon, but a series of battles or events that collectively comprise the war preceding the visible return of Jesus Christ. Perhaps they commence in today's Jordan, next move to the Mount of Olives, and finally to the Valley of Megiddo. The sequence is only partially clear. The description of these events is familiar to many readers, although what transpires in Jordan is much less known. Exactly how these events transpire is best left to another discussion; however, the Scripture teaches that Jesus returns first to those hidden away and protected "in the wilderness" and then over an extended period (perhaps ten days corresponding to the Ten Days of Awe from the time of Rosh Hashanah to Yom Kippur), may then move up what is today known as The King's Highway, from the Gulf of Aqaba (Eilat); then apparently to Jerusalem; then finally Megiddo to retake Israel from the occupying forces of Antichrist who has brought horrible destruction and martyrdom to two-thirds of Jerusalem's citizens.

The issue in our discussion is whether (1) Psalm 83 in fact constitutes a necessary pre-condition for the Battle of Gog and Magog, and (2) the proposed war remains "future" to our present day. Does a great war transpire between Israel and its neighbors? Does a major conflagration involving

Israel and the "inner ring" set the stage for the War of Gog and Magog? [113] Moreover, does the stage-setting still lie ahead? Or is it progressive?

IS PSALM 83 A PROPHETIC PASSAGE?

It is my opinion that Bill Salus deserves considerable credit for bringing to the attention of Bible prophecy students that Psalm 83 presents a prophecy *that will be or already is being fulfilled in our day.* [114] It is plainly apparent that Israel today remains surrounded by enemies on all sides. No one can doubt that Israel has been subject to "wars and rumors of wars" since it returned to its historic land and since the land was formally partitioned by the United Nations and granted to Israel in November, 1947 (with its official birth in May, 1948). There have been a series of famous wars in which Israel has expanded, as Bill Salus maintains, and each has led to increased security, prosperity, growth in its borders, and global esteem at least in the eyes of conservative Christendom. If we take the position that God has been reclaiming the ancient land of Israel on behalf of His ancient people through a steady process over the past sixty years, we have a strong case. If we take the position that there is yet another great war that will expand Israel's borders out to their equivalent at the time of Solomon, let alone the expansive land promised to Abraham by God (and that the Israel Defense Force [IDF] will accomplish this), we have a major uphill fight. [115]

My position is that Psalm 83 has a prophetic message and tells a story relevant to our day; however, I do not believe another great regional war is a necessary precondition to the War of Gog and Magog. And, therefore, there is no deferment to when the Gog and Magog war can commence (assuming we first need to wait for Israel to be "living securely" and "possess great wealth"). *These preconditions are the preconditions associated with the rationale for a still future, major, Psalm 83 war.* Israel, however, does not need to possess great wealth for Gog to be motivated to attack Israel to "take a great spoil". Gog will be hooked in his jaws and drawn in by God.

In this sense, we can speak of the War of Gog and Magog being "imminent" and "the next great war in the Middle East". Gog will be drawn into the Middle East, indeed has been drawn into the Middle East for one predominant reason: Gog seeks to protect his (Russia's) self-interest and his (Russia's) self-interest involves an alliance with Iran and Syria who just happen to be co-belligerents against Israel, Saudi Arabia, and the United States. The primary players are assembled and the play about set to begin. In other words, the only preconditions for the War of Gog and Magog are essentially *geo-political.* Israel is in the land. Russia has regained its military prowess and is a military threat to Israel (if Russia chose to engage in a war with Israel). The political situation could quickly turn against Israel and the U.S. in the Middle East as was documented in the first half of this book.

Perhaps ironically, but not inconsistent with my perspective, 2015 comes to a close with Turkey at odds with Russia. Not only is Turkey an unlikely candidate to be Gog, it is *unlikely to be associated with Gog whatsoever*, if Gog is Russia as I propose. Putin and Erdogan are hardly the best of friends. They are in fact engaged in a war of words and have been for quite some time. The downing of a Russian jet and a rescue helicopter, killing one Russian pilot in November 2015, has strained the relationship to a breaking point. While Turkey still remains a member of NATO, its probable support for ISIS, its antagonism and warring against the Kurds, and its hostility toward Russia make Turkey much more of a target for Gog than Israel is at the present time. Plus, it raises questions regarding whether the U.S. or the Europeans will come to Turkey's aid if Russia elects to attack the Turks.[116] Turkey could be expelled from NATO and find itself on its own. Of course, *should Turkey experience a regime change, the political situation could reverse itself almost overnight.* But then, those who have been campaigning for Erdogan as the best suspect for Antichrist would be proven wrong, at least in this one respect.

THE AGREED FRAMEWORK AND KEY POINTS OF CONTENTION

The timing of the War of Gog and Magog has been a matter for discussion and debate since I can remember, dating all the way back to 1970 and the intense interest in Bible prophecy that arose after the publication of *The Late Great Planet Earth* by Hal Lindsey.[117] In a nutshell, Bible scholars have taken varied positions. Of course, some indicate that the

War of Gog and Magog is the same as the final Battle of Armageddon. If true, the timing is simple: it is more or less simultaneous. But if we are dealing with two distinct wars (1. Gog/Magog, and 2. Armageddon) as the majority of Bible prophecy pundits believe we are), then the question naturally arises when one happens in relationship to the other. It is important to note that most prophetic teachers who are futurists assume that all seven years of Daniel's 70th Week (Daniel's key prophetic declaration beginning when Christ returns) still remains future. Some believe only the final three and one-half years remain. But they are in the minority. To expand on this, allow me to cite the key passage from Daniel 9:27:

> *And he shall confirm the covenant with many for one week: and in the midst of the week he shall cause the sacrifice and the oblation to cease, and for the overspreading of abominations he shall make it desolate, even until the consummation, and that determined shall be poured upon the desolate.*

This verse succinctly summarizes the final seven years, beginning with a *covenant* and concluding with the *consummation* (presumably of the Kingdom and the anointing of King Jesus). The midpoint event Daniel calls *"the abomination that maketh desolate"*. It should also be stipulated that the majority of these teachers agree there the seven years are split in two *almost equal* halves by this event (also understood as the revealing of the Antichrist). The event occurs halfway through the 70th week. I said *almost equal* because while the first half of the week is 1,260 days, the last half appears to be 1,290 plus 75 more days until the consummation of the Kingdom. This point pops out from a review of Daniel 12:11-12, which reads as follows:

> *And from the time that the daily sacrifice shall be taken away, and the abomination that maketh desolate set up, there shall be a thousand two hundred and ninety days. Blessed is he that waiteth, and cometh to the thousand three hundred and five and thirty days.*

The revealing of the *man of sin*, the *son of perdition* (2 Thessalonians 2:3-4), happens after the first 1,260 days of the seven years. The Apostle Paul amplifies this event with these words, indicating that this event can only occur after a "great falling away" has taken place, an *apostasia*:

> *Let no man deceive you by any means: for that day shall not come, except there come a falling away first [apostasia], and that man of sin be revealed, the son of perdition; Who opposeth and exalteth himself above all that is called God, or that is worshipped; so that he as God sitteth in the temple of God, shewing himself that he is God.*

After this *apokalyptō* of the Antichrist (the Greek word used by Paul which means the "revealing of what was formerly hidden"), we enter into the period known as *The Great Tribulation.* Note Paul's comment expressly states a Jewish Temple of some sort is in place. *That is a big precondition.* Jesus explained it using these words, referencing Daniel:

> *When ye therefore shall see the abomination of desolation, spoken of by Daniel the prophet, stand in the holy place, (whoso readeth, let him understand:) Then let them which be in Judaea flee into the mountains... For then shall be great tribulation, such as was not since the beginning of the world to this time, no, nor ever shall be.* (Matthew 24:15,16, 21)

In piecing together the various events, virtually all those who teach eschatology agree on the essential framework of the 70th week as follows:

1. There appears to be a prior covenant that is *confirmed* for a seven-year timeframe.
2. In the middle of the period of the covenant, the "he" (the Antichrist) causes the sacrifice and oblation to cease, and the covenant is thereby "de facto" broken.[118]
3. There is an "overspreading of abominations" by the Antichrist implying the Temple is completely contaminated by the abomination.[119]
4. After this event, the Great Tribulation ensues for 1,290 days.
5. At the end of the Great Tribulation, Jesus Christ returns during the "Campaign of Armageddon" when all the armies of the world are gathered together seeking to destroy Him – to kill God!

So when does the Battle of Gog and Magog occur? This is one of three major points of disagreement. Along with this issue is an even more contentious point of disagreement – *the timing of the rapture of the believers in*

203

Jesus Christ. Against the whole framework another question looms quite large. That is, "When is the Day of the Lord?" In my opinion these comprise the three toughest issues to plot on the timeline. To reiterate them here:

1. When does the Gog and Magog war occur?
2. When does the Rapture occur?
3. When does the Day of the Lord occur?

I will attempt to explain my position on all three matters and why there appears to be a connection between all three that provides a fully fleshed-out timeline. No doubt some readers will disagree with some aspect of my position – however, almost all readers will call me a coward if I don't try!

THE TIMING OF GOG AND MAGOG, VIS-À-VIS THE 70TH WEEK

At each junction of the seven-year framework, pundits pick one point or another when they believe the War of Gog and Magog transpires – in opposition to everyone else. In other words, experts identify a particular time when, based on their study, they believe Gog and Magog occurs. Thus, scholars can be grouped into one of five camps or *options* (as I refer to them – working from the end of the framework back to the beginning):

1. At the end of the Great Tribulation (simultaneous with the final battle at Megiddo, i.e., Armageddon).
2. During the Great Tribulation, *after* the midpoint (the abomination of desolation sets things in motion for Gog and Magog to occur).
3. Immediately prior to the midpoint (Gog and Magog enables the Antichrist to take power and enter the Temple to commit the Abomination of Desolation).
4. At the very beginning of Daniel's 70th Week, seven years before the return of Christ (Gog and Magog mark when Daniel's final week begins).
5. Some time prior to the beginning of Daniel's 70th Week, possibly three to three and one-half years before the final seven years begins.

I'm throwing out the very few experts who believe Gog and Magog takes place at the end of the Millennium (referencing Revelation 20 where Gog and Magog are mentioned leading one final rebellion against Jesus Christ).

When Gog and Magog Happens	Noted Eschatology Experts
1. **During or at the End of the Great Tribulation** (Commences the Armageddon Campaign/War and transpires for several months or years)	E.W. Bullinger David Dolan Clarence Larkin Harry Rimmer Robert Van Kampen
2. **At or After the Midpoint** (Upon the revealing of the Antichrist and his claim to divinity and global command – Gog and Magog rebel)	Hal Lindsey Noah Hutchings J. Vernon McGee J. Dwight Pentecost Jack Van Impe David Webber
3. **Just Prior to the Midpoint** (The seven-year covenant of peace breaks down. Gog attacks Israel and is defeated, clearing the way for Antichrist to rule.)	Ed Hindson Mark Hitchcock Salem Kirban Renald Showers John F. Walvoord Warren Wiersbe
4. **At the Beginning of 70th Week** (Gog rebels at the announcement of the seven-year covenant and attacks immediately. His weapons will be burned by Israel for seven years.)	J.R. Church Peter Goodgame Thomas McCall Charles R. Taylor Zola Levitt
5. **Sometime Before the 70th Week** (Israel has been gathered from the nations. Israel seeks protection and covenants with Antichrist. Gog attacks Israel and his defeat is major catastrophe for Islam, clearing the way for the Temple to be rebuilt.)	Arnold Fruchtenbaum Emil Gaverluk John Hagee Grant Jeffrey Tim LaHaye Chuck Missler Randall Price Chuck Smith

The number of scholars who take this position is a very small number, although one important one, Michael Heiser, takes this view.[120]

Otherwise, allow me to create another table plotting where the experts believe fall (on the following page). I have pulled together this table based upon my research with considerable help from the invaluable research in Douglas Berner's book, *The Silence is Broken.* It is important to stress, as Douglas Berner eloquently states, that the description of the War of Gog and Magog seems absent of any "awareness" of other crucial events in Bible prophecy. In other words, previous or concurrent actions or events associated with the apocalyptic period are not mentioned and do not appear to be presupposed. This list is impressive and sets the stage for adopting either options #4 or #5 as presented in the preceding table:

1. No mention of Satan, the Antichrist, the False Prophet, powers or principalities, demons, or the "mark of the beast".
2. No mention of ten kings empowering the Antichrist or nations outside of the Middle East/North Africa (Gog resides both inside and outside of the Middle East, i.e., within and beyond the Black Caspian Seas).
3. No mention of seven-year covenant between Israel and a "protector".
4. No mention of any army coming to the aid of Israel during this war (if Antichrist had covenanted with Israel, he fails to respond to war).
5. No mention that 144,000 sealed witnesses or Two Witnesses are active.
6. No mention of the Jewish Temple, that Temple worship has been reinstated, or the abomination of desolation has occurred.
7. No mention of the King of the north, King of the South, Babylon, Egypt, the Kings of the East, the drying up of the Euphrates River, or massing armies in the valley of Megiddo.
8. No reference to Valley of Megiddo, Armageddon, or Plain of Jezreel.
9. No mention of Jewish remnant holed up in Bozrah, or a war or jihad against Christians globally.
10. No mention of any miracles performed by forces of good or evil (Antichrist, False Prophet, Two Witnesses, Elijah, or the Messiah)
11. No reference to the great judgments of Revelation: the Seals, Trumpets, of Bowls of Wrath prior to, during, or after the war.

12. No mention of the Church, the rise and role of a one-world religion, one-world government, or one-world economic system (beast system).
13. No mention of Jesus Christ, Jewish Messiah, destruction of armies by the coming of the Messiah, the brightness of His coming, or His Word.
14. No reference to judgment of peoples, nations, and lake of fire.

When it comes to establishing the timing of the War of Gog and Magog and the relationship of this War with the rest of the apocalyptic scenario, the silence of Ezekiel's passage on these points cannot be discounted. Ezekiel, being both a priest and prophet, would certainly make reference to existence of a Temple (as he does immediately after the vision of the War) in Chapters 40-48. It would seem to be most illogical to suppose a prior temple had been built and existed during the Gog and Magog war and Ezekiel makes no reference to it. Likewise, it would seem highly improbable that the death of Gog, if due to the coming of the Messiah to commence His judgment of the peoples and the nations (the establishment of the Kingdom), would not be referenced either. For all these reasons, and many more implied from the prior list, the most likely timing for the War of Gog and Magog is prior to or at the immediate beginning of the seven-year period, i.e., Daniel's 70th Week. Therefore, options #4 and #5 stand out as the most likely scenarios for the timing of this event.

Next, we need to consider key factors that place the Gog prophecy *before* or at *the beginning* of Daniel's 70th week. Based upon careful examination, we detect several key issues presenting themselves in all scholarly arguments helping us determine which of these two scenarios are most biblical – as well as logical – when all factors are considered.

FACTORS THAT INFLUENCE THE GOG/MAGOG SCENARIO

Is Gog Daniel's King of the North?

One of the more interesting and challenging issues to consider is whether Gog of Ezekiel is the same as Daniel's king of the North (Daniel 11:40-45). If any given scholar believes they are one and the same, they adopt a scenario placing Gog within the seven-year timespan. If not, they are not compelled to do so. Berner relates, "This view directly identifies

Ezekiel's Gog of the land of Magog with Daniel's king of the North…
One of the variables is the exact timing of the initial invasion, involving
God and Magog or the kings of the South and North, which these authors
interpret as setting the rest of the sequence in motion." [121]

Those believing Gog and the king of the North are identical often assume
it is *Gog* that breaks the covenant through his attack on Israel, and therefore, his attack in Ezekiel 38 must be reconciled with Daniel 11's king of
the North. Allow me to cite the passage in Daniel 11 to demonstrate what
is said and what is not said about the King of the North:

> *36 And the king shall do according to his will; and he shall exalt him-
> self, and magnify himself above every god, and shall speak marvel-
> lous things against the God of gods, and shall prosper till the indig-
> nation be accomplished: for that that is determined shall be done.*

> *37 Neither shall he regard the God of his fathers, nor the desire of
> women, nor regard any god: for he shall magnify himself above all.*

> *38 But in his estate shall he honour the God of forces: and a god
> whom his fathers knew not shall he honour with gold, and silver, and
> with precious stones, and pleasant things.*

> *39 Thus shall he do in the most strong holds with a strange god,
> whom he shall acknowledge and increase with glory: and he shall
> cause them to rule over many, and shall divide the land for gain.*

> *40 And at the time of the end shall the king of the south push at him:
> and the king of the north shall come against him like a whirlwind,
> with chariots, and with horsemen, and with many ships; and he shall
> enter into the countries, and shall overflow and pass over.*

> *41 He shall enter also into the glorious land, and many countries
> shall be overthrown: but these shall escape out of his hand, even
> Edom, and Moab, and the chief of the children of Ammon.*

> *42 He shall stretch forth his hand also upon the countries: and the
> land of Egypt shall not escape.*

> *43 But he shall have power over the treasures of gold and of silver,
> and over all the precious things of Egypt: and the Libyans and the
> Ethiopians shall be at his steps.*

> *44 But tidings out of the east and out of the north shall trouble him:*

therefore he shall go forth with great fury to destroy, and utterly to make away many.

45 And he shall plant the tabernacles of his palace between the seas in the glorious holy mountain; yet he shall come to his end, and none shall help him.

Several key attributes of the king of the North are typically associated with the *Antichrist* – and NOT with Gog. By making note of these characteristics of the northern king, it clarifies that this king is *Antichrist* and *not Gog*.

- *"Speaking marvelous things against the God of gods"* – As Paul stated in 2 Thessalonians 2:4, " *Who opposeth and exalteth himself above all that is called God, or that is worshipped; so that he as God sitteth in the temple of God, shewing himself that he is God."*

- *"Neither shall he regard the God of his fathers"* (suggesting the King if Jewish in ancestry, at least in part);

- *"Nor the desire of women"* – Most often assumed to mean he is homosexual, but it could also infer either that (1) no woman would desire to be his mother (in contrast to Mary the mother of Jesus was grateful to be the handmaiden of the Lord); or most startlingly, (2) the seed of Satan and not "born of woman", being a hybrid creature, an "abomination" in his own right. That is a most frequent view we read today.

- *"Nor regard any god, for he shall magnify himself above all"* – Meaning that he is on the one hand, an atheist, but on the other, he asserts he is divine and the god of gods all humanity must worship. This aligns perfectly with 2 Thessalonians 2:4 as stated above.

- *"In his estate shall he honor the God of forces"* – Which likely does *not* convey a belief in pantheism (e.g., the "force" as in film, *Star Wars*); rather a commitment to the use of *force* or to fortifications as in *strongholds*, i.e., fortresses and military power. The forebears of the Jews trusted in the LORD – not in their military might.

- *"And he shall divide the land for gain."* – Here is a warning that dividing Israel constitutes an action of Antichrist and will be (and has been) deserving of God's judgment. America has experienced this judgment firsthand as many other authors have well-documented (Koenig, Brennan, et al).

Then there are inconsistencies between the actions and accomplishments of the two personages. For one thing, the king of the North successfully wages a campaign against Israel, passes through Israel into Egypt and Northern Africa (shades of Alexander the Great), but then returns to Israel because of rumors from the east and the north. In contrast, nowhere do we learn that Gog enjoys any success in his campaign against Israel. Nowhere are we told that God (the LORD) destroys the King of the North in the manner that the LORD destroys Gog. Additionally, we do not know Gog's attack constitutes the breaking of the covenant, although Lindsey and Pentecost seem to believe this is the case. (To clarify, Lindsey and Pentecost distinguish between Gog and Antichrist – unlike Richardson and Shoebat, but confuse Gog as the king of the North by superimposing the actions of Gog over the actions of the king of the North). Berner provides this insight:

> Pentecost concludes that the middle of the Tribulation is the only point that is consistent with this chronological pattern [that Gog/Magog happens before Armageddon]. *This conclusion is totally dependent upon the correct identification of Gog as Daniel's king of the North.* If Gog is not Daniel's king of the North, then Gog is not subject to Pentecost's' conclusion regarding the timing of the destruction of the king of the North. In that case, Pentecost's conclusion is completely incorrect regarding the timing of Gog's demise. [122]

What Must Happen Before the Temple Is Rebuilt

Another critical factor is the presence or absence of the Temple in Jerusalem. To put it simply, without a Temple to be desecrated there will be no revealing of the Antichrist. Closely tied to this factor is what must happen for the temple to be rebuilt. Berner strongly asserts, and I agree, "Israel must first undergo an event which literally shakes it out of its paranoid fear of the nations of the world and its apathy towards God. That event is the destruction of the invading forces of Gog and Magog." [123]

The issue is one of geopolitics. Berner points out firmly, "There is absolutely no way that the Arab Islamic nations, the Roman Catholic Church, or the other nations of the world would stand by and allow Israel to take full possession of the Temple Mount and rebuild a Temple on its ancient site under the present political, economic, and religious circumstances." [124] One could easily add other massive geopolitical entities and nation states which would forbid it such as the United Nations, the United States (under this or any foreseeable administration), the Europe Union, and the Russian Common-wealth of Independent States (CIS). Certainly, Shi'ites led by Iran, would declare war on Israel instantly as would Sunni Muslim states headed by Saudi Arabia. Berner rightly states that most Israelis within the country are opposed to rebuilding the Temple and certainly the Israeli government is not in any position to propose moving forward with the rebuilding of the Temple. Something dramatic must happen to change this situation. In short, a great war must occur. The question is, "which war?" Is it the *Psalm 83 war* or the *War of Gog and Magog*? Having ruled out the "Psalm 83 war" during our earlier discussion, from my perspective the only feasible alternative is the Gog/Magog war – an event so overwhelming and awe inspiring (which would also decimate the Islamic world to such a degree), that Israel would feel free to move forward with no earthly permission required. That act seems likely (in the best of cases) being inspired to rebuild the Temple sensing no palpable threat from its Muslim neighbors; or (in the worst case scenario) Israel would move ahead under the auspices of the Antichrist as one of the key terms of the seven-year covenant. Regardless, the point remains: *the Temple must be rebuilt before Antichrist is disclosed.*

The Burning of Gog's Weapons for Seven Years

We learn in Ezekiel 39 that after Gog and his army destroyed, that Israel would burn Gog's weapons for seven years and bury the dead of Gog for seven months. These details might seem inconsequential, but in fact they reign supreme in determining the timing of the Gog/Magog war. We read:

> *⁹ And they that dwell in the cities of Israel shall go forth, and shall set on fire and burn the weapons, both the shields and the bucklers, the bows and the arrows, and the handstaves, and the spears, and they shall burn them with fire seven years:*
>
> *¹⁰ So that they shall take no wood out of the field, neither cut down any out of the forests; for they shall burn the weapons with fire: and they shall spoil those that spoiled them, and rob*

those that robbed them, saith the Lord God.

11 And it shall come to pass in that day, that I will give unto Gog a place there of graves in Israel, the valley of the passengers on the east of the sea: and it shall stop the noses of the passengers: and there shall they bury Gog and all his multitude: and they shall call it The valley of Hamongog.

12 And seven months shall the house of Israel be burying of them, that they may cleanse the land.

13 Yea, all the people of the land shall bury them; and it shall be to them a renown the day that I shall be glorified, saith the Lord God.

14 And they shall sever out men of continual employment, passing through the land to bury with the passengers those that remain upon the face of the earth, to cleanse it: after the end of seven months shall they search.

15 And the passengers that pass through the land, when any seeth a man's bone, then shall he set up a sign by it, till the buriers have buried it in the valley of Hamongog.

16 And also the name of the city shall be Hamonah. Thus, shall they cleanse the land. (Ezekiel 39:9-16)

Arnold Fruchtenbaum makes a most interesting statement regarding this matter that might otherwise seem a needless detail pertaining to the aftermath of the Gog/Magog war. "These seven months of burying and seven years of burning are crucial in determining when this invasion occurs. For any view to be correct, *it must satisfy the requirements of these seven months and seven years.*" [Emphasis added] [125] These seemingly inconsequential details are key to determining when, in respect to the final Armageddon War and the return of Jesus Christ, the Gog/Magog war occurs.

Berner draws out the implications of this fascinating detail in Ezekiel's prophecy. Given that the second half of the Tribulation period comprises the worst period in human history (according to Jesus Christ), it is unlikely that the Jews will be in any position in the second-half of the Tribulation to be burying bodies and burning weapons. They will have fled from Israeli the areas of Bozrah and Petra to the hiding place prepared in the wilderness for those who heed the scriptural warning. Some authors attempt to get around this matter by indicating that the Scripture does not say that Jews from Jerusalem will be doing the burning, just persons living in Jerusalem. But cleansing the land doesn't seem to be a task non-Jews would be fit to conduct in response to God's glorious victory on behalf of Israel over Gog and the Islamic armies which appear to accompany him. Additionally, it would certainly seem this process would take a sizeable amount of peace and security to allow the cleaning of the land to transpire. If so, the point comes into focus *that the seven years must begin and end before the final three and one-half years of Daniel's 70ᵗʰ Week.* This puts the Gog/Magog event over ten years from the visible return of Jesus Christ to defeat the forces of Antichrist. In other words, the War of Gog could occur earlier, but must take place no later than ten years before Christ comes when "every eye shall see him". (Revelation 1:7) The math is inescapable.

A study of the history of eschatology yields an informative comment by Increase Mather, brother of the more famous Cotton Mather, and one of the early presidents of Harvard College. His assertion constitutes a not-so-subtle reminder that those called to Christ's Kingdom have been watchful and draw insight into the last days *from reading the very same scriptures we do today.* Mather stated in his *Dissertation Concerning the Future Conversion of the Jewish Nation* (1709), p. 15:

> Thus, when the World shall perish by fire, no saint shall be hurt by that fire, but sinners shall… We may not determine how long the conflagration shall last. Noah's Flood [flood] continued for many Days and Months, he was a whole year in the Ark. *The weapons of Ezekiel's Gog are seven years in burning…"*

Berner comments on the necessity of this "gap" between the Gog/Magog "conflagration" (to employ Mather's word) with this additional rationale:

> For the invasion of Gog and Magog to serve God's purpose of a wakeup call to Israel and the world to the presence and reality of God before the complete rise to power of the Antichrist and his total domination by Satan, there must be a gap of time between Gog's destruction and the Antichrist's betrayal of Israel at the

midpoint of Daniel's 70th Week. This gap of time must be long enough to allow Israel to respond to the God of its ancestors and for the people of the world to accept or reject the God of Israel. A portion of this period between the defeat of God and the Antichrist's self-declaration of being "God" will be used by God's true messengers, the two witnesses, and the 144,000 Jewish Servants of God, to proclaim God's case against Israel and the world regarding their rebellion against God, and the case for Jesus as the Son of God and the Messiah. A period of days, or weeks, or a few months would not be long enough. Most likely this gap of time will be three and a half years to seven years in length.[126]

VOICES AGREEING GOG OCCURS BEFORE DANIEL'S 70TH WEEK

Once again, Douglas Berner's research provides a great service to students of Bible prophecy (and this author in writing this book) by compiling the views of numerous reliable voices asserting what I have come to believe is the correct understanding of the timing of the War of Gog and Magog.

- Berner cites the late **Grant Jeffrey:** "I believe that the war of Gog and Magog will precede the seven-year treaty and create the preconditions that will allow Antichrist to consolidate his revived Roman empire in Europe." [127]

- **Randall Price**, one of the top Pre-millennial scholars today, Berner cites from Price's book, *The Battle for the Last Days' Temple:*

    I have opted for a pre-Tribulational setting on the basis that this best satisfies the majority of the temporal conditions described in Ezekiel 38:8-11 in relation to a people 'in the latter years' 'gathered from many nations' to a land that 'had been a continual waste' but is now inhabited and which was 'restored from the sword [domination]' and is now 'living securely' with enviable economic resources. All these descriptions can apply to modern-day Israel. [Comment in original] [128]

- **William Goetz**, as cited by Berner: "My own view is that the invasion will occur shortly after the Rapture, near the time the Antichrist makes his seven-year treaty with Israel – though I agree it could possibly be as early as three and one-half years before." [129]

- Berner provides **Tim LaHaye's** important opinion as well: "Since it will take seven years to burn them, when will they do it? Certainly not the first seven years of the millennial kingdom, for after the Battle of Armageddon, which ushers in the millennial kingdom, swords will be beaten into plowshares (Isaiah 2:4), not burned! The only conclusion we can draw is that Russia will attack Israel before the tribulation." [130]

- The words of **Emil Gaverluk** are cited as follows:

  Since the Antichrist is not there, this invasion takes place before the Tribulation period and before Antichrist arises as Dictator of Earth... We do not see the revived Roman Empire of Europe in this grouping in Ezekiel 38. There is no Antichrist on the scene yet. If the invasion by Russia and her satellites is [sic] in the first three-year period of the seven-year Tribulation, Ezekiel 38 would have portrayed this presence. This is an excellent point as to why Russia must attack Israel before the seven-year tribulation period. [131]

- **Arnold Fruchtenbaum** provides additional justification for this view:

  The *before the Tribulation view* is the only one which has no problems with either the seven months or seven years. The Jews continue to dwell in the Land after this invasion and remain there until the middle of the Tribulation. Hence, the seven months of burial is no problem. The seven years also create no problem since they would begin before the Tribulation and can extend as far as the middle of the Tribulation if at all necessary. According to this view, this invasion must take place at least 3 ½ years or more before the Tribulation starts. [132]

- Then Berner provides a lengthy quotation from **Chuck Missler**:

  However, there are also some of us who believe that the Ezekiel 38 event precedes, and perhaps leads to, or sets the stage for, the events during the 70th Week of Daniel. This view attempts to reconcile the absence of mention of Egypt, Babylon, and the Coming World Leader (the 'Antichrist') which are so prominent in the other passages concerning the '70th Week," and yet are conspicuously absent in the Ezekiel 38 passage. Furthermore, technicalities in the analysis of Daniel 11 also seem to present problems to some, in considering Ezekiel 38 as a parallel passage. [Meaning that Gog cannot be the king of the North in Daniel's prophecy]. [133]

215

In summary, the considered opinion of many of today's top scholars no longer holds that the War of Gog and Magog must happen within Daniel's 70th Week. For the most part, the opinions of many noted experts coincide: Gog and Magog happens BEFORE the seven-year period many popularly identify as The Tribulation.

DOES THE DAY OF THE LORD BEGIN WITH GOG AND MAGOG?

In seeking alignment between the various events in Bible prophecy, one of the most confounding issues is settling on what the Bible means by the designation of *The Day of the Lord.* This topic deserves a study all on its own. We shall touch on it but briefly here.

Isaiah uses the phrase on several occasions:

- *For the day of the LORD of hosts shall be upon every one that is proud and lofty, and upon every one that is lifted up; and he shall be brought low:* (Isaiah 2:12)

- *Behold, the day of the LORD cometh, cruel both with wrath and fierce anger, to lay the land desolate: and he shall destroy the sinners thereof out of it.* (Isaiah 13:9)

- *In that day shall Egypt be like unto women: and it shall be afraid and fear because of the shaking of the hand of the LORD of hosts, which he shaketh over it.* (Isaiah 19:16).

Likewise, Jeremiah also employs the phrase: *"For this is the day of the Lord GOD of hosts, a day of vengeance, that he may avenge him of his adversaries: and the sword shall devour, and it shall be satiate and made drunk with their blood."* (Jeremiah 46:10). And Joel famously uses the same words, *"And the LORD shall utter his voice before his army: for his camp is very great: for he is strong that executeth his word: for the day of the LORD is great and very terrible; and who can abide it?* (Joel 2:11)

The Book of Zephaniah deals with the *Day of the Lord* in all three of its chapters and concludes with the promise of bringing Israel together again: *At that time will I bring you again, even in the time that I gather you: for I will make you a name and a praise among all people of the earth, when I turn back your captivity before your eyes, saith the Lord.* (Zephaniah 3:20) For Zephaniah, the Day of the Lord relates to the salvation of Israel. His words predict punishment for those that have no regard for the LORD:

> *12 And it shall come to pass at that time, that I will search Jerusalem with candles, and punish the men that are settled on their lees: that say in their heart, **The Lord will not do good, neither will he do evil.***
>
> *13 Therefore their goods shall become a booty, and their houses a desolation: they shall also build houses, but not inhabit them; and they shall plant vineyards, but not drink the wine thereof.*
>
> *14 The great day of the Lord is near, it is near, and hasteth greatly, even the voice of the day of the Lord: the mighty man shall cry there bitterly.*
>
> *15 **That day is a day of wrath, a day of trouble and distress, a day of wasteness and desolation, a day of darkness and gloominess, a day of clouds and thick darkness,***
>
> *16 A day of the trumpet and alarm against the fenced cities, and against the high towers.*
>
> *17 And I will bring distress upon men, that they shall walk like blind men, because they have sinned against the Lord: and their blood shall be poured out as dust, and their flesh as the dung.*
>
> *18 Neither their silver nor their gold shall be able to deliver them in the day of the Lord's wrath; but the whole land shall be devoured by the fire of his jealousy: for he shall make even a speedy riddance of all them that dwell in the land.* (Zephaniah 3: 12-18) (See also Zephaniah 1:7 and 1:14)

And Zechariah provides one of the more familiar passages regarding this turbulent period of time, a time when the LORD delivers His people:

> *8 In that day shall the Lord defend the inhabitants of Jerusalem; and he that is feeble among them at that day shall be as David; and the house of David shall be as God, as the angel of the Lord before them.*
>
> *9 And it shall come to pass in that day, that I will seek to destroy all the nations that come against Jerusalem.*

> *¹⁰ And I will pour upon the house of David, and upon the inhabitants of Jerusalem, the spirit of grace and of supplications: and they shall look upon me whom they have pierced, and they shall mourn for him, as one mourneth for his only son, and shall be in bitterness for him, as one that is in bitterness for his firstborn.* (Zechariah 12:8-10) (See also Zechariah 14:1)

Finally, we can add that other so-called "minor" prophets speak of it too. Amos does so in 5:18; Obadiah in verse fifteen.

THE TWO PROGRAMS IN THE ECONOMY OF GOD

The Day of the Lord focuses on both the wrath of God and the deliverance of God. As far as the Old Testament is concerned, it deals just with Israel.

The teaching of *Dispensationalism*, which is the backbone for most Premillennialists in America and their views on eschatology, distinguishes between God's plan for *the Church* and for *Israel*. The LORD created the Church as a peculiar people called out for the name of Christ. The concept of the Bride of Church is regarded as a mystery (in Greek, a mystērion), a hidden truth only revealed by the Apostles (primarily Paul) during the first century. Pure Dispensationalism remains quite rigid regarding the periods of these two programs from the standpoint they cannot overlap or be concurrent. Traditionally, dispensationalists have argued that the Rapture of the Church occurs prior to the seven-year period of Daniel's 70th Week or precisely at its commencing. The sequence: (1) God focuses on the Church. (2) The Rapture occurs. (3) God shifts focus to Israel. The Rapture constitutes the line that separates the two programs. Anthropomorphic language aside, the point to be made: What the world *witnesses* (observes) regarding the plan of God, moves from one emphasis to another. This is God's doing.

My personal perspective remains that the two programs are distinct. The notion that God has a specific plan in mind for the Church seems consistent with the "hiddenness" of the Church in the Old Testament and the emergence of the plan of God to go "global" with the gospel to gentiles after the nation of Israel failed to receive Jesus as the Messiah. I reject the idea that the Church replaces Israel. I reject that there is no distinct plan of God to restore Israel to its land. Likewise, I reject the view that the Kingdom of God does *not* include the Messiah reigning from Jerusalem on this earth upon David's Throne – that there is no earthly Messianic Kingdom or literal Millennium. There is. While true that during (what is known to dispensationalists as) "the Church Age" there is no distinction between Jew and Gentile (Romans 10:12); likewise, there seems to be an obvious work of God in the world today that relates to the Israel as a nation. The return of the Jews to Israel is, in my view, a miracle and a "mega-sign" that the last days are indeed upon us and the "two programs" are in a real sense distinctive and both in force at this time (I believe the programs overlap in a specific sense). God continues to work through the Church while He is restoring Israel. This is obvious. To assume Israel came together as a nation in 1948 because of a Zionist conspiracy beginning in the nineteenth century, or that the Jews of today are not in any sense special in the economy of God during this aeon (before its conclusion), or that what has happened thus far has no relation to the culmination of the age during the time we call Daniel's 70th week, is – from my vantage point - a prejudiced view that borders on anti-Semitism. It certainly slights one of the LORD's most providential and miraculous acts – the restoration of Israel to its land. The restoration began almost seven decades ago. It will conclude one day not too far from today.

Many draw the connection between the Antichrist's covenant with Israel (seven years before Christ's return to this earth), with the LORD's refocus on national Israel, as if the covenant of Antichrist is what causes the LORD to tend to Israel. If this were accurate, then the War of Gog and Magog occurring several years before the Antichrist makes his presence known, would not have anything to do with Israel's restoration and their acknowledgement of God (for they were be exalting the Antichrist, not glorifying God), which stands in direct conflict with the express intention of the Gog and Magog War, as Ezekiel's very words testify:

- *So will I make my holy name known in the midst of my people Israel; and I will not let them pollute my holy name any more: and the heathen shall know that I am the LORD, the Holy One in Israel.* (Ezekiel 39:7)

- *So the house of Israel shall know that I am the LORD their God from that day and forward.* (Ezekiel 39:22)

- *Then shall they know that I am the LORD their God, which caused them to be led into captivity among the heathen: but I have gathered them unto their own land, and have left none of them any more there. Neither will I hide my face any more from them: for I have poured out my spirit upon the house of Israel, saith the Lord GOD.* (Ezekiel 39:28-29)

That is why Berner says,

> Ezekiel's prophecy does not reflect this type of timing. Gog's invasion and God's intervention is the turning point – when God again focuses His attention on Israel as a nation prophetically. That is the main point of Ezekiel 38-39 as a prophecy. The invasion of Gog and Magog becomes the beginning point which marks the "latter days" of Israel's age! Is it possible that Israel's latter days could begin prior to the beginning of Daniel's 70th Week? Yes – this is clearly possible if the Day of the Lord and Daniel's 70th Week do not begin at the same point in time or with the same prophetic event.

Some have suggested that no "Last Day's prophecy" can be fulfilled until Daniel's 70th Week begins. But if Ezekiel's account of the "dry bones coming back to life" (Ezekiel 36-37) stands out as a prophecy pertaining to the last days, and if this fulfillment began in the twentieth century (with the key events of 1917, 1948, 1967 bringing about the restoration of Israel, each playing no small part), plainly that "rule" does not comprise a worthy biblical principle. Thus, I am correct to say that the War of Gog could happen *prior to* Daniel's 70th Week and still be counted *an enormous fulfillment of Bible prophecy.*

All of these events are in Israel's "latter days". Before World War II the Jews in Israel numbered less than 500,000. Israel's Jewish population now exceeds six million. One could easily imagine that it would balloon dramatically after Gog's defeat and after a covenant of peace is completed (with the supposed Messiah aka Antichrist) when the Temple begins its construction. All of these events would signal the Messianic Age has begun. Of course, we who study eschatology know that this additional "re-gathering" will continue to be *without* relationship between Israel *and its true Messiah.* We reckon that the Jews who make Aliyah will eventually face the assault of the Antichrist. Many will flee to Bozrah, to Aqaba, to Petra, and to Edom. Gog's defeat will prove to be a strong motive for Jews to return to their ancient land. For those not experiencing faith in the true Messiah, they will have been lured back to Jerusalem to face yet another Holocaust. For those who *do* find true faith, they will have been brought back to Israel making their flight into the wilderness practicable.

But does this mean that the day of the Lord actually begins with the War of Gog and Magog? The answer appears to be "Yes". Berner points out that Ezekiel uses a particular phrase repeatedly – "on that day" – in 38:10, 14, 18, 19, and 39:11. "On that day" (recall that *yowm* – day – is variable) appears to be the same day I have argued in which Gog attacks Sheba and Dedan, the Merchants of Tarshish, and it's Young Lions. (Recall too the modern equivalents are Saudi Arabia, the United States, and England). *"Behold, it is coming and it shall be done, declares the Lord God. That is the day of which I have spoken."* (Ezekiel 39:8) However, what exactly is the *day of the Lord?* Berner provides this quick summation:

> It is a sudden, violent, and unexpected onslaught of supernatural catastrophes initiated by God bringing judgment upon the entire world. The Time of the End, marked by the unveiling of the Day of the Lord, will be initiated with the big bang of "Sudden destruction." *"Moreover, man does not know his time: like fish caught in a treacherous net and birds trapped in a snare, the sons of men are ensnared at an evil time when it suddenly falls upon them"* (Ecclesiastes 9:12). [134]

Paul writes of this *time of sudden destruction,* but indicates that this is not a time for Christians to be afraid.

> *For yourselves know perfectly that the day of the Lord so cometh as a thief in the night. For when they shall say, Peace and safety; then sudden destruction cometh upon them, as travail upon a woman with child; and they shall not escape. But ye, brethren, are not in darkness, that that day should overtake you as a thief.*

> *Ye are all the children of light, and the children of the day: we*
> *are not of the night, nor of darkness. For God hath not appoint-*
> *ed us to wrath, but to obtain salvation by our Lord Jesus Christ.*
> *(1 Thessalonians 5:2-5, 9)*

The world will be caught be complete surprise. But those who are watchful and expectant for the coming of Christ will not be surprised by the destruction that comes upon the world. Events that comprise the War of Gog and Magog quickly become one major cataclysmic event that "goes global". The *day of the Lord* has begun. As Berner testifies, "I believe that God is saying that the War of Gog and Magog is the event that actually initiates His prophetic period of judgment – the Day of the Lord." [135] The words of Ezekiel clearly state that the events of Ezekiel 38 and 39 "scream" judgment to the world. God has broken His silence! God's wrath has been displayed; and yet, this is not the wrath of Revelation's *trumpets and vials.* But could it relate to one or more of the *seals?*

THE GREATEST EARTHQUAKE AND THE RAPTURE

Berner notes that one Sherlock Bally takes the position that the Rapture of the Church occurs during the invasion of Gog and Magog.[136] For those that believe in the Pre-Tribulation Rapture of the Church, there are some strong reasons to select this specific timing. But could it be so? Given the Jews living in the Holy Land at that time appear not to suffer loss of life, could it be Christians living around the world are safeguarded when "an evil thought comes into the mind of Gog" and he attacks the United States, England, and Saudi Arabia? Before Gog attacks his enemies, even as the missiles are launched, might it be when the church is rescued through the Rapture? Ezekiel speaks of God's wrath, and in particular, a massive shaking that occurs during this tumultuous moment when God judges Gog's armies:

> *And it shall come to pass at the same time when Gog shall come*
> *against the land of Israel, saith the Lord GOD that my fury shall*
> *come up in my face. For in my jealousy and **in the fire of my***
> ***wrath have I spoken,** Surely in that day there shall be **a great***
> ***shaking in the land of Israel;** So that the fishes of the sea, and the*
> *fowls of the heaven, and the beasts of the field, and all creeping*

*things that creep upon the earth, and **all the men that are upon the face of the earth, shall shake at my presence, and the mountains shall be thrown down,** and the steep places shall fall, and every wall shall fall to the ground.* (Ezekiel 38: 18-20)

We know that this is a time of judgment, but not for Israel nor for the Church. Ezekiel 39:6 tells us, *"And I will send a fire on Magog, and among them that dwell carelessly in the isles: and they shall know that I am the LORD."* And likewise, in Ezekiel 39:21, *"And I will set my glory among the heathen, and all the heathen shall see my judgment that I have executed, and my hand that I have laid upon them."* It would seem reasonable to connect these events from Ezekiel 38:18-20 with Ezekiel 39:6 and its explanation in 39:21. The event consists of fire and brimstone and includes a great earthquake that not only occurs in Israel, but takes place globally.

Where else do we see a global earthquake in scripture? Yes. Does it have anything to do with the Day of the Lord? It certainly does. There is one very familiar passage which comes to mind. It has everything to do with the moment when the Day of the Lord begins – *the breaking of the Sixth Seal*:

> *[12] And I beheld when he had opened the sixth seal, and, lo, there **was a great earthquake**; and the sun became black as sackcloth of hair, and the moon became as blood;*
>
> *[13] And the stars of heaven fell unto the earth, even as a fig tree casteth her untimely figs, when she is shaken of a mighty wind.*
>
> *[14] And the heaven departed as a scroll when it is rolled together; and **every mountain and island were moved out of their places.***
>
> *[15] And the kings of the earth, and the great men, and the rich men, and the chief captains, and the mighty men, and every bondman, and every free man, hid themselves in the dens and in the rocks of the mountains;*
>
> *[16] And said to the mountains and rocks, Fall on us, and hide us from the face of him that sitteth on the throne, and from the wrath of the Lamb:*
>
> *[17] **For the great day of his wrath is come**; and who shall be able to stand?* (Revelation 6:12-17)

On a number of occasions, I have referenced my friend David Lowe and his book, *Then His Voice Shook the Earth*. I wrote a foreword for David's most recent edition of this much-underappreciated book (that I encourage you to read as soon as possible!) David's thesis: that *earthquakes always accompany the resurrections documented in the Bible.* It constitutes a curious observation indeed. He proposes the Rapture of the church will be accompanied by a great earthquake – in fact, the greatest earthquake since the time of the rumblings atop Mount Sinai when the LORD God came down upon the mountaintop during the giving of the Law by God to Moses. The writer to the Hebrew (who I believe was the Apostle Paul) speaks of this momentous event and the earth shaking sign that accompanied it in Hebrews 12:18-21. Moses was so frightened that he trembled exceedingly! The children of Israel begged Moses to ask God to stop the sound of the trumpet (note… a trumpet accompanies the event).

Paul goes on to admonish his readers: *"Whose voice then shook the earth: but now he hath promised, saying, Yet once more I shake not the earth only, but also heaven."* (Hebrews 12:26)

The giving of the Law was the beginning of the dispensation of the Law. It occurred on Pentecost, the same day that the Holy Spirit was given to the Church, likewise beginning another dispensation, that of Grace. Of course, we recall that especially great signs accompanied the coming of the Spirit of Christ too when the "men of Galilee" began witnessing to Jews from around the world gathered together in Jerusalem to celebrate Pentecost. The witness was of the great deeds of the LORD and spoken in languages and with dialects that made the apostles and believers "speaking in tongues" without a Galilean accent, sounding native to those that heard!

Lowe goes into detail (which I will not do here) regarding what physical action transpires causing the earth to quake when a resurrection occurs. He suggests that if one assumes the pattern repeats at the time of the greatest resurrection (when perhaps over one billion resurrections occur simultaneously – both those in the graves and those alive at that moment), it should not be surprising that "a whole lotta shakin's goin' on" which not only knocks down every wall, but moves mountains and islands out of their

224

place. He asserts it is at "the sound of the trumpet" of the archangel and the voice of God when the resurrection/rapture occurs. According to Hebrews 12:26, *only once more* (besides the giving of the Law) will God's voice speak in such a way that it will shake both the earth and the heavens. *"Whose voice then shook the earth: but now he hath promised, saying, Yet once more I shake not the earth only, but also heaven."* Lowe proposes that this is "the last trump" of 1 Corinthians 15:52, *"In a moment, in the twinkling of an eye, at the last trump: for the trumpet shall sound, and the dead shall be raised incorruptible, and we shall be changed."*

The exclamation in Revelation 6:17 confirms unequivocally that this is the moment *when the Day of the Lord begins.* Lowe proposes that it is at this moment when the rapture occurs.

> *For the Lord himself shall descend from heaven with a shout, with the voice of the archangel, and with the trump of God: and the dead in Christ shall rise first: Then we which are alive and remain shall be caught up together with them in the clouds, to meet the Lord in the air: and so shall we ever be with the Lord.* (1 Thessalonians 4:16-17)

I would propose that this also comprises when the great earthquake of Ezekiel 38:18-20 takes place. Berner most certainly agrees:

> This earthquake in Ezekiel 38 will be the same earthquake that is described as a great earthquake in the breaking of the sixth seal in Revelation 6:12. This is the first earthquake reference in the book of Revelation which will occur throughout the Seal, Trumpet, and Bowl Judgments of the Day of the Lord. Both passages describe people all over the planet shaking in fear at the sudden presence of God. But this is not the immediate presence of Christ in His Glory that will be manifested at His second coming to do battle at the end of the Tribulation. This is the awakened presence of an angry God who is shaking the earth from a distance and who will not allow anyone to ignore His presence any longer. The sixth seal specifically notes that the people believe that the great day of God's wrath has come.[137]

WHAT DAY MIGHT THIS OCCUR?

Perhaps the Day of the Lord is ten years in length and the War of Gog and Magog occurs at its beginning. Perhaps this is the day when the Church of Jesus Christ is raptured, even as sudden destruction seems ready to break upon the earth. We cannot know for certain – but we have considered a plethora of reasons to cautiously anticipate this could be the case. If so, this is not because America deserves special consideration (as many have supposed, arguing that America contains so many Christians, the rapture would decimate America). Rather, it occurs because this is the time that God has selected. It is grace. As Christians, we should recognize America may be judged before the Rapture transpires, but it does not mean that there is no Pre-Tribulation Rapture. The judgment of America and the timing of the Rapture do not necessarily have any bearing on one another. So often, American Christians believe we will be sparred God's judgment on our nation. That is a fanciful understanding. Our nation deserves judgment more than most! (Of whom much is given, much is required). *When the Rapture occurs is timed based upon what God's plan for Israel is... and what His time for the Church is... not what His plan for America is!*

Grant Jeffrey makes an intriguing observation about when the attack might take place – what specific day of the year it might happen. It amounts to speculation but it has a strong scriptural basis. He predicted that the day of the attack would be on the 24th day of Chisleu, which is the day before *Hanukkah*, a date of deliverance for the Jews.

> Although Scripture does not indicate the exact year in which this invasion and defeat will occur (Ezekiel 38-39), the prophet Haggai (Chapter 2) gives us a strong indication of the actual day of the year on the Jewish calendar, when this prophecy will be fulfilled. Haggai 2 reveals that *on the 24th day of the ninth month of Chisleu, the day before Hanukkah, god will deliver Israel as he did twice before on this anniversary date:* (1) the defeat of the Syrian army and re-capture of the Temple in 165 B.C. and (2) the capture of Jerusalem from the Turks in 1917 A.D.

> *The prophet Haggai declares:*

*The Word of the Lord came unto Haggai, in the four and twentieth day of the month (Chisleu), saying... **I will shake the heavens and the earth**; and I will overthrow the throne of kingdoms and i will destroy the strength of the kingdoms of the heathen; and I will overthrow the chariots, and those that ride in them; and the horses and their riders shall come down, every one by the sword of his brother* (Haggai 2:20-22).

This description and the exact language are uncannily like that of Ezekiel 38 and 39, which describes Russia's defeat. The interesting point is that it names the exact day of the year on which this will occur. Since so many other prophecies have been so precisely fulfilled to the day, there is a strong likelihood that this event will also occur on its appointed day. *"Behold, it is come, and it is done, saith the Lord God; this is the day whereof I have spoken"* (Ezekiel 39:8)." [138]

And the fact should not be lost on the reader, that when the writer to the Hebrews cites the prophecy of God speaking *only once more in such a way to shake the heavens and the earth*, he is quoting Haggai, the very same prophet and prophecy that Grant Jeffrey references, in relation to the salvation day for Israel when God saves Israel's from utter destruction. Could the day of deliverance be the 24th of Chisleu, the day before Hanukkah, in some not too distant year?   Could this also be the day of the Rapture of the Church?

Only time will tell. Our LORD, however, does love to fulfill His most important prophecies on sacred dates that underscore His power and total providence over all that happens on His earth. This is the character and power of the God of the Bible. He has the whole world in His hands. And He holds each of us dear, if we trust in Him.

Should we place our trust in Him, *our destiny is not a day of judgment, but to eternal life in the Kingdom of God and of His Christ.* That is the good news – the Gospel – good news that in our dark days we need to relish and upon which we must, more than ever before, place our hope.

Appendix A: The Climax of Colonialism and Roots of Jihad

"A lot of the problems we are having to deal with now, I have to deal with now, are a consequence of our colonial past... The Balfour declaration and the contradictory assurances which were being given to Palestinians in private at the same time as they were being given to the Israelis—again, an interesting history for us but not an entirely honourable one." Former British Secretary, Jack Straw (2002)

ROOTS OF THE ARAB-ISRAELI CONFLICT

Almost exactly 100 years ago (May 1916), a process began which would conclude with the creation of the modern state of Israel – and in the process generate non-stop worldwide controversy from that moment forward. Indeed, the present-day crisis in Syria and Iraq between ISIS (aka ISIL), the United States, and the governments of Iraq and Syria links to this treaty signed a century ago, less one year.

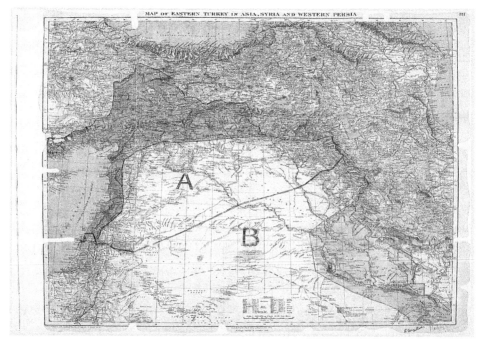

Figure 20 – Sykes Picot Agreement 16 May 1916 Map of the Middle East

The event was the inking of the *Sykes-Picot Agreement* (May 16, 1916). This secret agreement focused on settling how the French, British, and Russians would divvy up the Ottoman Empire post-World War I should the "entente" prevail. However, because this agreement was made with the Czarist government of Russia (the treaty being concluded before the Communist Revolution of 1917 when that government was ousted), the terms of what Russia was to receive would be revoked as Lenin and Trotsky took control.

How relevant is Sykes-Picot at the present moment? The leader of ISIS, Abu Bakr Al-Baghdadi, vowed in *July 2014* at Mosul's Great Mosque of al-Nuri "this blessed advance will not stop until we hit the last nail in the coffin of the Sykes–Picot conspiracy." [139] While this brief narrative hardly comprises a defense for ISIS, it does underscore the Arab world rightly believes the British and the French betrayed it long ago and their present status owes in part to the colonial miscalculations of London and Paris.

This point, however, remains lost in the clamor (sometimes violently so) against Zionism. ISIS and radical Islam blames Jewish Zionism much more than the British for the structure of the Middle East as it stands today in which Israel exists and the Palestinians remain a people without a country. The Islamists assume Zionism was at the center of British and French interests. The facts argue their motives were mostly power plays.

Indeed, a close look at the confusing series of events from 1915 to 1922 shows a different reality than what is advocated by the "Palestinian argument." In effect, the Middle East of today was structured by British geo-political maneuvers in order to protect its empire. Britain often acted unilaterally without French counsel, without American advice, and without regard to promises made to the Arab leaders at that time. Furthermore, in contrast to what we commonly hear today, Zionism was much less influential in arriving at the overall structure of the Middle East. Finally, British actions resulted from secret communiqués and were enacted without consensus among British leadership. Demonstrated all too well in this historical series of events is the old adage: "The tangled web we weave when we practice to deceive."

Figure 21 - Abu-Bakr-Al-Bagdadi

Wikipedia supplies a succinct description of the Sykes-Picot Agreement:

> The agreement effectively divided the Arab provinces of the Ottoman Empire outside the Arabian Peninsula into areas of future British and French control or influence. The terms were negotiated by the French diplomat François Georges-Picot and Briton Sir Mark Sykes. The Russian Tsarist government was a minor party to the Sykes–Picot agreement, and when, following the Russian Revolution of October 1917, the Bolsheviks exposed the agreement, "the British were embarrassed, the Arabs dismayed and the Turks delighted." [140]

Sykes-Picot actually was a renunciation of an earlier treaty (*Règlement Organique*) signed by the Ottoman Empire (the Turks) along with the British, French, Russians, and Austrians in 1860 (and confirmed again in 1864). Importantly, it conflicted with a series of correspondences beginning in July 14, 1915 and concluding in January 30, 1916, between the British High Commissioner in Egypt, Henry McMahon, and the Sharif of

231

Mecca (the most distinguished leader of the Arab world at that time) through which the British encouraged the Arabs to move ahead with their existing plan to revolt against the Ottoman Empire. [141]

The British (supposing that their Commissioner did not act on his own initiative), provided this clandestine piece of encouragement to put pressure on the Turks. As mentioned above, the correspondence not only conflicted with the agreements from 50 years prior, it also sidestepped the French, conflicted with the Sykes-Picot plan, and contradicted the later Balfour Declaration of 1917. These secret letters, along with the de facto renunciation of the 1860 agreement with the Ottoman Empire, increased the geo-political inconsistency of the British. Moreover, it proved a prime example of commitments broken by the British (and indirectly their French ally) to the Arab Emirs who had sought independence from the Turks for an indeterminable number of years. Clearly, at minimum, there was a lack of coordination within His Majesty's Government and *this uncoordinated effort that fueled the Arab-Israeli conflict even before 1920.*

ZIONISM AND ITS INFLUENCE ON THE SYKES-PICOT TREATY

Zionism (founded by Theodore Herzl in the late nineteenth century) was known disparagingly as "the Jewish problem" by the British and French. This movement would endure a multitude of political machinations leading to a series of Treaties and Agreements from 1916 with Sykes-Picot until the League of Nations Mandates in 1922. It would, however, finally yield the formation of a Jewish homeland in Palestine in 1948.

After Herzl's death in 1904, Chaim Weizmann was the most notable public figure driving Zionism – during the period leading up to World War I – and he tirelessly campaigned for the cause throughout the next four decades. (Weizmann eventually would become the first president of Israel in 1949). But it was a British Cabinet member, the lesser-known Herbert Samuel, who would pave the path for the creation for an Israeli homeland.

Working behind the scenes, Samuel (the very first Jewish member of the British Cabinet) would engage his fellow Cabinet members arguing for the creation of a Jewish homeland. His paper, *The Future of Palestine*, [142] made an important contribution (and comprises a key document to read even today) that delivered the argument for why Britain would be well-served to support Jewish aspirations. On February 27, 1916, Samuel personally delivered a plan to Sykes via a memorandum Sykes committed to memory and then destroyed. Later Sykes would make the following comments:

> By excluding Hebron and the East of the Jordan there is less to discuss with the Moslems, as the Mosque of Omar [the easily recognized golden domed sanctuary in Jerusalem] then becomes the only matter of vital importance to discuss with them and further does away with any contact with the Bedouins, who never cross the river except on business. I imagine that the principal object of Zionism is the realization of the ideal of an existing centre of nationality rather than boundaries or extent of territory. [143]

Figure 22 – Herbert Samuel: First High Commissioner of Palestine 1920-1925

Today, the issue of Israel's boundaries stands right at the forefront of global geo-political affairs. How interesting that borders were not well defined by any of the aforementioned treaties. From a whitepaper written by Winston Churchill in 1922, we learn that boundaries were not particularly important in the early stages—Samuel had not demanded them. Israel was to be a "Jewish Center" for inspiration to the Jews globally— *not a nation state.*

According to another Wikipedia article on Churchill's white paper:

> Contrary to popular belief, the borders of Palestine were not defined in the texts of the Balfour Declaration of 1917, The San Remo conference, The Treaty of Sèvres, the Treaty of

Lausanne, or even by the British Mandate for Palestine. The preamble of the Mandate read:

The Council of the League of Nations:

Whereas the Principal Allied Powers have agreed, for the purpose of giving effect to the provisions of Article 22 of the Covenant of the League of Nations, to entrust to a Mandatory selected by the said Powers the administration of the territory of Palestine, which formerly belonged to the Turkish Empire, **within such boundaries as may be fixed by them…** [144]

The Balfour Declaration so often cited by evangelicals who support Israel's right to exist, was accompanied by a memorandum from Lord Balfour refuting the Sykes-Picot Treaty (note: this was penned within one year of Sykes-Picot signing) and other British or French assurances both before and after providing for Arab independence. Instead, Balfour stated bluntly that the Allies were committed to Zionism. [145] As events would soon demonstrate, his bold statement was out of order and in contradiction to many other commitments made by the British and the French.

TRYING TO MAKE THINGS RIGHT

Indeed, the awareness of Balfour's position created another political stir that required some considerable "walking back." No doubt that Balfour's point of view reflected attitudes among some British leaders, but it was hardly common to all parties, especially British allies across the English Channel. This would lead to another declaration in 1918 by the British and the French promising they would assist setting up indigenous governments in Syria and Mesopotamia (at that time, Syria included Jordan and Palestine) and support self-rule. Neverthe-

Figure 23 - Lord Arthur Balfour

less, soon there would be an uprising in Damascus due to Syrian rejection of newly reinstated French rule. To quell the revolt, French troops would be needed. Enter the French Foreign Legion.

Soon another conference would be called in San Remo in 1920. More conflicts and intrigue would transpire. But eventually, order was restored and the British and French mandates in the Middle East were officially sanctioned by the League of Nations in 1922 confirming British authority over Palestine, today's Jordan, as well as most of Iraq – with French rule in Syria and today's Lebanon. Herbert Samuel, who had been the voice advocating Zionism in the British Cabinet leading to the Sykes-Picot agreement, became the High Commissioner of Palestine in 1920 continuing until 1925 (perhaps calling to mind the counsel "be careful what you wish for.") Although Samuel would do his best to be fair to both Israeli and Arab interests, no constituency in Palestine appreciated his administration. Eventually, he would go home to England likely wondering if his earlier efforts had been worth it.

During that same period, the British leaders continued to argue among themselves and with the French as to what commitments had really been made, which ones had been broken, and what agreements would be put in place for the future. *On March 27, 1923, Lord Grey,[146] who had been foreign minister, called for all secret agreements to be made public, thereby admitting that there were various factions within the British government negotiating with the Arabs, the French, and the Zionists during the timeframe from 1915 to 1918.* Essentially, it had become clear that the policies of the His Majesty's Government were at best inconsistent, and at worst, intentionally deceptive.

In a 2002 interview in *The New Statesman*, then British Foreign Secretary Jack Straw provided this assessment: "A lot of the problems we are having to deal with now, I have to deal with now, are a consequence of our colonial past... The Balfour Declaration and the contradictory assurances which were being given to Palestinians in private at the same time as they were being given to the Israelis—again, an interesting history for us but not an entirely honourable one." Straw should be awarded Grand Master of Understatement.

ANALYSIS AND CONCLUSION

Perhaps one of the most provocative issues today can be summarized in this question: "Should the Palestinians cite Zionists for advancing who truly possesses the strongest claim to Middle Eastern lands?" And then there is the century-old conspiracy debate: "Was there a cabal headed by Lord Rothschild to create the State of Israel as part of a plan for Jewish domination of the world?" Of course, this sentiment was the subject of the deservedly maligned and blatantly anti-Semitic *Protocols of the Elders of Zion.*

In contrast to prevailing anti-Israel opinions, *the historical evidence plainly implicates the British, and to a lesser extent the French, as the responsible parties for dividing the territories of the Middle East with blithe indifference for both Arab and Jewish independence.* The borders drawn up in the 1920s were generally arbitrary and intended to accommodate not the Jews nor the Arabs, but the Allies of World War I. Although it is another story, many conjecture the operative factor behind British and French actions was access to Mesopotamian oil and the ability to move petroleum to various ports in Israel and Jordan for shipment back to Europe. This too is probably too conspiratorial. More likely, promises which had been made and broken were chiefly motivated by the desires of Europe's rulers to gain strategic advantages in World War I and the geopolitical situation afterwards.

In the final analysis, England was the principal culprit. It promised Arab leaders their independence if they fought alongside the allies against the Turks. Certainly, this was the well-known promise made by *T.E. Lawrence (Lawrence of Arabia) to the Arabs during WWI.* It was the promise made in official British correspondences to *the Sharif of Mecca.* The British also encouraged Zionism, less overtly until the Balfour Declaration, in order to gain support of worldwide Jewry against the Austro-Prussian Empire (Germany) and the Ottoman Empire (Turkey). Without question, it made contradictory promises simultaneously. In part, these promises were in conflict due to competing factions within the British government. Additionally, promises may have been made as a result of certain leaders deciding to "lie now and pay later."

In any event, the initial leader within the British government, Herbert Samuel, sought to create a "Jewish commonwealth" which was protected by Britain, promised access by Christian pilgrims to holy sites in Palestine, and would be amenable to Arab inhabitants living in Palestine. Samuel had commented in his paper, *The Future of Palestine,* that it might be 100 years before "Aliyah" [147] would lead to enough Jewish immigrant transplants in the new homeland such that an independent government should be established. Meanwhile, it was understood that this Jewish homeland could not protect itself. It would need support of Western powers forever. *Samuel was wrong on both counts.*

Zionists that pushed for Jewish independence in the decades that followed rushed well ahead of what Herbert Samuel, Mark Sykes, and Lord Balfour anticipated. In this wake, the "neutral" status of Israel would be forsaken so that a permanent and sovereign nation state could be formed. Sykes-Picot was indeed one significant step toward creating an independent Israel; but it hardly stood alone as there were many treaties, commitments, and conflicts involving all the major parties between 1915 and 1948.

Concerning the allegation mentioned at the beginning of this article, ISIS stands historically mistaken. But much more important than historical accuracy, in contrast to the typical blasts directed at Israel's sympathizers, as far as the alignment of nations in the Middle East, Zionism played but a small part in motivating the principal actions of the major players during the years of World War I and the years that immediately followed. Arab sentiments were considered no more and no less than Jewish ones. All things considered, no one was particularly happy.

As far as those living in Israel at the time, the Arab wasn't consulted and neither was the Jew. Concerning the subsequent borders that were "drawn in the sand", this author surmises the Turks and the Prussians

(Germans) were the least happy of all among the parties involved. *One wonders how much the betrayal of Sykes-Picot plays on the minds of Turkish leaders today.*

Appendix B:
Is the U.S. the "Daughter of Babylon"?

[From the book, "Is Russia Destined to Nuke the U.S.?"]

JUDGMENT IS COMING TO THE DAUGHTER OF BABYLON

FROM THE PERSPECTIVE OF BIBLE PROPHECY, THERE SEEMS TO BE A DARK OUTCOME TIED TO THE SPARRING BETWEEN RUSSIA AND THE UNITED STATES TODAY. IN ORDER TO PLACE THIS IN THE CONTEXT of what the Bible says about the last days, it is necessary to determine whether the U.S. comprises what the Bible calls the *daughter of Babylon*.

This entity (a city, a nation-state, an empire), known as *the daughter of Babylon*, stands destined for a consuming judgment. In fact there are over 220 verses in the Bible focused on the daughter of Babylon, and a large subset of those verses dealing with its catastrophic destruction by enemies from the "north." In many cases, Babylon and the daughter of Babylon are considered one and the same. Listen to these words from the Bible:

- **Daughter of Babylon**, *who art to be destroyed; happy shall he be, that rewardeth thee as thou hast served us. (Psalm 137:8)*

- *Come down, and sit in the dust, O virgin **daughter of Babylon**, sit on the ground: there is no throne, O daughter of the Chaldeans: for thou shalt no more be called tender and delicate. (Isaiah 47:1)*

- *Sit in silence, go into darkness, **daughter of the Babylonians**; no more will you be called the queen of kingdoms. (Isaiah 47:5)*

- *And **Babylon**, the glory of kingdoms, the beauty of the Chaldees' excellency, shall be as when God overthrew Sodom and Gomorrah. It shall never be inhabited, neither shall it be dwelt in from generation to generation. (Isaiah 13:19-20a)*

- *They shall hold the bow and the lance: they are cruel, and will not shew mercy: their voice shall roar like the sea, and they shall ride upon horses, every one put in array, like a man to the battle, against thee, O **daughter of Babylon**. (Jeremiah 50:42)*

239

- *For thus saith the LORD of hosts, the God of Israel: "The **daughter of Babylon** is like a threshing floor, it is time to thresh her… the time of her harvest shall come." (Jeremiah 51:33)*

- *Deliver thyself, O Zion, that dwellest with the **daughter of Babylon**. (Zechariah 2:7)*

From the verses above, we note that this prophecy originates from more than one prophet – at least four different Bible prophets sound the alarm. This collection of seers indicates the daughter of Babylon constitutes a rich nation that once supported Israel, but turns its back on the people of God. Zechariah directs the nation he calls Zion to free itself from its alliance (its "dwelling") with the daughter of Babylon. That much we can infer from these selected passages.

THE TOP TEN CLUES THE U.S. IS THE DAUGHTER OF BABYLON

But there are many more attributes of the daughter of Babylon that make its identity easy to determine. Consider these ten attributes (Note: there are no less than 30, but here we touch on only the most clear-cut characteristics):

1. It is "the hindermost" of nations (youngest and last in a series— Jeremiah 50:12). It appears to be the world's final empire before the reign of Jesus Christ in His Millennial Kingdom.

2. Jeremiah calls it "the hammer of the whole earth." (Jeremiah 50:23) This nation possesses the most powerful military in the world.

3. It is the richest nation in the world (Jeremiah 50:12, 37; Jeremiah 51:13). This nation dictates economic terms worldwide.

4. It is composed of a "mingled people." (Jeremiah 50: 37) It is not a single race of persons—but a nation known as "a melting pot."

5. It is a nation living on many waters (Jeremiah 51:13). This likely means it is surrounded by oceans and traversed by large rivers and great lakes of fresh water.

6. This nation has "mounted up to the heavens." (Jeremiah 51:53) Even "the sky is no limit." It is known by its program to transcend the atmosphere with its advanced technology.

7. The nations of the world "flow unto him... stream unto him." (Jeremiah 51:44) All the nations of the world meet in this city/nation.

8. It was once a golden cup in the hands of the Lord (Jeremiah 51:7). But it is now identified with sin and immorality—a cup of filthiness.

9. The people of God are warned several times to "flee Babylon." (Jeremiah 50:8, 28, 51:6) This suggests that Babylon contains many Jews. Of course, the United State has a Jewish population about equal to that in Israel. This command may also be intended for God's new covenant people (Christians) that live in Babylon.[148]

10. It has betrayed the people of God and it will collapse as a result. We see this in Jeremiah 51:49 where the prophet contends, "Babylon must fall because of Israel's slain, just as the slain in all the earth have fallen because of Babylon."

NORTHERN POWERS DESTROY THE DAUGHTER OF BABYLON

As this author has argued elsewhere, notably in the book, *The Final Babylon,* (and many of my colleagues in the eschatology community), that the U.S.A comprises this nation. This prospect weighs heavy since Isaiah and Jeremiah are predicting how peoples (many peoples) "from the north" will destroy our nation one day. Of course, Russia occupies the northern most land (excusing Canada from the argument for somewhat obvious reasons). Russia could be joined by a number of other northern nations (North Korea, China to name but two).

Yet, the prophets of the Bible make this very clear—a great northern power is indeed destined to destroy the daughter of Babylon. Note the consistent and crystal clear testimony from the verses in Jeremiah, chapter 50:

*   *"For, lo, I will raise and cause to come up against Babylon an assembly of great nations from the north country: and they shall set themselves in array against her; from thence she shall be taken: their arrows shall be as of a mighty expert man; none shall return in vain"* (verse 9). Could this refer to missiles that perfectly hit their targets?

*   *"Your mother shall be sore confounded; she that bare you shall be ashamed: behold, the hindermost of the nations shall be a wilderness,*

a dry land, and a desert" (verse 12) Does this reference England as a survivor since "she is confounded"?

- *"Because of the wrath of the LORD it shall not be inhabited, but it shall be wholly desolate: every one that goeth by Babylon shall be astonished, and hiss at all her plagues"* (verse 13). Is this the same as saying that America will be destroyed by fire and brimstone as was Sodom and Gomorrah? (Isaiah 13:19) Is this a reference to nuclear weapons being used on America? Like Isaiah, Jeremiah employs the same analogy (the destruction of Sodom and Gomorrah) in predicting what happens to the daughter of Babylon (see Jeremiah 50:40)

- *"A sound of battle is in the land, and of great destruction"* (verse. 22). What is happening to Babylon aka the daughter of Babylon? Jeremiah tells us it can be nothing other than war and the outcome is total devastation for the daughter of Babylon.

- *"How is the hammer of the whole earth cut asunder and broken! How is Babylon become a desolation among the nations!"* (verse 23) Here we see that Jeremiah refers to the daughter of Babylon simply as *Babylon*. Despite the fact *Babylon* has the mightiest of militaries, we learn that she experiences total destruction.

IS IT TOO LATE TO CHANGE COURSE AND SAVE AMERICA?

I believe the Bible predicts the destruction of the United States by a great northern power (or powers). I cannot say exactly when this prediction may come to pass. So this infers there may be something we can do.

The first step: *recognizing that we are at grave risk.* Will the persons and powers that lead our great nation heed the warning and take action? Or will they dismiss the prophecies assuming they have no application to the U.S.A.? Americans should do what they can to warn their representatives and senators of what is in store for our country if we (1) do not change our Middle East policy, and (2) do not establish an effective deterrent to a "first strike" from threatening nation states and from terrorists that could strike us with so-called "suit-case nukes and dirty bombs".

In the final analysis, the protection of the United States (and the United Kingdom) has more to do with spiritual matters and not military ones.

As a people, we must repent of our national sins and change the moral direction in our culture. For if we continue to "sow in the wind, we will reap the whirlwind (Hosea 8:7)

* * * * * *

Do you know Jesus Christ? Perhaps the only thing you can do now is to take responsibility for your life and those you love. *"Believe on the LORD Jesus Christ and thou shalt be saved, and your household."* (Acts 16:31) Invite Him into your heart right now and thank Him for dying for you that you might live with Him for eternity! Share with your family what you have done. Encourage them to consider their decision as well.

Then, as God as enables you, influence your community and your church, encourage those you know to pay attention to the political and spiritual issues at stake in these turbulent times. Remember: we are to be involved in our communities and in our government. Two of the Bible's most important personalities, Joseph and Daniel, were governors. Joseph in Egypt and Daniel in Babylon, were each the "number two" leader in these respective empires that ruled the world during their lifetimes. We need no other precedent than the lives and witness of these two great men.

May the LORD God of the Bible, through His indwelling Spirit (the Spirit of Jesus Christ) empower you to live victoriously for Him and to bring others to an awareness that time is short and that Jesus comes soon.

The final words of the Book of Revelation provide the proper mindset for believers to profess and affirm daily. We see awesome events approaching and the likelihood of coming persecution and frightful difficulties we may face. Despite these challenges, our prayer must remain, *"Even so, come Lord Jesus."* Our hope lies in Him. Let us continue to embrace the "blessed hope" of resurrection upon our death or our rapture if we are alive when Jesus returns. (Titus 2:13)

My final thought for you the reader are expressed in these two passages:

243

- *The Lord knows how to rescue godly people from their trials, even while keeping the wicked under punishment until the day of final judgment.* (2 Peter 2:9, New Living Translation)

- *These things I have spoken unto you, that in me ye might have peace. In the world ye shall have tribulation: but be of good cheer; I have overcome the world.* (John 16:33)

So be of good cheer! Christ has overcome the world. Even if we must face persecution or even martyrdom, He will be with us. He can and will equip us to be "overcomers" too, as we trust in Him.

ENDNOTES

[1] "The situation of South Africa is particularly precarious with an external debt which is almost three times its central bank reserves. What this means is that these three BRICS member states are under the brunt of their Western creditors. Their central bank reserves are sustained by borrowed money. Their central bank operations (e.g. with a view to supporting domestic investments and development programs) will require borrowing in US dollars." See http://www.globalresearch.ca/brics-and-the-fiction-of-de-dollarization/5441301.

[2] See the article in Wikipedia for a nice overview of this theological teacher and expert in ancient languages of the Middle East. https://en.wikipedia.org/wiki/Wilhelm_Gesenius.

[3] The word Rosh itself is controversial with biblical scholars divided over whether it in fact is the basis for the proper noun and familiar name, Russia. Citing from Douglas Berner's study on Ezekiel's Gog and Magog, *The Silence is Broken* (2006), p. 33:

> "If Rosh is an ethnic and national entity separate from or in addition to a title description for Gog, as I believe the weight of the arguments support, then we are left with Daniel Block's question, "who then is this Rosh?" H.W.F. Gesenius, a Hebrew language expert and lexicographer, whose Gesenius' Hebrew-Chaldee Lexicon was published posthumously in 1847, specifically identified the Rosh of Ezekiel 38-39 with Russia. Gesenius states that Rosh is a proper name: "of a northern nation, mentioned with Tubal and Meschech; undoubtedly the Russians, who are mentioned by Byzantine writers of the tenth century, under the name of [written in Greek letters, THE ROS] "dwelling to the north of Taurus, and described by Ibn Fossian, an Arabic writer of the same age, as dwelling on the river Rha. (Wolga) [the Volga]"

This issue is taken up later in the book, in Chapter 9: The Sons of Japheth.

[4] *"For, lo, I will raise and cause to come up against Babylon an assembly of great nations from the north country: and they shall set themselves in array against her; from thence she shall be taken: their arrows shall be as of a mighty expert man; none shall return in vain."* (Jeremiah 50:9)

[5] Jonathan Master, "How Powerful is Russia's Military," *Defense One*, November 14, 2014. See http://www.defenseone.com/threats/2014/11/how-powerful-russias-military/99062/.

[6] Dave Majumdar, "Not So Scary: This Is Why Russia's Military Is a Paper Tiger", *National Interest,* October 20, 2015, see http://nationalinterest.org/blog/the-buzz/not-so-scary-why-russias-military-paper-tiger-14136?page=2.

[7] David Axe, "Russia's Navy: More Rust than Ready," Reuters.com, May 27, 2015. See http://blogs.reuters.com/great-debate/2014/05/27/russias-navy-more-rust-than-ready/.

[8] Garret I. Campbell, "Russian Military Proving Western Punditry Wrong," Brookings Institute, October 23, 2015. See http://www.brookings.edu/blogs/order-from-chaos/posts/2015/10/23-russian-military-capabilities-syria-campbell.

[9] Ibid.

[10] Dave Majumdar, "Russia's Half-baked War in Syria," *The National Interest,* October 6, 2015. See http://nationalinterest.org/blog/the-buzz/russias-half-baked-air-war-syria-14022.

[11] Patrick J. Lyon, "Russia's Kalibr Cruise Missiles, a New Weapon in Syria Conflict," *New York Times,* October 8, 2015. See http://www.nytimes.com/2015/10/09/world/ middleeast/russias-kalibr-cruise-missiles-a-new-weapon-in-syria-conflict.html.

[12] Steven Lee Myers and Eric Schmitt, "Russian Military Uses Syria as Proving Ground and West Takes Notice," New York Times, October 14, 2015. See www.nytimes.com/2015/10/15/world/middleeast/russian-military-uses-syria-as-proving-ground-and-west-takes-notice.html?_r=0ttp.

[13] Ibid.

[14] Ibid.

[15] Marina Koren, "Russia is Now Hitting ISIS with Pinpoint Strikes," November 18, 2015, *The Atlantic*, cited in *Defense One.* See http://www.defenseone.com/threats/2015/11/ russia-now-hitting-isis-pinpoint-strikes-syria/123814/?oref=d-dontmiss.

16 Polina Tikhonova, "Russia Military Is a Lethal Threat to the U.S.", *Value-Walk*, October 25, 2015, see http://www.valuewalk.com/2015/10/russia-military-is-a-lethal-threat-to-the-us/.

17 Jonathan Master, "How Powerful is Russia's Military," *Defense One*, November 14, 2014. See http://www.defenseone.com/threats/2014/11/how-powerful-russias-military/99062/.

18 Myers and Schmitt, op. cit.

19 Ibid.

20 Andrey Biryukov, "The Secret Money Behind Vladimir Putin's War Machine," Bloomberg Business, June 2, 2015. See http://www.bloomberg.com/news/articles/2015-06-02/putin-s-secret-budget-hides-shift toward-war-economy

21 "America's got a whole lot of challenges. Russia is a regional power that is threatening some of its immediate neighbors — not out of strength, but out of weakness." President Obama in response to question from ABC reporter. Wall Street Journal, March 25, 2014. See http://blogs.wsj.com/washwire/2014/03/25/obama-russia is-just-a-regional-power-not-top-u-s-foe/.

22 Master, op. cit.

23 Dmitry Gorenburg, *"Countering Color Revolutions Russia's New Security Strategy And Its Implications For U.S. Policy,* PONARS Eurasia, Policy Memo No. 342, September 2014. See http://www.ponarseurasia.org/sites/default/files/policy-memos-pdf/Pepm342_Gorenburg_Sept2014.pdf.

24 S. Douglas Woodward, *Is Russia Destined to Nuke the U.S.?* Faith-Happens, July, 2015.

25 Polina Tikhonova, "Russia vs. NATO – It's War Time," *ValueWalk,* August 12, 2015. See http://www.valuewalk.com/2015/08/russia-vs-nato-its-war-time/.

26 Terry Moon Cronk, "Breedlove Warns Congress of Russian Aggression," DOD News, April 30, 2015. See http://www.defense.gov/News-Article-View/Article/604550.

[27] Benjamin Baruch and J.R. Nyquist, *The New Tactics of Global War, Reflections on the Changing Balance of Power in the Final Days of Peace*, Coeur d' Alene: Scribe Publications, (2015), pp. 13-14.

[28] S. Douglas Woodward, *Is Russia Destined to Nuke the U.S.?*, Oklahoma City, Faith-Happens, (2015) p. 12.

[29] The core elements of the START Treaty in effect at this time are as follows:

1. 1,550 warheads. Warheads on deployed ICBMs and deployed SLBMs count toward this limit and each deployed heavy bomber equipped for nuclear armaments counts as one warhead toward this limit. This limit is 74% lower than the limit of the 1991 START Treaty and 30% lower than the deployed strategic warhead limit of the 2002 Moscow Treaty.

2. A combined limit of 800 deployed and non-deployed ICBM launchers, SLBM launchers, and heavy bombers equipped for nuclear armaments.

3. A separate limit of 700 deployed ICBMs, deployed SLBMs, and deployed heavy bombers equipped for nuclear armaments. This limit is less than half the corresponding strategic nuclear delivery vehicle limit of the START Treaty.

This list is cited from http://www.cfr.org/nonproliferation-arms-control-and-disarmament/new-start-treaty/p21851. Published by the CFR on April 8, 2010.

[30] Master, op. cit.

[31] Ted Koppel, *Lights Out: Cyberattacks, a Nation Unprepared, Surviving the Aftermath*, Crown Publishers. Cited in a review by New York Times contributor Walter Russell Mead, November 20, 2015. See http://www.nytimes.com/2015/11/22/books/review/lights-out-by-ted-koppel.html?_r=0.

[32] Baruch and Nyquist, op. cit., p. 20.

[33] Eland is Senior Fellow and Director of the Center on Peace & Liberty at the Independent Institute. He received an M.B.A. in applied economics and a Ph.D. in Public Policy from George Washington University. He has been Director of Defense Policy Studies at the Cato Institute.

[34] Ivan Eland, "Is a 'Resurgent' Russia a Threat to the United States?" November 2, 2008, *Independent Institute*. See http://original.antiwar.com/eland/2008/11/01/is-a-resurgent-russia-a-threat-to-the-united-states/.

35 Mark Riebling, *The Wedge: The Secret War Between the FBI and CIA* (New York: Alfred A. Knopf, 1994), p. 408.

36 David Adesnik, "A Strong Defense is No Luxury," *U.S. News and World Report*, February 27, 2015. See
http://www.usnews.com/opinion/blogs/world-report/2015/02/27/budget-control-act-sequestration-defense-cuts-must-be-reversed.

37 *The Daily News*, Sept. 25, 2015,
http://www.dailynews724.com/politics/russians-syrians-and-iranians-setting-up-military-coordination-cell-in-baghdad-h579245.html.

38 Chris Good, "President Obama's 'Red Line': What He Actually Said About Syria and Chemical Weapons", ABC News, August 26, 2013,
http://abcnews.go.com/blogs/politics /2013/08/president-obamas-red-line-what-he-actually-said-about-syria-and-chemical-weapons/

39 Lucas Tomlinson, "Russia Adding Second Airbase in Syria, Pursuing 'Expansion' in Military Capability," *Fox News,* December 1, 2015. See
http://www.foxnews.com/politics/2015/12/01/russia-adding-2nd-airbase-in-syria-pursuing-expansion-in-military-campaign.html.

40 The May 23, 2015 episode of the PBS production, *Front Line* entitled "Obama at War," documents these facts along with the assessment of the experts supporting most views stated here.

41 Nabila Ramdani, "Ghaddafi is gone but Libya is More Dangerous than Ever", July 29, 2014, *The Guardian.*
See http://www.theguardian.com/world/2014/oct/28/muammar-gaddafi-death-impact-libya.

42 James Miller, "Putin in Syria: Russian Airstrikes Begin, but ISIS is not the Primary Target," *The Interpreter*, September 27, 2015. See
http://www.interpretermag.com/russian-su34s-tracked-from-russia-to-syria/.

43 Barbara Star, "U.S. Delivers 50 Tons of Ammunition to Syrian Rebels," CNN, October 12, 2015. See
http://www.cnn.com/2015/10/12/politics/syria-rebel-groups-ammunition-50-tons/.

44 Nancy A. Youssef, Michael Weiss, and Tim Mak, "We can't Protect Syrian Allies from Russia's Bombs," *The Daily Beast*, October 1, 2015,

See http://www.thedailybeast.com /articles/2015/10/01/u-s-admits-we-can-t-protect-syrian-allies-from-russia-s-bombs.html.

45 Ibid.

46 Ibid.

47 Paul Craig Roberts, "CIA May Assassinate Putin," Interview on Alex Jones Show, October 15, 2015. See https://www.youtube.com/watch?v=silx1DL8H_Y.

48 Luis R. Miranda, "Putin is in Substantial Danger of Assassination," *The Real Agenda News*, October 16, 2015, See http://real-agenda.com/putin-is-in-substantial-danger-of-assassination/.

49 Putin: "Who Created ISIS?" Sept. 25, 2015, see https://www.youtube.com/watch?v= VbZDyr2LkdI.

50 Ibid.

51 Ibid.

52 Michael Pearson and Laura Smith-Spark, "Iran nuclear deal: What's at stake, what it means, what happens next," *CNN*, July 14, 2015. See http://www.cnn.com/2015/07/14/ politics/iran-nuclear-deal-up-to-speed/index.html.

53 Herbert London, "Why the Iran Deal," *Family Security Matters*, November 25, 2015. See http://www.familysecuritymatters.org/publications/id.19020 /pub_detail.asp #ixzz3szebRkQD

54 Ibid.

55 Ibid.

56 Fyodor Lukyanov, "Why the West Should Now See the Sense in Russia's Mideast Policies," *Russia in Global Affairs*, published in *The Huffington Post*, November 24, 2015. See http://www.huffingtonpost.com/-fyodor-lukyanov/west-russia-middle-east-policy_b_8631388.html.

57 Sciutoo, Perez, Liptak, Wolf, "Why did Obama declare ISIS 'contained' the day before Paris attack?" CNN, November 11, 2015.

58 Ibid.

[59] Obama originally indicated that the U.S. would "degrade and then destroy" ISIS in 2014 after America James Foley was beheaded by ISIS on video seen widely across the Internet. For various reasons, most likely because bombing alone could not destroy ISIS and ground forces would be required, the policy shifted to "contain" ISIS which happened to play into the hand of U.S. strategists who believed ISIS could be helpful in the new policy as it would create constant pressure on Assad to resign. The plan might have worked, but Russia determined they could not let they ally go under. Russia spoiled the Obama plan when Russian pilots began bombing U.S.-trained rebel groups intended to overthrow Assad.

[60] See https://www.whitehouse.gov/blog/NewBeginning/transcripts.

[61] Christiane Amanpour, Terry Moran, Nasser Atta, Huma Khan, Obama Hails Mubarak's Resignation: "Egypt Will Never Be the Same, " February 11, 2011. See http://abcnews.go.com/International/obama-hails-hosni-mubaraks-resignation-egypt/story?id=12891572

[62] See http://www.huffingtonpost.com/2013/08/14/allen-west-muslim-brotherhood_n_3758303.html.

[63] Jim Emerson, "Afghanistan Asking Russia for Help?" *Coach Is Right Blog*, October 31, 2015. See http://www.coachisright.com/afghanistan-asking-russia-for-help/?subscribe=success #blog_subscription-2.

[64] Joe Giambrone, "Why ISIS Exists: The Double Game," *International Policy Digest*, November 29, 2015. See http://www.internationalpolicydigest.org/2015/11/29/why-isis-exists-the-double-game/.

[65] Zack Beauchamp, "The Russians Say they are Bombing ISIS in Syria. This Map Shows they are Lying," October 7, 2015, *Vox*, See http://www.vox.com/2015/10/7 /9471271/ russia-syria-bombing-map.

[66] We know the early Huns and Mongols were a nomadic Siberian horse-riding peoples who would eventually travel west to conquer, subsequently leaving Asian tribes to populate the region known today as Mongolia. We also know that the Huns became today's Turks (Turkic peoples), and the Scythians are today's Russians. As noted earlier, these people groups would eventually populate present-day Eurasia, including Russia, Siberia, the numerous republics north of Israel as precisely described in Ezekiel 38 and 39." See http://www.soundchristian.com/magog/ for an extensive and compelling treatment of the racial dispersion throughout Asia of Japheth's

descendants. This topic is addressed in depth in Chapter 9: The Sons of Japheth.

[67] Here we think of Hitler and his interest in Nordic folklore, of Thor, of Thule and Hyperborea.

[68] Regarding this possibility, but the inference seems biblically valid and stunning to consider.

[69] We should recognize that Scofield Bible was published before Russia's Marxist revolution when it became the Soviet Union. The Russian "Bear" had been characterized as the enemy of the West during the so-called *Great Game* between Britain and Russia which began circa 1807 and continued until the First World War when the two empires became allies against Germany. Ironically, today, Germany and Russia are becoming so cozy that it threatens the unity of NATO.

[70] Mark Langfan, October 5, 2015, Israel Nation News.

[71] Eerik-Niiles Kross and Molly K. McKew, "The Dangerous Link between Syria and Ukraine," Politico, September 22, 2015. See http://www.politico.com/magazine/story/2015/09/putin-syria-ukraine-213173#ixzz3tC6o7cwK.

[72] Thomas Grove and Ali A. Nabhan, "Iraqis Urge Russia to Strike ISIS," Dow Jones Business News, October 7, 2015, See more: http://www.nasdaq.com/ article/iraqis-urge-russia-to-strike-isis-20151007-00037#ixzz3tC8cFtt9.

[72] *Caphtor* appears to be referencing Crete or Cyprus. It is generally thought that the Philistines originated from the Minoans on the island of Crete, whose ancient civilization dates back to 3,000 B.C. which was destroyed when a massive volcanic explosion occurred in 1627 B.C. on the nearby island of Santorini (the volcano Thera – whose volcanic ash has been radiocarbon dated to this time and piled up over 21 meters high in lands east of the volcano).

There was only a remnant of the natives of this island that survived the volcanic eruption estimated to have been ten times more powerful than the Krakatoa event of 1869. (The Krakatoa shockwave traveled around the world three times before relenting!) Above is a map showing the depth of volcanic ash that fell from the eruption of Thera in the Eastern Mediterranean.

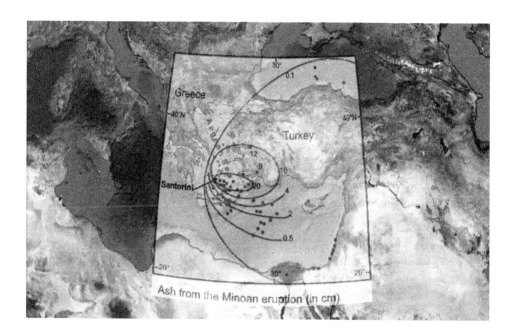

Ash from the Minoan eruption (in cm)

[74] Taimoor Kahn, "How Syria Sees U.S. – Russian Tug of War," ValueWalk October 9, 2015. See http://www.valuewalk.com/2015/10/how-syria-sees-us-russian-tug-war/?utm_source=mailchimp&utm_ medi-um=email&utm_campaign=EMAIL_DAILY&utm_content=quick_link

[75] See http://en.wikipedia.org/wiki/Caliphate#Sharifian_Caliphate_.281924.E2.80.9325.29. The Sharifian Caliphate existed right after the Turkish caliphate was dissolved, but did not gain widespread recognition. The Ahmad-iyya Caliphate was founded by an Indian, Mirza Ghulam Ahmad in 1908 and continues to the present with perhaps ten to twenty million followers out of Islamic population of well over one billion. In this instance it has come to be seen only as a spiritual office.

[76] From Wikipedia:

The Christian population of the empire, owing to their higher educational levels, started to pull ahead of the Muslim majority, leading to much resentment on the part of the latter. In 1861, there were 571 primary and 94 secondary schools for Ottoman Christians with 140,000 pupils in total, a figure that vastly exceeded the number of Muslim children in school at the same time, who were further hindered by the amount of time spent learning Arabic and Islamic theology. In turn, the higher educational levels of the Christians allowed them to play a large role in the economy. In 1911, of the 654 wholesale companies in Istanbul, 528 were owned by ethnic Greeks.

See https://en.wikipedia.org/wiki/Ottoman_ Empire#Defeat_and_dissolution _.281908.E2.80.931922.29.

[77] Biographical information offered by Shoebat: "Walid Shoebat was born and raised in Bethlehem, Israel by an Arab father and an American mother. His paternal grandfather was an associate of Haj-Ameen Al Husseni, the Grand Mufti of Jerusalem, who was an ally of Adolph Hitler who conspired with the Nazis during the holocaust." While I disagree with Walid's position on Antichrist and Gog and Magog, I count him a brother in Christ and a courageous man that stands opposed as few do against the insanity of jihad.

[78] Selected evangelical groups support both while others consider them false prophets. For our purposes, I assume they are sincere and teach from conviction and in good faith. I have not met either but certainly hope to sometime in the future. They are avid Christians and deserve respect. My challenges to their point of view are in no means personal attacks.

[79] Richardson, Joel, *The Islamic Antichrist: The Shocking Truth about the Real Nature of the Beast, 2009,* Midpoint Trade Books. Kindle Edition. (p. 96).

[80] Walid Shoebat, "Turkey as the Antichrist Nation – Seven Scriptural Proofs", *Stichting Vrienden van Israel*, August 3, 2012. See http://www.vriendenvanisrael.nl/?p=2155.

[81] Joel Richardson, "6 Reasons Why Gog is Antichrist", WorldNet Daily, 8,26,2012. See http://www.wnd.com/2012/08/6-reasons-why-gog-is-the-antichrist/#ZIUeV47 POLhdpkbh.99.

[82] Craig C. White, "What is Erdogan Up To?" June 7, 2015, *High Time to Awake.* See http://hightimetoawake.com/what-is-erdogan-up-to/

[83] See http://www.breitbart.com/national-security/2015/11/02/world-view-erdogans-party-in-turkey-wins-landslide-victory/.

[84] "The Antichrist was Just 'Outed' by a Tweet," *The Right Scoop*, March 19, 2015. See http://therightscoop.com/turkey-akp-ruling-party-official-just-outed-the-antichrist-in-a-tweet/#ixzz3uSzkTLyv.

[85] See http://www.trackingbibleprophecy.com/antichrist.php

[86] All the citations are from the web site studies in multiple parts. These quotations are from the third such segment of the study. Read all at: http://www.redmoonrising.com/Giza/raiders3.htm.

[87] Peter goes on to explain away another objection, that he is misidentifying who Asshur is because there are two Asshurs listed.

> Another objection that is raised against equating Asshur with Nimrod is that this would mean that there are two "Asshurs" in Genesis 10—one a descendent of Ham and the other a descendent of Shem. However, this is a superficial objection. Just because Asshur is named as a descendent of Shem does not mean that Ham could not have had a descendent with *the same name*. The fact is there are many such cases in Genesis 10. There are two Meshechs—one from the line of Japheth and one from the line of Shem; there are two Shebas—one from Ham and one from Shem; and there are two Havilahs—again one from Ham and one from Shem. There is also the curious case of the Ludites descending from Ham, but Lud himself descending from Shem. The truth is that the descendants of Shem and the descendants of Ham shared several names in common and **Asshur** is simply another one of these cases.

From http://www.redmoonrising.com/Giza/raiders3.htm.

[88] Tom Horn has explored the connection between Nimrod, Apollo, Osiris, and Orion, extensively in his most important book, *Apollyon Rising 2012*. My conclusion is that there is absolutely a connection of their personages (both real and mythical) to *the spirit of antichrist.* Peter's conclusion – that the Antichrist is resurrected perhaps from DNA of the ancient Nimrod – may be going a step too far. However, this is no longer a scientific impossibility and is a breathtaking theory. Peter is another wonderful brother and I count it a privilege to have worked with him on occasion at conferences.

[89] Farrell, Joseph P. (2015-07-30). *The Third Way: The Nazi International, European Union, and Corporate Fascism* (Kindle Locations 2205-2210). Adventures Unlimited Press. Kindle Edition. Farrell's study deserves considerable attention, more than the scope of this book will allow.

[90] Douglas Berner, *The Silence is Broken, God Hooks Ezekiel's Gog and Magog* (2006), pp. 88-89.

[91] Ibid., p. 82.

[92] Ibid., p. 81.

[93] Ibid., p. 81.

[94] Ibid. p. 208.

[95] Stuart Rolio, "Turkey's Dangerous Game in the Middle East," Wall Street Journal, December 29, 2015. See http://www.aina.org/news/20151229010 213.htm.

[96] Most teachers today speculate that this perfection had to do with the purity of his human DNA, having not been corrupted by "angelic entanglement" when the Sons of God came into the daughters of men. (Genesis 6:4)

[97] This is the modern dating. Eratosthenes, the famous Greek mathematician and principal librarian of the library at Alexandria living in the third century B.C., dated the war between 1194–1184 B.C. Eratosthenes was the first person to calculate the circumference of the earth and possibly the distance to the sun. He stands as another example of how humankind has gained and lost knowledge as civilization has waxed and waned through the ages.

[98] ttp://artsales.com/ARTistory/Ancient_Ships/11_solomons_navy.html.

[99] The possibility exists that the refugees were the giants of Canaan and were the targets of Joshua's conquest. When the walls of Jericho feel, the whole land of Canaan (future Israel) quaked. The giants knew their days were numbered. They set sail for safer places. Steven Quayle and L.A. Marzulli have studied these matters extensively. The archeological evidence for giants in America is becoming a well-documented fact. It may be another twenty years however before the scientific community in the U.S. is willing to accept it, simply because it challenges current understandings of evolution and the development of the human race.

[100] Berner, op. cit., p. 34. These citations are from Michael Heiser, *Islam and Armageddon*, pp. 70-71. Despite disagreeing with Dr. Heiser in this book on the topic of Gog and Magog, Heiser is a true scholar and strong advocate for the biblical worldview and evangelical theology. I appreciate his work very much. His contribution to conservative scholarship is enormous. I recommend visiting his new website and reading his books. See http://drmsh.com.

[101] Ibid., p. 55. Citing Heiser, p. 32, 75.

[102] Ibid., p. 56, Citing Heiser, p. 75.

[103] Ibid., p. 58.

[104] Ibid.

[105] Methinks the NIV has taken a bit too much liberty here, i.e., eisegesis par excellence.

[106] See Berner's discussion from which this citation is listed on page 28.

[107] Berner, op. cit., pp 28-29. Citation from Heiser is from his aforementioned book, *Islam and Armageddon*, p. 103-104. Comment: Heiser is truly an expert in ancient Semitic languages. Of course, academics can never be wrong in drawing conclusions, especially when it allows them to impress others with their area of special expertise. I'm not saying that Heiser is being unnecessarily sarcastic or patronizing, but it does seem so here since the tone of his argument casts more aspersions on a view he deems not-so-scholastic.

[108] Ibid., p. 30, citing Jon Mark Ruthven, *The Prophecy That Is Shaping History*, Xulon Press, 2003, p. 24.

[109] Ibid., p. 31, citing from Mark Hitchcock and Thomas Ice, *The Truth Behind Left Behind*, Multnomah Publishers, 2004, p. 50.

[110] Ibid., p. 33.

[111] Joel Richardson, "The Psalm 83 War?" *Joel's Trumpet*, November 17, 2013. See http://www.joelstrumpet.com/?p=5731.

[112] Ibid.

[113] Related to this is the "Burden of Damascus", the passage in Isaiah 17, which indicates that in one day Damascus will be reduced to rubble.

[114] David Regan in his newsletter and website, several years ago hosted a debate of sorts between Dr. Tommy Ice and Bill Salus which is recommended reading Ice criticizes Salus for "speculation" regarding Psalm 83 and claims that Bill cannot be correct because all prophecies for a "true futurist" must be fulfilled only during the period of the Tribulation, aka Daniel's 70th Week, and Salus' contention is that the Psalm 83 war occurs prior to Gog and Magog, which Ice believes lies within the time period of Daniel's 70th week. As we will discuss later, I believe Dr. Ice is quite wrong to challenge Salus based upon his "futurist" principle and in regard to Salus "speculating" outside the bounds of good biblical research and sincere intent to expound the meaning of God's word. I may disagree with Bill's exposition, but I heartily endorse the authenticity of his effort and quality of his work. This debate is preserved and available for review here: See http://www.lamblion.com/enewsletter1/new_enewsletter_template_140326.html.

[115] There is a growing point of view among evangelicals that rejects the notion that today's Israel represents the "mega-sign" of the last days. Some are questioning whether a nation comprised of so many atheists could be considered worthy of God's mission to redeem the ancient people. This perspective is accompanied by a denial of Israel being "God's people" in the form of what is called "replacement theology", i.e., the Church replaces Israel that crucified the Messiah Jesus Christ. I reject their rejection and worry that Christians are being led into a new mode of anti-Semitism.

[116] Why is Turkey so at odds with Russia? Primarily, because Russia supports the Shi'ite cause rather than the Sunni one.

> "Turkey soon joined the other Islamic countries in their opposition against the Assad regime in Syria and the promotion of a Sunni-majority; the movement is driven by a desire to weaken both Syria and the Shiite-centric Iran and by extension, the Lebanese Hezbollah. To quote Mercier, "Saudi Arabia, Qatar, the Emirates and Turkey became staunch allies to promote, including by force, a Sunni agenda in the region... Regime change in Syria became the top priority on the Sunni axis agenda, mainly to weaken and isolate Shiite Iran". Religious organization has given way to political changes and military action and Mercier argues that there "exists countless evidence to establish the direct involvement of Turkey and the Gulf states in the creation of the entity with many names (ISIS, ISIL, Daesh, etc.)."

> See http://www.valuewalk.com/2015/12/will-nato-expel-turkey-over-recent-aggressiveness/2/.

[117] Lindsey stated the following in his book, *The Late Great Planet Earth* which teed up the issues combining a particular interpretation of the "seven seals" (the first four being the so-called "four horsemen of the apocalypse") and an understanding of Soviet Union policy and mindset:

> Almost immediately after the Antichrist declares himself to be God, God releases the dreaded second of the four horsemen of the Apocalypse. This is a figure of the unleashing of war upon the earth. That beautiful balance of power established by the Antichrist is suddenly ruptured. God begins to show man that the Antichrist's promises cannot stand. The thing which man feared most, an all-out war, now rushes upon him.... Russia and her allies use this occasion to launch an invasion of the Middle East, which Russia has longed to do since the Napoleonic Wars.

> Cited by Berner, op. cit., p. 301, quoting Hal Lindsey, *The Late Great Planet Earth* (1970), p. 142.

[118] Some argue the "he" is Christ and his sacrifice caused the oblation to cease.

[119] Which is the Hebrew word *kânâph*, meaning "wings" but used in the sense of a garment which hides every inch of what it covers, from one extreme point to the other, almost literally top to bottom and side to side.

[120] Heiser asserts,

> The clear references to Ezekiel 38-39 in Rev. 20:7-9 completely rule out any occasion for this battle prior to the second coming of Christ... I believe that Revelation 20:7-9 is perfectly clear that the ultimate fulfillment of Ezekiel 38-39 occurs after the millennial period, when the nations of the world, referred to as Gog and Magog, are empowered by Satan to attack Jerusalem. However, I also believe that the Gog prophecy has had several previous fulfillments. **Hence Ezekiel 38-39 is part of the 'already but not yet' paradigm that dominates biblical prophecy.** [Emphasis in original]

> From Berner, op. cit. p. 283, citing Heiser, *Islam and Armageddon*, pp. 93, 95, 97.

[121] Berner, op. cit., p. 294.

[122] Ibid., p. 306.

[123] Ibid., p. 298.

[124] Ibid.

[125] Ibid., p. 274. Citing Fruchtenbaum, *Footsteps of the Messiah: A Study of the Sequence of Prophetic Events*. P. 117.

[126] Berner, op. cit., p. 307.

[127] Ibid., 314, citing Grant Jeffrey, *Messiah: War in the Middle East and the Road to Armageddon*, p. 68.

[128] Ibid., 314, citing Randall Price, *The Battle For the Last Days' Temple*, p. 265.

[129] Ibid., p. 314, citing William Goetz, *Apocalypse Next*, pp. 146-147.

[130] Ibid., p. 315, citing Tim LaHaye, *The Beginning of the End*, p. 80.

[131] Ibid., p. 315, citing Emil Gaverluk, *The Rapture before the Russian Invasion of Israel*, pp. 125, 132.

[132] Ibid., p. 315, citing Arnold Fruchtenbaum, *Footsteps of the Messiah*, op. cited, p. 122.

[133] Ibid., p. 315, citing Chuck Missler, *The Magog Invasion*, p. 281.

[134] Ibid., p. 320.

[135] Ibid., p. 322.

[136] Berner cites Bally's "The Battle of 'Gog and Magog'", Bally's Prophecy Perspective, 2001.

[137] Berner, op. cit., p. 195.

[138] Grant Jeffrey, *Armageddon: Appointment with Destiny*, pp. 106-107

[139] See http://www.liveleak.com/view?i=8da_1404587611.

[140] See http://en.wikipedia.org/wiki/Peter_Mansfield_(historian).

[141] From Wikipedia:

> The McMahon–Hussein Correspondence, or the Hussein–McMahon Correspondence, was an exchange of letters (14 July 1915 to 30 January 1916) during World War I, between the Sharif of Mecca, Husayn bin Ali, and Sir Henry McMahon, British High Commissioner in Egypt, concerning the political status of lands under the Ottoman Empire. The Arab side was already looking toward a large revolt against the Ottoman Empire; the British encouraged the Arabs to revolt and thus hamper the Ottoman Empire, which had become a German ally in the War after November 1914."

See http://en.wikipedia.org/wiki/McMahon–Hussein_Correspondence.

[142] Read the paper at http://en.wikisource.org/wiki/The_Future_of_Palestine.

[143] Roland Sanders, *The High Walls of Jerusalem, A study of the Balfour Declaration*, Holt, Reinhart, and Winston, p. 346.

[144] See http://en.wikipedia.org/wiki/Churchill_White_Paper.

[145] Document 242, Memorandum by Mr.Balfour (Paris) respecting Syria, Palestine, and Mesopotamia, 11 August 1919, in E.L.Woodward and Rohan Butler, *Documents on British Foreign Policy*, 1919–1939. (London: HM Stationery Office, 1952), ISBN 0-11-591554-0, p.340–348.

[146] Lord Earl Grey – the namesake of the *tea* we often enjoy.

[147] *Aliyah* is the Hebrew word (and program) for the immigration of Jews from the diaspora to the land of Israel (*Eretz Yisrael*).

[148] See also Revelation 18:4. Revelation 18:8 predicts that Babylon is destroyed in one day. Revelation 18:17 states that her destruction, as seen by the merchants of the earth, is in one hour. Could one reflect the entire nation and the other 'that great city' that serves as the icon for the nation as a whole?

CPSIA information can be obtained
at www.ICGtesting.com
Printed in the USA
LVOW04s1212071116

511952LV00001B/386/P

9 781523 230068